"In *The Betrayal Bind*, Michelle Mays uses attachment theory to explain, educate, and empower hurting partners. Through her compassionate use of storytelling, Mays shares profound insights, normalizes partner's experiences, and provides encouragement and support. It is a must read for any person experiencing betrayal."

—**Stefanie Carnes, PhD,** President of the International Institute for Trauma and Addiction Professionals and author of *Courageous Love*

"Mays speaks the unvarnished truth about the impact of intimate betrayal with warmth and compassion as she guides the reader on a hero's journey from pain to grace. She accurately describes the emotionally harrowing, complex experience of betrayal trauma without pathologizing either party. With neuro-scientific accuracy, Mays explains why fear, shame, and powerlessness drive attachment ambivalence and how to shift out of it. *The Betrayal Bind* illuminates a clear and empowering path forward toward creating safety, sexual healing, and reclaiming an authentic sense of self."

—**Alexandra Katehakis,** author, *Mirror of Intimacy: Daily Reflections on Emotional and Erotic Intelligence*

"Michelle Mays weaves personal insight, beautiful writing, current attachment science, and clinical expertise to share this gift with us. With gentle respect for the busy brain, *The Betrayal Bind* reaches her reader where the heart is, guiding us to a deeper understanding of why sexual betrayal is so devastating. I recommend this book for not only those swimming in the deep water of sexual betrayal, but also for adults living with the intimate betrayal that happens when our first caregivers are abusive."

—**Kelly McDaniel, LPC,** trauma therapist and author of *Ready to Heal* and *Mother Hunger*

"In this landmark text, Michelle Mays provides a path to healing from the pain of relationship betrayal. She candidly shares her personal experience of recovery and renewal from the trauma of partner betrayal. This transformation provided her with the understanding and empathy she expresses as a therapist, speaker, and author. *The Betrayal Bind* offers new hope for individuals and partners seeking to move beyond the hurt of their past to experience the life and relationship they desire."

—**Dr. Mark Sanna,** Breakthrough Coaching

"One of the most useful and comprehensive books on identifying and healing emotional betrayal. Michelle Mays' examination of these painful issues is laced with generous doses of practical advice and hope for the future. Relying on her personal and professional experience, she has created a must-read for betrayed partners, cheating loved ones, and the therapists who treat them."

—**Robert Weiss, PhD,** author of *Prodependence: Beyond the Myth of Codependency* and *Sex Addiction 101*

"Michelle provides a well-grounded process for healing and restoration following one of the most devastating life events possible: the intimate betrayal by a loved one. Such a trauma shatters everything, including a sense of self, sense of safety, sense of connection with self and others and our higher power or God. Betrayed partners will find hope within this comprehensive book that provides well-grounded tools and a pathway toward healing and post-traumatic growth following betrayal."

—**Dr. Barbara Steffens,** coauthor of *Your Sexually Addicted Spouse: How Partners Can Cope and Heal* and founding President of the Association of Partners of Sex Addicts Trauma Specialists (APSATS)

THE BETRAYAL BIND

THE BETRAYAL BIND

*How to Heal When the Person
You Love the Most Hurts You the Worst*

MICHELLE MAYS

RELATIONAL RECOVERY PRESS LLC
LEESBURG, VIRGINIA

Relational Recovery Press LLC

© 2023 by Michelle Mays

All rights reserved. Published 2023. Printed in the United States of America.

No part of this publication may be reproduced, stored in a retrieval system, or transmitted in any form or by any means, electronic, mechanical, photocopying, recording, or otherwise, without the written permission of the publisher.

Names: Mays, Michelle, author.

Title: The betrayal bind : how to heal when the person you love the most has hurt you the worst / Michelle Mays.

Description: Relational Recovery Press LLC | Includes bibliographical references. | Summary: "Introduces new language, concepts, and imagery to explore the crucial relational dilemma that betrayed partners face when their significant other is unsafe to connect to, yet connection is the key to healing" -- Provided by publisher.

Identifiers: ISBN 978-0-9988434-4-5 (paperback) | ISBN 978-0-9988434-5-2 (ebook)

Photo of Michelle Mays by Julie Fischer McCarter. Used with permission.

Publisher's Note

The information contained herein is not medical advice. This book is not an alternative to medical advice from your doctor or other professional healthcare provider.

Our books represent the experiences and opinions of their authors only. Every effort has been made to ensure that events, institutions, and statistics presented in our books as facts are accurate and up-to-date. To protect their privacy, the names of some of the people, places, and institutions in this book may have been changed.

Cover design and interior by Kern Collective.

To all those who have braved hope after betrayal

TABLE OF CONTENTS

INTRODUCTION:
We've Come a Long Way, Baby *1*

CHAPTER ONE:
And So It Begins *11*

CHAPTER TWO:
What's So Complex about Partner Betrayal? *23*

PART 1

INTRODUCTION:
The Attachment Injury at the Heart of Betrayal *41*

CHAPTER THREE:
We Are Family: Getting Attached *45*

CHAPTER FOUR:
I Love You, I Love You Not: The Dilemma of Attachment Ambivalence *57*

CHAPTER FIVE:
Shamed If You Do, Shamed If You Don't: Understanding the Shame Bind Created by Betrayal *75*

CHAPTER SIX:
Attachment-Focused Trauma Symptoms *93*

CHAPTER SEVEN:
Healthy Coping Strategies That Support Our Attachment Systems ... 105

PART 2

INTRODUCTION:
The Emotional and Psychological Injury at the Heart of Betrayal ... 121

CHAPTER EIGHT:
Liar, Liar, Pants on Fire: The Four Types of Gaslighting ... 125

CHAPTER NINE:
A Horse and Water: When You Can't Make Someone Tell the Truth ... 143

CHAPTER TEN:
See No Evil, Hear No Evil: Understanding Betrayal Blindness ... 161

CHAPTER ELEVEN:
Going Blind: Patterns of Betrayal Blindness ... 177

CHAPTER TWELVE:
Getting Stuck: Fear, Shame, and Powerlessness ... 189

PART 3

INTRODUCTION:
The Sexual Injury at the Heart of Betrayal ... 207

CHAPTER THIRTEEN:
Sex and Attachment: Meeting Our Needs for Belonging and Significance ... 211

CHAPTER FOURTEEN:
Killing the Sexy: Common Patterns in Relationships with Hidden Cheating ... 225

CHAPTER FIFTEEN:
Losing the Sexual Self: The Impact of Betrayal
on Partner Sexuality ... *241*

CHAPTER SIXTEEN:
Sexual and Emotional Safety: Part One ... *257*

CHAPTER SEVENTEEN:
Sexual and Emotional Safety: Part Two ... *267*

PART 4

INTRODUCTION:
The Attachment-Focused Partner Betrayal Model ... *281*

CHAPTER EIGHTEEN:
Relational Recovery: Attachment-Based
Treatment for Partner Betrayal ... *283*

CHAPTER NINETEEN:
Braving Hope after Betrayal:
The Six Phases of Healing ... *299*

CHAPTER TWENTY:
The Braving Hope™ Process: Imagining a New Life ... *319*

CHAPTER TWENTY-ONE:
Don't Waste a Good Crisis: Endings and
New Beginnings ... *337*

ACKNOWLEDGMENTS ... *347*

ENDNOTES ... *351*

> Helplessness and isolation
> are the core experience
> of psychological trauma.
> Empowerment and reconnection
> are the core experience
> of recovery.
>
> — JUDITH HERMAN

INTRODUCTION

WE'VE COME A LONG WAY, BABY

Back when I was married to a sex addict and seeking help, there were almost no books addressing sexual betrayal from the perspective of the betrayed partner. Patrick Carnes had written his seminal volume, *Out of the Shadows*, in 1983. Carnes introduced the public to the concept of sex addiction, but, as with most new ideas, it was many years before sex addiction entered our common lexicon. Even though my story unfolded in the mid-to-late 1990s and early 2000s, there were still very few resources for me to reach for.

When I did search for help, I found books that told me because I was married to a sex addict, I was automatically dealing with my own disease of co-addiction/codependence. Some of these early books contributed mightily to my healing, and I am grateful to have found them. The first one that dealt with being the partner of a sex addict was Laurie Hall's *An Affair of the Mind*, and it blew the doors off my denial. I also found comfort, solace, and identification in Jennifer Schneider's *Back from Betrayal* and Charlotte Davis Kasl's *Women, Sex, and Addiction*.

However, as Maya Angelou and Oprah have said, "When you know better, you do better." And therapists, as a field, now know better and are doing better when it comes to treating betrayed partners.

In 2006, Barbara Steffens and Robyn Rennie published a seminal research study examining the traumatic nature of betrayal for partners of sex addicts.[1] This was followed by her book, *Your Sexually Addicted Spouse*, published in 2009 with Marsha Means, which altered our understanding of what happens to partners of sex addicts—moving us from a shared disease (co-addiction) model to that of a traumatic experience rooted in being separated from emotional and relational safety through betrayal in our primary relationship.[2]

One of the key findings of Steffens's research was that 69 percent of partners of sex addicts meet all but Criteria A1 (the criteria regarding life-threatening circumstances) for a diagnosis of Post-Traumatic Stress Disorder (PTSD). Steffens's research allowed the fields of sex addiction treatment and trauma treatment to, for the first time, link their understanding of the origins, manifestations, and treatment of post-traumatic stress to individuals impacted by adult sexual betrayal.

This was a significant leap forward in our understanding of the hurricane of symptoms and reactions partners experience following betrayal. It opened the door for the therapeutic community to use treatment approaches that had proven effective in treating trauma in their work with betrayed partners. Instead of being labeled codependent or co-addicted, partners began to be seen as individuals experiencing a traumatic event and responding accordingly. This was progress.

Despite the enormous gifts the trauma model has brought to our understanding of partner betrayal, the traumatic stress model still falls short of helping us thoroughly understand the internal (emotional) and external (behavioral) patterns that betrayed partners commonly experience.

To move our understanding forward, I want to introduce you to Jennifer Freyd, PhD. In 1996, Freyd introduced Betrayal Trauma Theory (BTT). Freyd's work, rooted in attachment theory, focuses on childhood and adult traumas that are relational or sexual in nature. BTT transformed our understanding of trauma because it placed betrayal—a relational dynamic—at the center of the experience. Birrell, Bernstein, and Freyd have stated that BTT, "is a theory of psychological response to trauma that proposes that an individual's cognitive encoding of and response to trauma depends not only on the terror or fear of a specific event, but also on the event's social betrayal."[3] In this context, social betrayal refers to being betrayed by someone you are close to and often dependent upon. BTT holds that the closer and more important the relationship is (such as a parent or a spouse), the more severe the sense of betrayal and thus the traumatic impact will be.

One of Freyd's critiques of the traditional understanding of traumatic stress is that it emphasizes pathological fear as the central experience that creates symptoms. Freyd argues that it is not just fear but the attachment dynamics and injuries inherent in relational betrayal that drive the experience of trauma.[4]

By shifting the existing understanding of traumatic betrayal from a fear paradigm to a relational paradigm, Freyd altered our understanding of "meaning-making." The trauma treatment field agrees that one of the biggest tasks of what occurred, and integrating this new understanding of events, ourselves, and others into our life narrative.

Because traumatic events often interrupt or contradict our assumptions about the world and our place in it, a new understanding must be processed and integrated. For example, prior to discovering cheating, you may have thought that if someone were to cheat on you it would be unforgivable and would mean the relationship must end. But when you actually experience cheating, you may find yourself trying to forgive and allow your partner to repair the relationship. These shifts in assumptions and perceptions require you to rethink what you value, believe, and want. This shattering of assumptions and rebuilding of understanding is part of all traumatic experiences.

Freyd argues that when betrayal is at the center of the traumatic experience, the process of meaning-making changes. Instead of focusing only on the cognitive experience of rebuilding or remaking shattered assumptions, finding meaning expands to include healing the core wound at the heart of betrayal—relational disconnection.

Betrayal always creates relational disconnection. We feel disconnected from ourselves and who we knew ourselves to be, from our significant other and who we thought they were, from friends and family who we suddenly feel alienated from as we struggle with deep pain and sadness, and from our higher power or larger systems of meaning that suddenly seem unsafe and unpredictable. As Freyd succinctly puts it: "Those traumas that involve betrayal cut us off from connection with others and even a basic sense of 'being' within ourselves."[5]

Betrayal does this because it changes the story we thought we were living in. In an instant, we move from a state of relative safety, connection, and congruence to a state of fragmentation, fear, shame, and powerlessness. This new story does more than just alter our thinking and perceptions. It changes us at the level of our attachment systems and the way we experience our relational bond with others and ourselves.

This experience of relational disconnection lies at the root of all symptomatic behaviors betrayed partners display in the aftermath of betrayal. Looking through the lens of attachment theory changes not only our understanding of what is happening to betrayed partners but our understanding of what is needed to treat partner betrayal trauma.

Recognizing that betrayal is at the heart of traumatic experience shifts meaning-making from a cognitive task to a relational task. If the heart of betrayal trauma is a profound relational disconnection, then the heart of healing must be profound relational *connection*.

The graphic below helps us locate relational disconnection as the starting point for the distress, emotional dysregulation, and trauma symptoms that betrayed partners experience after betrayal. These trauma symptoms are *all* relational at the core. They serve a relational purpose and are driven by the distress our attachment systems feel when we experience the danger of relational disconnection.

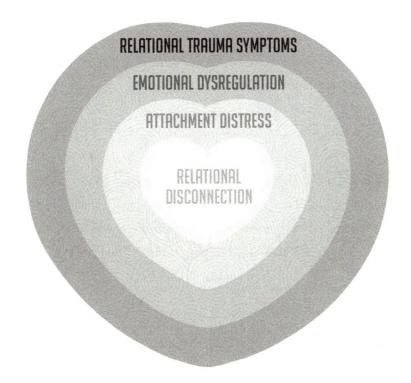

Without understanding this core issue—how a partner's attachment system functions in the wake of sexual betrayal—we are missing a vital element in recognizing why partners do the things they do and how to effectively treat them. We also miss the key to unlocking true long-lasting transformation: relational connection. If betrayal happens in relationship, then it makes sense that our healing and restoration must also happen in relationship with others and with ourselves.

In the following pages, I am going to introduce you to new language, concepts, and imagery to explore the crucial relational dilemmas that betrayed partners face when their significant other is unsafe to connect to, yet connection remains the key to healing. This relational bind—the dynamics it creates—and the path to healing form the heart of this book.

If you are reading this book, you may be a betrayed partner or the cheating partner. You may be a therapist, sponsor, friend, or family member. Whatever your role in the drama that surrounds sexual betrayal, my hope is that this book will enlighten, inspire, and motivate while providing a proven path to healing.

This book is written for anyone who has dealt with cheating or adult sexual betrayal in their romantic relationship. It doesn't matter if the cheating is the result of a single affair, multiple affairs, compulsive pornography use, or a pattern of problematic sexual behavior that adds up to addiction. The traumatic impact is similar regardless of the shape the behaviors take. I have tried to use examples from both traditional forms of cheating (i.e., an affair) as well as from relationships dealing with sex addiction.

Also, in our culture, we are seeing how we bond and who we bond with change and broaden its shape and form from traditional monogamy to open relationships, polyamorous relationships, and more. Cheating and the betrayal accompanying it pertain to all these varied permutations because cheating is about violating the sexual and emotional agreements that create safety and trust within a relationship, regardless of its form. In my experience, clients from non-monogamous relationships are just as devastated when a partner violates the relationship agreements as clients in traditionally monogamous relationships. Betrayal creates a universal loss of trust and safety and that is what this book seeks to address.

Throughout the book you will notice that I use the language of *cheating partner*, *betrayer*, *unfaithful partner*, etc., to describe the person who has betrayed the relationship agreements. This is not intended to be a pejorative label but is simply to help us keep the two partners in the relationship clear by identifying them as cheating partner or betrayed partner. In the same way, I use the language of *relationship*, *marriage*, and *partnership* to describe varying forms of long-term romantic relationships.

In addition, there is always a conundrum about how to write about populations that include, well, everyone. Anyone in a romantic relationship can experience cheating regardless of where you identify in terms of gender, orientation, sex, etc. To avoid the clumsiness and limitations of *he* or *she* I have used *they*, *their*, or *them* as often as possible when talking about the various individuals involved.

If you are a betrayed partner who is thinking about leaving your relationship or have already left, I encourage you to read this book. Much of what we are going to explore is about the dynamics that unfold within you and within the relationship with the cheating partner after discovery of the cheating. Even if you are no longer with the cheating partner, much of your healing hinges on understanding the relational and emotional patterns that developed for you because of the cheating.

These patterns can become part of what you believe about yourself and others and impact your behaviors, choices, and responses. The goal is to become conscious of the way cheating impacted your sense of self and your expectations for relationships so that you can change the patterns that block you from creating the life and relationships you long for.

As always, in the specific stories, quotes, or case studies that I offer, client information has been combined and details have been added or omitted to ensure that no identifying information is shared.

Last, you will notice that I occasionally reference God or higher power throughout the book. My belief is that relational trauma impacts our relationship with ourselves, our relationships with others (especially our partners), and our relationship with our higher power or larger systems of meaning. For me, my higher power is God and so I have written from that perspective particularly when sharing a part of my story. Please feel free to think about higher power in whatever way is best for you.

ADDITIONAL RESOURCES FOR YOU

The 5-Step Strategy to Take Back Your Life After Betrayal is a free online masterclass by Michelle Mays.

Discover a step-by-step game-plan to heal sexual betrayal by reducing trauma symptoms, restoring your personal power, and grounding your healing in authentic hope that creates *real change*.

Visit michellemays.com/masterclass to watch
The 5-Step Strategy to Take Back Your Life After Betrayal.

ADDITIONAL RESOURCES FOR THERAPISTS & COACHES

 For information about training and certification in **The Attachment-Focused Partner Betrayal Model: Attachment-based healing for partner betrayal** developed by Michelle Mays LPC, CSAT-S please visit michellemays.com/professionals.

The life you are negotiating to save, after all, is your own.

ELIZABETH GILBERT

CHAPTER ONE

AND SO IT BEGINS

Nothing can prepare you for the moment you discover that the person closest to you, the person you count on the most, has betrayed you. As that realization slams home, heat and adrenaline rush in. Your hands shake, your knees buckle, your heart races; your mind skips like a damaged record, jumping from one bad moment to another. The thoughts come too fast to even think, flying by in a kaleidoscope of remembered conversations and events, color, and sound, all mixed together in a shower of lies. Your body turns cold; your heart slows; a deep, brick-like dread fills your stomach and chest. The tears come. More tears than you had any idea you could cry.

At least that was what it was like for me.

The discovery of my spouse's extracurricular sexual activities spun me into sheer terror. The pain of the betrayal knocked me to the floor, and I did not get back up for a long time. Like many people, I got married believing I had found the partner who would make me safe, content, and happy.

I entered marriage naïve about life, marriage, sex, relationships, and myself: a twenty-three-year-old baby playing at being an adult and thinking I was grown up. And for a while, all went well. Marriage was fun, life was good, we were young and in love and having a good time. I relaxed into the relationship, let my guard down, trusted that I was finally "home," and was vulnerable and open with my spouse.

When I discovered that all was not as I thought and that my husband was struggling sexually and behaving in ways that shocked me, the pain was unbearable. It ripped through me, and, in a flash, everything changed. The part of me that had let my guard down, trusted, and opened up . . . that part of me curled into a teeny ball in the corner of my heart and whispered, "You foolish, foolish, girl. Now protect yourself." Like Alice falling down the rabbit hole, my world shifted, and suddenly all that I thought was true and could count on was gone.

If you have experienced sexual betrayal, you probably recognize the type of pain I am describing. There really are no words, are there? It hurts to your core. Along with the pain is an incredible amount of fear, panic, anxiety, and anger. Sexual betrayal, whether it springs from sexual addiction or typical cheating and infidelity, puts your entire relationship on the line. All that felt certain and sure is suddenly unclear and unpredictable. This is the experience of partner betrayal trauma.

I remember the moment when I finally recognized that my spouse's behavior—the lies and secrets—added up to sexual addiction. I was standing at my kitchen window watching dust particles float in the early morning light when suddenly two and two collided and for the first time equaled four. I realized that if what I was putting together was true, it meant something compulsive was going on for my husband with sex. When I understood that there was something driven and obsessive about his behavior, it broke through my confusion and connected the dots for me. I wandered aimlessly from the kitchen through the apartment, turned very far inside of myself. I ended up standing in the middle of my bedroom where, for the first time, I uttered the words *sexual addiction* to myself and believed them.

It was not the first time I had heard the term. Others had used that language to describe my spouse. Each time I heard the words spoken, it was like water that washed over me and evaporated into thin air, gone before it had any chance to sink in. I was not ready for all that those words implied.

Up to this point in my marriage, I had been careening between blindness to the problem versus high-energy alarm and preoccupation. I would spend months pretending all was well, minimizing and rationalizing away all indications of troubling behavior. *My husband is not doing anything. He says he is not doing anything, and I believe him. Things are fine.* Then, a random clue or new betrayal would surface and yank me into reality. Reality was so awful, so scary and painful that then I would flip into a raging, controlling, confronting zealot determined to somehow make this problem and my pain go away. I call this painful loop "circling the drain"—a common place where partners can get stuck after discovering betrayal.

During this time, I did not understand addiction, let alone sexual addiction. I did not know how to handle my pain and fear. I did not know that it was possible to be okay even amid all that was happening. I thought the only way to survive emotionally was to eliminate the problem.

As a result, I was not open to hearing about recovery. I did not want to hear about a PROCESS, or a JOURNEY, thank you very much. I didn't have time to walk a PATH or to GROW or MATURE or DEVELOP. I needed it to GO AWAY. So I spent years cycling through my personal trauma loop, wearing myself out as I swung wildly from blindness to hypervigilant control and back again. It wasn't until I had thoroughly exhausted myself and repeatedly proved that my efforts were not changing anything that I was ready to accept that I needed a new path out.

THE VERY BOTTOM

Very soon after recognizing and accepting the presence of sexual addiction in my relationship, I was given a mysterious and wonderful gift: I hit bottom. In recovery lingo, the bottom is when the pain of how you are living overwhelms your fear of change and you become willing to step into the unknown. The reality that something is terribly wrong breaks through, and you finally recognize that what you are doing is not working, not going to work, never will work, and you must find another way. Another brand new, never-tried-before way.

Often, that new way feels scarier than staying stuck. This is why it can take some time to hit bottom. The devil we know is at least the devil we know. Making a bid for change by seeking out the unfamiliar, untried, and untraveled is risky and scary.

I found my bottom without a lot of fanfare. One morning I was lying in bed after recently moving to Seattle to enter graduate school for my master's in counseling. I still didn't know my way around. School had not yet started, and I was as miserable as I have ever been. That morning, as I lay in bed listlessly looking out the window, watching it drizzle, this thought entered my mind: *Something is wrong with me.*

Until then, I had been very sure there was something wrong with my husband. I was equally sure there were a million things wrong with me. Deep in my heart, I believed *I* must be doing something to cause my husband's sexual behavior; I thought that if I could just fix myself, I could fix him, too. I had been working like a hamster trapped on a wheel of self-improvement, trying to figure out how my own actions were causing our marriage to be such a disaster. The idea that there was something wrong with me was not new. That belief had been living in me for most of my life.

But this thought that crept in was different. This time, I realized that something was wrong in a different way. This new idea did not have to do with a search for more proof of dysfunction; instead, it focused on what was good in me—my dignity and worth as a child of God. This thought was about the daring notion that perhaps what was wrong was that it felt normal to live in so much pain. That perhaps I was created to live differently. Perhaps I was worthy of a different type of life and relationship. Perhaps I shouldn't be living with and enduring and putting up with all that I had been living with and enduring and putting up with.

This was a very different way of thinking, and it created a crack in my defenses—a way for the light to begin to stream in, illuminate the darkness, and transform my situation. This new thought made me curious. It was a tantalizing taste that left me longing for more. What if it were true? What if a steady diet of love, kindness, care, and attention was available to me? What if I were worthy of that? Could it be possible?

A NEW WAY

This strange new thought woke me to the possibility of something different and potentially wonderful. Suddenly I was looking around with new eyes, taking in information in a new way. Slowly, things began to change as clarity replaced confusion and hope replaced despair.

For the first time, I became able to stay in my reality and learn to live there. The hope streaming in gave me the courage to look head-on at my situation and, for the first time, to recognize that the betrayal I was experiencing was not my fault and ultimately not about me at all. I began to understand that my spouse was trapped in the cunning, baffling, and powerful clutches of a spiritual, emotional, mental, and physical problem. While the betrayal was still painful and hurt me, I stopped experiencing it as a referendum on my worth and lovability. I began to see that my worthiness was separate from my relationship, separate from the betrayal, separate even from my own failings and struggles. It was instead rooted in something immovable, permanent, and dependable. It was inherent within me, and no one could take it away.

My oh-so-tentative grasp on this new truth also inspired a willingness and ability to look honestly at myself and humbly acknowledge my own unhealthy behaviors. When my faults and failings no longer added up to a deeply unconscious yet mighty conviction that, somehow, I *deserved* betrayal, I became able to look at my faults and failings in ways that allowed them to heal and be transformed.

This new perspective and understanding resulted in my willingness to get on a damn path and walk a journey after all, even though I only had a few answers at a time and most of my questions required that I wait, walk, and live into them step by step. I had been camped for so long in such a dark, dank, narrow space, when everything in me was screaming for light and air and freedom. And I found that. Inch by inch, the darkness receded, the light came in, and fresh air began to flow.

It was still hard. In fact, it was excruciating. But part of that pivotal moment of change was the realization that the only way out of the pain and anguish was through the pain and anguish. Once I discovered that,

I began to pray what may seem like an odd prayer. It went something like this: "Okay God, if I must go through this mind-numbingly shitty experience anyway, then I ask that it not be wasted. Use it to change me, heal me, grow me, and make me into more of who I am supposed to be." In a way that I still don't fully understand, I found a place of courage and fight inside myself where I was determined to be the hero of my own betrayal story.

THE UNWANTED CALL

Everybody is called at some point (and most of us are called several times throughout life) to go through something so challenging that we think it will break us. We are called out of our place of comfort and are asked to go to a new place, a place of challenge and change. We are asked to walk through the fire or to brave the sea, to navigate the dark woods or to conquer the sky. When we finally accept that yes, we must go forward and face the challenge, take it on and move through it, we are changed. Like the caterpillar that must battle the cocoon to break free and live into its glory as a butterfly, so too must we go through the struggle required to achieve our own metamorphosis.

And that is what happened. My journey took me from that desperate moment lying in bed to healing and flourishing. It took me through graduate school, where I received a Master's in Counseling, into private practice, where I started working with sex addicts and their partners. This led me to get trained as a Certified Sex Addiction Therapist and Supervisor (CSAT-S) and to specialize in some of the most difficult and rewarding work I can imagine. Along the way, my husband and I separated and eventually divorced. This is a heartbreak I would wish on no one, but it was a necessary and vital part of my healing.

My journey brought me such long-lasting freedom and joy that today I can say that I would go through it all again if necessary to be who I am. I am not the only one who would tell you this. I have had many of my clients, survivors of adult sexual betrayal, walk their own road of healing and eventually, as they've experienced the gifts of the journey, they too have said, "It was hell, but it was worth it."

DECISIONS, DECISIONS

In countless fairy tales, legends, and folk stories, the hero of the tale starts out as just a normal person, minding their business, living their life, just like you and I were before betrayal rolled in. Then, in some unforeseen way, life suddenly presents them with a grand challenge. This challenge requires them to make a choice. They can refuse the challenge and stay where they are, or they can accept the challenge and embark on an unknown journey. Refusing the challenge means giving up the benefits that the journey may offer and the possibility that it may change their life forever in wonderful ways. But they get to stay safe and life remains familiar and known. They do not have to risk losing anything.

Another way to think about this is that life has suddenly plopped you down at a crossroads. In one direction is the familiar, worn path that loops around on top of itself, creating an endless ring. You already know this path. You know where it leads, you know what it looks like. You've been there time and time again, going round and round. This might look like ignoring the signs of cheating and staying in a place of blindness about what is unfolding out of fear of losing your relationship. Or it might look like discovering that your partner is a sex addict and immediately filing for divorce and moving on without ever stopping to find out how you might need to grow and heal yourself. Rather than considering that for this moment life is serving up betrayal as a teacher and a very unlikely source of growth, you decide to stick with what you know. You sacrifice potential for safety, curiosity for certainty, the unknown for the status quo. Fear wins.

On the other side of this fork in the road is a new path. This one doesn't loop around on itself. Instead, it stretches out into the distance. You can't see very far down it. It's unclear where it leads, how long it will take to travel it, and what you will encounter on the way. But this path also seems to represent opportunity. Your old path brings you back to the same place over and over again. This other path appears to at least go somewhere new and provide a chance for things to change.

MAKING THE CHOICE

So, you stand at the crossroads and deliberate. You have not asked for this challenge; you did not want to find yourself at this fork in the road. This challenge has in many ways picked you. Nobody volunteers to be a betrayed partner. Most partners are just like I was at the start—trying hard to find the quickest way out of the pain. In fact, it may be that I am just making you angry with all my talk of growth and accepting the challenge. I would have been angry, too, if someone talked to me about that at the beginning. Eventually, however, I needed to hear about hope, healing, and freedom. I needed to understand that I was in the middle of a process that eventually would be worth every dreadful, horrible, excruciating minute. Without that, I couldn't have kept putting one foot in front of the other.

For betrayed partners, the crisis of betrayal is the crossroads where you are presented with the call and must make a decision. A pivotal life-altering decision. You must decide *how* you will go through the crisis. You can keep your head down, play it safe, avoid vulnerability, and sacrifice courage in the hope that it will all be over soon. Or you can brave hope, gather courage, take a deep gulp, and step forward in faith, believing that this crisis will not destroy you but instead enlarge you in unimaginably good ways.

How will you go forward?

Will you take a leap of faith toward believing that despite betrayal and all its trauma, despite shocking losses and unbelievable pain, there is a way through that will not destroy you but will strengthen you, free you, and give you the most precious gift of all—the gift of your true self? Will you make room for the possibility that the cascading shitstorm your life has become is about much more than surviving betrayal? It is about you finding your true power, owning your voice, connecting your heart to the hearts of others, and grounding deeply in your inherent worth.

You stand at the fork in the road, facing this moment of choice. You consider your options. You consider the cost. And then you reach deep down inside and grab hold of courage you didn't even know you had. You nod once to yourself firmly, and then slowly, tentatively, take your first steps onto the new path.

This is where it gets interesting.

In all the legends and stories of old, the hero encounters guides and helpers on the journey. Often, these guides and helpers are unlikely sources of assistance: random fairies, talking animals, bushes that burn, wart-covered strangers. But help is always there, providing the hero with whatever they need to climb the next rise and to eventually reach the end of their quest.

This will be true for you as well. What I want to say to you as clearly as possible is that there is hope and healing for you as a betrayed partner. Sometimes it's easy to think that the path is mysterious and that only the lucky few stumble onto it, but this is not true. The path is well-trodden. Many others have walked it before you, and they've left plenty of markers and arrows pointing the direction. There is lots of help to be had as you go along, and friendship, love, and care to support you on the way.

My hope is that this book will be a key support on your journey. This book is written from my heart to yours. It is the information and support I wish someone had given me when I stepped onto my own new path. It is a compilation of the wisdom, information, and encouragement that I found vital for my own healing. My vision is that we might together embrace the hero's journey that takes us out of the old and into the new, out of self-doubt and into self-trust, out of shame and into self-compassion, out of disconnection and into the beauty of connection.

Let's start our journey together by looking at what happens when we first discover and experience sexual betrayal.

**Dante placed
Judas and Brutus
in the lowest circle of hell
to show that betrayal
is the worst of sins.**

DAVID RICHO

CHAPTER TWO

WHAT'S SO COMPLEX ABOUT PARTNER BETRAYAL?

Betrayal makes us feel like we are losing our minds. It yanks our sense of security out from under us and puts us in a state of emotional free fall. It is severely emotionally distressing, and until you have experienced it, you really can't imagine how truly life-altering it can be.

To heal from sexual betrayal, we must first understand what has happened to us, our partner, and our relationship. Over the past twenty years, as I have worked with thousands of betrayed partners, I have developed an attachment-based treatment model that captures the experience of betrayal and the resulting relational trauma. In this chapter, we take a step-by-step tour of this model, because starting with the big picture always helps us better locate ourselves when we get lost in the details of our experience.

THE ATTACHMENT-FOCUSED PARTNER BETRAYAL MODEL

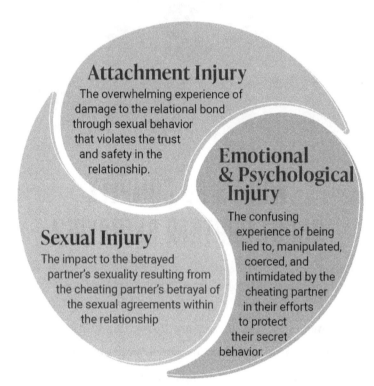

Our understanding of The Attachment-Focused Partner Betrayal Model begins by identifying the three core injuries that all betrayed partners experience. Regardless of whether the cheating partner had one affair or a lengthy history of compulsive sexual behavior, these three inuries are present for each betrayed partner. See if you resonate with the description of these traumatic injuries.

- **Attachment injury:** The overwhelming experience of damage to the relational bond through sexual behavior that violates the trust and safety in the relationship.

- **Emotional and psychological injury:** The confusing experience of being lied to, manipulated, coerced, and intimidated by the cheating partner in their efforts to protect their secret behavior.
- **Sexual injury:** The impact to the betrayed partner's sexuality resulting from the cheating partner's betrayal of the sexual agreements within the relationship.

For betrayed partners, these three injuries weave together, creating an overlapping, intertwining braid of betrayal that often touches the nerve center of all three experiences simultaneously.

BETRAYAL: SHOT TO THE HEART

Attachment Injury
The overwhelming experience of damage to the relational bond through sexual behavior that violates the trust and safety in the relationship.

Emotional & Psychological Injury
The confusing experience of being lied to, manipulated, coerced, and intimidated by the cheating partner in their efforts to protect their secret behavior.

Sexual Injury
The impact to the betrayed partner's sexuality resulting from the cheating partner's betrayal of the sexual agreements within the relationship

Betrayal

At the heart of each of the injuries is betrayal. Betrayal winds its way through the sexual behavior, the lying, the secrets, and the destruction of trust and security in the relationship.

Over the past few years, the term *betrayal trauma* has begun to enter our common lexicon. As we start to hear and use this terminology more, it is essential that we don't become numb to the term *betrayal* and the world of significance contained within that single three-syllable word. Betrayal is *the* thing that separates relational trauma from other types of traumas, changing the nature of the experience for those impacted.

Betrayal is a form of disloyalty or unfaithfulness to someone we've promised, explicitly or implicitly, to be loyal and/or faithful to. At the heart of this disloyalty are issues of dependence, vulnerability, and trust. When we are dependent on another person, whether that person is a spouse, a parent, or a trusted friend, inherent in that dependence is vulnerability and trust. By relying on that person, we have made ourselves vulnerable. We have shown our soft underbelly, trusting that they will understand and treasure the gift that our vulnerability is, holding it with faithful, dependable kid gloves.

It is this vulnerable, dependent entrusting of ourselves to the care of another that betrayal shatters. Betrayal is the metaphorical experience of having someone ask us to leap off the cliff, promising to catch us when we do, and then, after much hesitation and checking and many promises and reassurances, we jump—only to have that person step away at the last moment, letting us crash. Our bodies will be bruised and broken, but our biggest wound will be the betrayal—the shattering of our belief and trust in the other person.

This experience—finding that our dependency, vulnerability, and trust have been broken—is at the heart of betrayal. And it is this experience that makes betrayal trauma so challenging to heal.

A DYNAMIC MULTIDIMENSIONAL RODEO

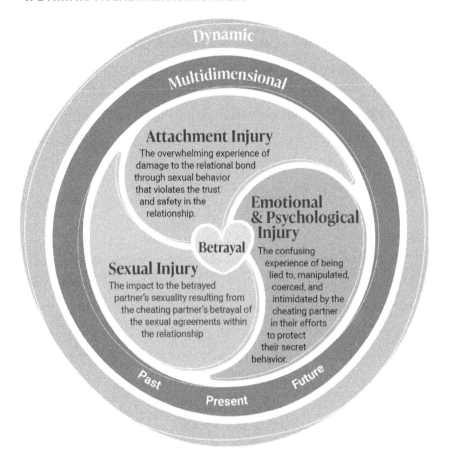

If you are a betrayed partner, you may have heard the diagnosis of Post-Traumatic Stress Disorder used to describe the symptoms and reactions you are experiencing. Although I believe this diagnostic category is often the most appropriate interpretation of the symptoms that typically follow the discovery of sexual betrayal, I also believe that sometimes when we use the language of post-traumatic stress, we mislead ourselves about the dynamics that we are dealing with.

Allow me to explain.

When I first dragged myself to therapy after discovering my spouse's extracurricular sexual behaviors, I didn't know about sexual addiction. I didn't know about compulsivity, brain chemistry, neuropathways, arousal templates, trauma issues, attachment styles, emotional regulation issues, and all the other things that make up our current understanding of addiction. What I did know was that I was in pain and that my husband's behaviors had violated the trust and safety in our relationship at the deepest levels. I also knew I wanted out of the pain, so I went to therapy to see if we could fix what had happened and move on.

I tried. We tried. Our therapist tried. It didn't work. You know why? Because that was only the beginning.

The beginning of more discoveries, more lying, more tearful conflicts, and more rounds of betrayal. I thought I was going to therapy to deal with what had happened and move past it. Instead, while I was sitting on that couch week after week, more rounds of broken promises, lies, and secret behavior came to light, leaving me shocked and reeling.

My experience was not unusual. Even if what you are dealing with is not sexual addiction but an affair or another form of infidelity, there is still a process of ongoing discovery that most partners experience in which information, secrets, and lies are uncovered over time.

As a result, when betrayed partners enter therapy after the initial discovery of betrayal, they are not dealing with *post*-traumatic stress. Instead, they are *mid*-trauma. They are in the middle of an unfolding nightmare of betrayal that seems to have no end. Betrayed partners are dealing with what they have already discovered (the past), what they just found out this week or a few hours before they walked into the therapist's office (the present), and the enormously threatening fear that their cheating partner's behavior may continue or happen again (the future).

The multidimensional nature of betrayal trauma has serious implications for healing and treatment. To heal from traumatic experiences, emotional and physical safety are required. As Freyd has said, "Because during trauma it is usually not safe or possible for individuals to consciously access their emotional reactions or experiences, awareness often emerges after trauma ceases."[1] Betrayed partners often enter therapy or seek healing before emotional and sometimes physical safety have been acquired. This complicates the healing process and can create a one-step-forward-two-steps-back dynamic in treatment as both the partner and their helpers attempt to deal with the ongoing revelations, sense of threat, and lack of emotional safety created by repeated rounds of discovery or fear of future betrayal.

Not only are partners in the middle of a multidimensional trauma, but they are also dealing with a situation that is incredibly *dynamic*, shifting shape and form from minute to minute as new information is revealed, dots connect, and new understanding dawns.

The dynamic nature of sexual betrayal creates a situation in constant flux, as there are changes in significance, severity, and impact with every new discovery. As details of the sexual behaviors surface, some partners face health or legal issues. Others discover devastating financial consequences. Some face public scrutiny and shame if the cheating partner's behavior was revealed through an employer, a church community, social media, or some other public forum. These unfolding consequences repeatedly alter the landscape of betrayal.

The multidimensional and dynamic nature of sexual betrayal means that partners do not yet know how to find the edges of their traumatic experience. When someone's house burns down and they lose everything, as horrible as that is, there is a sense that the event is over, the level of damage and loss can be assessed, and the rebuilding process can begin.

Not so with betrayal trauma. Betrayal trauma often feels uncontained, as though there are no edges. Betrayed partners can't figure out when the lying and cheating began, are panic-stricken that it may never end, and feel hope drain away as the hits of discovery keep coming. Coping capacities become overwhelmed and they enter a state of long-term chronic insecurity and emotional and psychological danger.

The multidimensional dynamic nature of betrayal trauma makes it a unique type of trauma to both experience and treat. Therapists and clients are joining together not to deal with something that has ended and that both parties can wrap their hearts and minds around and begin to address; instead, therapists and clients join in an unfolding shape-shifting experience that changes daily, hourly, and even minute-by-minute.

WHAT MAKES TRAUMA COMPLEX?

A simple definition of trauma comes from Dr. Norman Wright, who defined trauma as a separation from safety. This elegantly sums up what happens when we experience betrayal. We are instantly separated from our sense of safe connection with our significant other, who has suddenly become dangerous and painful. Author Tara Brach offers another definition, saying, "Trauma is when we have encountered an out of control, frightening experience that has disconnected us from all sense of resourcefulness or safety or coping or love." This expands our understanding by pointing out that trauma separates us from safety with our partner, but it also separates us from ourselves as we are suddenly disconnected from our usual resources and coping skills.

Judith Herman, in her book *Trauma and Recovery* in 1992, was the first to define *complex* trauma. Since then, others have built on her original concepts, further developing our understanding of this important topic. Complex trauma is most often associated with children who experience various types of relational and repeated violations during key developmental moments. However, it can also be applied to cumulative adversities experienced by cultures, groups, and communities. *And* it can be applied to adults who have experienced chronic relational trauma (for instance, ongoing sexual and emotional betrayal) that destroys the foundational trust in their primary relationship.

Herman and other researchers identified seven traumatic stress reactions resulting from complex trauma. These reactions are: 1) Alterations in regulation of affective impulses; 2) Alterations in attention and consciousness; 3) Somatization and/or medical problems; 4) Alterations in self-perception; 5) Alterations in perception of the perpetrator; 6) Alterations in relationship to others; 7) Alterations in systems of meaning.[2]

I believe these seven symptoms fall into two broad categories of impact for betrayed partners: 1) emotional dysregulation, and 2) relational disconnection. Let's take a closer look at these below.

Emotional Dysregulation

Our brains and our bodies are in a co-regulating dance every minute of every day. When we become emotionally activated, whether through fear, excitement, or something else, our Autonomic Nervous System (ANS) signals changes to our breathing, heart rate, blood pressure, etc. As a result, emotions are felt first in the body as affect. Affect is important to understand because we are so programmed to live in our mental minds that we often forget that before our minds recognize we are feeling something, our bodies have already responded.

For example, I have a phobia of spiders. I can handle the little guys but if they get past a certain size, I am unable to function in the face of them. If I were to see a big spider crawling across my desk, I would respond as though someone had just pulled the pin on a grenade under me. My brain would immediately send signals to my body that I am in danger! My body would respond. My heart would pound, my face would flush, my breathing would elevate, I would scream, and I would jump as far away as possible (can you tell this has happened before?). Only then would I consciously register fear and panic as the emotions I am feeling. This would all happen in a split second, but notice the order in which it happens. The brain registers danger, the body responds, and then the mind registers what is happening and gives it the meaning of "I'm terrified of spiders."

Betrayal creates distressing and disruptive affective states that interrupt our normal functioning. Once we are dysregulated, our minds get involved by interpreting our body's distress and giving it meaning. A stomach full of butterflies may be interpreted as "I'm afraid" by one person and "I'm excited" by another. The meaning we give to the sensations and signals our body sends us following betrayal are based on what we already believe about ourselves, our partner, our relationships, and our place in the world.

When trauma occurs, the ANS shifts into high gear almost instantly and the body ratchets up into a state of threat preparedness. The body registers danger and sends signals throughout preparing to fight back, run away, or, if those are not possible, to freeze or shut down. The body is created to respond to stress in this way and then to calm itself back into a balanced state of being—alert yet relaxed.

The ANS has two branches; both branches are involved in different ways in how we regulate ourselves throughout the day. The Sympathetic Nervous System (SNS) is the branch that amps up in response to threat and danger. It connects from our brain, down through our spinal cord, and out to the different organs in our bodies. When activated, the sympathetic branch sends us into a hyper-aroused or hypervigilant affective state as our body prepares to either fight the threat or flee and seek safety. When we are in a hyper-aroused affective state, we can be anxious, revved up, hyper-alert, enraged, and agitated.

The other branch of the ANS is called the Parasympathetic Nervous System (PNS). Think of this system as your brakes. The PNS helps us to calm down, to be in a state of rest and relaxation. When our sympathetic branch gets activated and sends us into fight or flight, the parasympathetic system responds by pumping the brakes and sending out its own set of signals and hormones to help the body to calm back down. Breathing and heart rate return to normal and the body once again enters a state of alert restfulness.

Our PNS plays one other important role in responding to threat. Dr. Stephen Porges's Polyvagal Theory identifies the PNS as a key actor in the third common threat response: *freeze*. Instead of being revved up we are going to shut down. As the sense of danger and threat overcomes our body's coping capacities, it puts our physical system into a state of freeze to manage the overwhelm. When this happens, numbness, depression, paralysis, denial, avoidance, and dissociation shape our experience of trauma.

When infidelity occurs, betrayed partners enter a state of prolonged emotional threat and danger. Because of the multidimensional and dynamic nature of sexual betrayal, the threat response system repeatedly activates. Instead of acting as an emergency brake system, this state of high activation becomes chronic. Because of this, betrayed partners often find themselves attempting to handle life with a chronically activated threat system. This creates profound emotional dysregulation that often lasts many weeks, months, or even years.

Below are the three key symptoms of complex trauma that contribute to chronic emotional dysregulation.

1. **Alterations in regulation of affective impulses.** What this means in plain language is that we are now riding an emotional rollercoaster where our emotions are big and change rapidly and often. Our ability to remain calm and to not be swept away by these heated emotions is limited thanks to the chronic state of activation in our bodies.
2. **Alterations in attention and consciousness.** When our body's threat response system is activated, it impacts our prefrontal cortex—the part of our brain that helps us to pay attention, focus, make decisions, and assign meaning to what is happening. As a result, betrayed partners report difficulty in concentrating, remembering things, tracking information, and staying present.
3. **Somatization and/or medical problems.** Prolonged stress impacts health significantly. Betrayed partners report an astonishing array of health problems surfacing after discovery of betrayal, ranging from diagnosable ailments such as gastritis, chronic fatigue, high blood pressure, adrenal failure, etc., to clusters of mystery symptoms that no one can accurately diagnose but that the betrayed partner feels acutely in the form of bodily-based pain and discomfort.

Author and researcher Dan Siegel coined the term *window of tolerance* to define the state we are in when our nervous systems are well-regulated. When we are in our window of tolerance, we can access our thinking and reasoning, connect to our resourcefulness, problem-solve, and make decisions. We take in information, process it, and integrate it into our lives. We can meet challenges and function well.

When our sympathetic or parasympathetic systems fire in response to threat and danger we can stay within our window of tolerance and respond if the threat is something we can handle. Someone cutting us off in traffic may momentarily make us stressed, but most of the time, we can frown or say a few choice words and go on our way without it truly disrupting us.

Other stressors or traumas, like sexual betrayal, can overwhelm our coping capacities, and when that happens, we are bumped out of our window of tolerance. When we leave our window of tolerance, our functioning can be compromised, and we can begin to reach for ways to cope that may surprise us. Being bumped outside our window of tolerance is a neurobiological event. Our body, brain, and mind all move into dysregulation.

Relational Disconnection

I believe that at its core all trauma is relational. Whether that trauma results from a car wreck, a tornado, a wartime event, or being cheated on, it impacts at a minimum our relationship with ourselves. Often, it also impacts our relationship with our higher power (or our larger sense of safety and trust in the world around us) and our relationship with others, especially our spouse, close friends, and family.

When we experience betrayal, it shatters our assumptions and perceptions about how the world or our relationships operate. This creates relational disconnection, as we begin to feel that we cannot trust ourselves, others, or our higher power to operate the way we have come to expect. The new scary events separate us from safe connection with ourselves, others, and larger systems of meaning.

Below are the four complex trauma symptoms that fall under the category of relational disconnection.

1. **Alterations in self-perception.** Betrayed partners sustain loss after relational loss. We not only lose the partner we thought we had, but we lose ourselves. In the aftermath of betrayal, when emotional dysregulation has impaired our functioning and elevated our anxiety to crippling levels, it can feel like the joyful person we thought we were no longer exists, as we are now frequently fearful, restricted, isolated, exhausted, alienated, and depressed.

2. **Alterations in perception of the perpetrator.** When our significant other cheats on us and systematically lies and manipulates to cover it up, they become a stranger to us. We thought we knew who they were. But discovery shatters the front-facing life of our significant other and reveals a hidden double-life. This discovery permanently alters our understanding of who our partner is, and we can become preoccupied with trying to sort out our relationship to this new stranger in our lives.

3. **Alterations in relationship to others.** Experiencing relational trauma that has betrayal at its core makes us want to curl up in a ball and protect our heart. Doubts about our ability to accurately perceive who others are make it easy for us to distance ourselves in relationships. After all, we were wrong about the person closest to us, so maybe we are wrong about others, too. Feelings of doubt and mistrust about others' motives and authenticity can cause us to drift toward isolation.

4. **Alterations in systems of meaning.** For some of us, discovery challenges our faith in the goodness or reliability of our higher power. How could such pain be part of a loving higher power's plan? For others, grief about the loss of the relationship we thought we had colors our ability to feel hopeful about the

rest of life. All aspects of life seem tainted by the betrayal, and we can feel hopeless and despairing about whether life will ever again feel meaningful, purposeful, or joyful.

This is our roadmap for understanding the experience of sexual betrayal. We start with the three injuries (the attachment injury, the emotional and psychological injury, and the sexual injury), knowing that betrayal lies at the heart of each. We understand that our experience is multidimensional and dynamic, affecting the past, present, and future as new discoveries cause our reality to shape-shift over and over again. Lastly, it is a complex trauma negatively impacting both emotional regulation and relational safety and connection.

My hope is that this big-picture perspective will help you begin to put words to your experience. Being given language to describe your internal world can help make things feel more manageable and contained.

In the remainder of the book, we are going to deeply explore the three injuries identified above. We start with the attachment injury because it lays the foundation for all that follows.

PART ONE

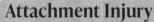

INTRODUCTION

THE ATTACHMENT INJURY AT THE HEART OF BETRAYAL

I wish that when I was going through the many rounds of betrayal I experienced, I knew then what I know today. More information would have helped me feel normal, and I would have been able to be kinder to myself when my emotions and behavior felt out of control. At the time, I did not understand the science and theory behind the way that we pair-bond and what happens when that attachment is damaged. I only knew that discovering sexual betrayal in my relationship changed me overnight.

Every betrayed partner is dealt two blows at once when they discover the cheating partner's sexual behavior, and I was no different. Blow number one was the gut-punch of betrayal—a breathtaking breach in trust that changed my relationship in permanent ways. Blow number two was the shocking realization that my spouse had been extravagantly and expertly lying to me and manipulating my reality.

While no one physically hit me, those blows still smashed into my heart and instantaneously changed my life.

That moment of discovery became a demarcation point, a streak in the sand separating my life into before and after. Before, I felt secure in my relationship. I trusted my spouse, felt hopeful about our future together, and found joy, laughter, and connection with him. After, I felt anxious, revved up, stressed out, fearful, disorganized, and emotionally chaotic.

My experience was not unusual. When betrayal occurs, it severely injures our sense of safe connection to our partner. The abrupt loss of safety creates enormous desperation for those who have been betrayed. This feeling of desperation cannot be overstated. It is a tsunami rolled inside a hurricane and spun up inside the center of a tornado. Betrayed partners report feeling unhinged with grief, pain, and anger in the aftermath of discovery. As they are unmoored from their primary relationship, they are set loose upon a sea of danger, and their bodily-based attachment system goes into unmitigated stress and distress over the loss of their safe connection.

In Part One of the book, we dive into the information I wish had been available to me when suffering my own perfect storm of betrayal. This section explores the science behind the emotions and reactions that create the attachment injury at the heart of betrayal.

We begin by looking at what it means to become attached to our partner and the attachment styles we develop in early childhood that shape our relational bonds. We will explore the binds that betrayal creates as our attachment systems are caught in a no-win situation. Then we wrap up with an exploration of three behavior patterns stemming from partner reactions to the attachment injury: battling for empathy, repudiating shame, and declawing the tiger.

Love does not begin
and end the way we seem
to think it does.
Love is a battle, love is a war,
love is a growing up.

JAMES BALDWIN

CHAPTER THREE

WE ARE FAMILY:

Getting Attached

Our number one survival tool is our ability to bond with others. We are wired with an instinctual drive that motivates us to seek relational connection and, from that relational connection, to experience a sense of safety, security, and protection from danger.

It is important to understand that how we are attached to our significant other is not something we create only with our rational minds. Attachment happens at a physiological level and involves our bodies, our minds, and our emotions. John Bowlby, the father of attachment theory, considered attachment to be a psychobiological system made up of two parts: our body's emotional and physical ability to form attachments, and the behaviors we exhibit in our primary relationships.[1]

When we pair up into long-term relationships, we begin a process of bonding with one another that is a beautiful and profound intertwining of our lives. In this mysterious attachment, we start to physically operate as one biological organism. As Amir Levine and Rachel Heller state in their groundbreaking book *Attached,* "Numerous studies show that once we become attached to someone, the two of us form one physiological unit. Our partner regulates our blood pressure, our heart rate, our breathing, and the levels of hormones in our blood."²

While we experience relational connections to numerous others—friends, co-workers, family members—our primary attachment figures occupy a singular place in our lives. They are our parents initially. Later, they are our primary partner, the person we turn to for support, protection, and to be emotionally held within a felt sense of connectedness.

According to attachment theorists, we look to our attachment figures for four key things:

1. **Proximity:** We want to be near them or in their presence frequently.
2. **Safe Haven:** They provide us with a sense of comfort, support, protection, and relief when we need it.
3. **Secure Base:** They are the home from which we launch into the rest of life and to which we return at the end of the day.
4. **Separation Distress:** When we feel disconnected from them either emotionally or physically, we begin to feel distress and seek reconnection.³

We used to believe that as we grew up, we became independent and no longer needed people. In fact, this idea of independence is deeply embedded in our American cultural psyche. We often hold independence as the key marker of what it means to be a mature adult both individually and in our relationships.

Yet attachment research regarding how we bond and how those bonds impact us has shown that we've based this belief on a profound misunderstanding of how humans are wired. We now know that our dependency needs don't go away as we mature. They stay with us and are transferred from our caregivers to our adult relationships. As adults, we are no longer physically and emotionally dependent in the same ways we were as children, but we are still vulnerable in our relational connections. And our most important adult relationship is the one we share with our spouse or significant other.

In the 1980s, attachment researchers Mario Mikulincer and Phillip Shaver found that "infants' bonds with parents and romantic or marital partners' bonds with each other are variants of a single core process." Their research showed that "for every documented feature of attachment there is a parallel feature of love, and for most documented features of love there is either a documented or a plausible infant parallel."[4]

This means that our needs for proximity or physical closeness, for a safe haven and secure base with our adult attachment figures (our romantic partners), are similar to our needs as children with our parents or caregivers. We do not outgrow our relational needs for safety and secure attachment with others. They are with us throughout our lifespan.

In adulthood, as our bond grows, perhaps through getting married, combining our homes, having children together, and working toward common goals, we become more and more interdependent with our partner. This is not codependency. This is healthy, normal, mutual dependency. It is what makes relationships fulfilling and sought after.

By entrusting ourselves to our partner in these profoundly important ways, we make ourselves deeply vulnerable to and emotionally dependent on that person. We give our partner the keys to parts of ourselves that no one else gets to access. We invite our partner into the most sacred parts of who we are.

We all want this special someone to attach to and intermingle our lives with. In fact, attachment researchers often talk about the paradox of attachment: attachment to and dependency on another person strengthens us as individuals.

The better our relationships are in terms of providing us with a sense of "I can depend on you," the more we are able to move fully into the rest of our lives, face insecurity, and take risks. In this way, our adult relationships mirror our relationship with our parents as children; both, when functioning well, provide us with a secure base from which we can enter the wider world with confidence. As Levine and Heller so beautifully say, "The more effectively dependent people are on one another, the more independent and daring they become."[5]

YOUR ATTACHMENT STYLE

One of the biggest tasks we face throughout our lives is learning how to balance our need for connection with our need for autonomy. As Mikulincer and Shaver state, "When attachment relationships function well, a person learns that distance and autonomy are completely compatible with closeness and reliance on others."[6]

This task—balancing connection with individuation, and how well we manage this task throughout our lifespans—is primarily determined by the level of security in the bonds we form with our parents or primary caregivers when we are infants and children.

In their article, "Treating Attachment Injured Couples," Sandra Naaman and colleagues offer two core questions that summarize our attachment needs:

- Am I worthy of love and care?
- Can I count on others in times of distress and need?

How we answer these questions determines how we attach to and relate with others over the course of our lives.[7] And how we answer these questions also determines how we see ourselves: as worthy or unworthy of consistent love, care, and protection.

Bowlby talked about the "internal working models" of attachment that we all develop and apply to both ourselves and others. These internal working models are the assumptions and expectations we develop based on the experiences we have with others and how they respond to us. Their response to us, especially early in life, creates our sense of value and worthiness.

My client Sally grew up with a mother who was intermittently available, sometimes providing attention and care but sometimes preoccupied, ignoring Sally's needs. Through repeated experiences of inconsistent availability, Sally learned that others are not dependable, and she can only focus their attention and get her needs met if she behaves in certain ways.

Sadly, for Sally, this lack of consistent secure attachment with her mother left her with an unconscious but rooted belief that she is not worthy of secure connection with others. Deep down, she believes there must be something defective in her that caused her mother to be unresponsive to her needs as a child. As a result, she enters her adult relationships with unconscious shame about herself that creates self-doubt and insecurity about whether anyone will ever love her the way she desperately longs to be loved. Her assumptions from childhood—that others will not be there for her the way she needs them to because there is something defective or unworthy in her—are the model that she carries into the world and her adult-life relationships.

Like Sally, we all have working models of attachment based on what we experienced with our parents or primary caregivers. These working models tend to fall into three primary patterns called attachment styles. As Mikulincer and Shaver state, attachment styles are the "patterns of expectations, needs, emotions, and social behavior that result from a particular history of attachment experiences, usually beginning in relationships with parents."[8]

We each have an attachment style that grew out of how we first attached to our parents. These patterns are referred to as secure, anxious, and avoidant attachment.[9]

Secure Attachment

Secure attachment is created when an infant/child is responded to consistently by their parents or other primary caregivers with safety, comfort, protection, and guidance. When the distress of disconnection occurs, it is quickly repaired, and safety is restored. This child will grow into a securely attached adult who is able to be both intimately bonded with others and to function with autonomy when appropriate.

Here is the script that might guide the internal world of a securely attached adult: "If I encounter an obstacle and/or become distressed, I can approach a significant other for help; they are likely to be available and supportive; I will experience relief and comfort as a result of proximity to this person; I can then return to other activities."[10]

A child who experiences secure attachment is likely to become an adult who approaches relationships expecting that their needs will be met most of the time and that when they are not, they will be okay because they can adapt and care for themselves until they are able to reestablish connection. The important thing to note about securely attached individuals is that their internal working model *assumes* or *expects* that their needs will be met most of the time. They believe they are worthy of love, attention, and protection, and that others will be responsive when reached for. Best of all, their assumption of worthiness allows them to rely on and trust their abilities to care for themselves when others cannot be there for them. According to attachment studies, about 50% of the population is securely attached.[11]

Anxious Attachment

We can become anxiously attached if, as an infant/child, we experience intermittent caregiving where sometimes our needs are met and sometimes not; sometimes we are paid attention to and sometimes ignored; sometimes our distress is comforted and sometimes it is not. Thus, we learn our needs may or may not get met.

Anxious attachment comes from activation of the fight response as the child attempts repeatedly to capture the attention of caregivers so they can get their needs met consistently. Because sometimes their efforts work and their caregiver responds, they are motivated to continue this hyper-activated response to distress as a means of attempting to restore safety and security through reconnection.

A child who learns this type of anxious, hyper-activated attachment strategy will often become an adult who is anxious about their closeness to others, preoccupied with their partner's availability, and uses fight or pursuit behaviors to protest the distress experienced from real or anticipated disconnection from their partner.[12]

An anxiously attached adult has an internal working model built around doubt about self and others. First, there is doubt that the self is worthy of consistent care, attention, and protection. Then there is doubt that others are able or willing to provide that care, attention, and protection. Anxiously attached adults bring this assumption of insecurity to their relationships, and when their doubt is triggered, they will fight or pursue their partner to try to get a response that alleviates the pain of self-doubt.

Another way of saying this is, "My connection to you means I am worthy. My disconnection from you means I am not worthy. Therefore, any feeling of disconnection sends me into anxiety and distress and stirs shame. I must get connection reestablished to alleviate my anxiety and shame, and I will invest enormous energy in pursuing you to get reconnected."

This is called anxious attachment. About 20% of the population falls into this category.[13]

Avoidant Attachment

If, as an infant or child, we grow up with caregivers who disapprove of, punish, or withdraw when we express our neediness or vulnerability, we can learn to hide or repress these needs so that we have a better chance of staying connected to our caregiver. This coping mechanism activates the flight response, and we learn to deal with attachment needs and insecurities alone.[14] Bowlby refers to this coping strategy as compulsive self-reliance, which beautifully articulates the core of this attachment style.[15]

A child who experiences this type of deactivated attachment strategy will often grow into an adult with an avoidant attachment style. These individuals have the same attachment needs and core relational desires as everyone else. However, because they were not responded to when they expressed their needs as children, they learned to repress or disconnect from these needs. As adults, they may not recognize their need for connection and secure bonding because they have become so used to dissociating from and repressing those needs. Again, what is important to remember about the avoidant attachment strategy is that these individuals feel the same arousal (need for connection) of their attachment system when disconnection or threat occurs; they have simply learned to repress or dissociate from it.

Avoidant individuals' internal working model assumes that closeness will bring pain, danger, or overwhelm. As a result, avoidant individuals may not register emotional disconnection in their relationships, as they learned early on to tolerate disconnection as the normal state of things. They may also have learned to dissociate from the distressing feelings that disconnection brings. They may actively avoid connection due to fear that the connection will be fleeting and then vanish or that the connection will only bring conflict or pain. Individuals with an avoidant attachment style make up about 25% of the population.[16]

Anxious Avoidant Attachment

There is a fourth attachment style called anxious avoidant attachment; about 5% of the population falls into this category.[17] We will explore this attachment style more in the next chapter.

ATTACHMENT STYLES AND BETRAYAL

Our attachment systems operate at an unconscious, bodily-based level that is deeply intertwined with our threat response system. The way we react to betrayal is impacted by our attachment system and the style of coping we have developed to manage disconnection and relational threat. For those who are insecurely attached (whether anxious or avoidant), the experience of betrayal will activate old fears and assumptions about both ourselves and our partner, significantly exacerbating our level of distress and trauma symptoms.

Even if we began our adult life and relationships with a secure attachment style, this can change when we encounter significant relational trauma like sexual betrayal. If it is true that when we attach to someone who is healthy and functional, it feels good and provides a sense of security, grounding, safety, and wholeness, then the opposite can also be true. When we attach to someone who is cheating on us or is sexually addicted, it can affect our physical, mental, emotional, and spiritual health in teeth-rattling ways. Instead of feeling grounded, we are in free fall. Instead of security, we experience fear. Because of the betrayal, our partner now feels like a threat to our well-being rather than a source of comfort. As a result, even those with a secure attachment style will experience significant distress when encountering sexual betrayal. For a while, it may feel like we are operating the way an insecurely attached person might. This is normal, and we are going to see why as we move forward in our exploration of the attachment injury caused by betrayal.

ARE WE REALLY ATTACHED?

One of the questions betrayed partners frequently ask is, "How can I be attached to someone who is not actually available for emotional intimacy or connection?" They also say, "I might be attached to my spouse, but they are not attached to me. They are attached to their sexual addiction or their affair partner, but they haven't been available for connection with me for years, so they aren't attached to me at all."

This question and the follow-up statement make perfect sense. If you haven't felt able to emotionally connect to your significant other in months or years and haven't felt that they really "had your back," then how can you be truly attached to them? And how can they be attached to you?

The fact is that our attachment system is psychobiological. In other words, our attachment system includes our minds, emotions, and bodily-based reactions. We attach to our significant other not just with our minds and emotions but also with our bodies (remember, we even regulate each other's bodily-based systems like heart rate, blood pressure, and hormone levels).

What this means is that being attached to our significant other is separate from that attachment feeling good. We can have attachment relationships that feel bad and fall anywhere along a continuum from challenging to toxic to dangerous. This has to do with how the attachment bond in the relationship is functioning and whether we have secure or insecure attachment with our partner. Even if the bond does not feel good or is not functioning well, we are still attached.

Now that we understand how we attach and what attachment styles are, let's explore the core issue for betrayed partners: attachment ambivalence. Understanding attachment ambivalence—what it is, why it happens, and the reactions it creates—is vital to understanding partner betrayal and treating it effectively.

ADDITIONAL RESOURCES FOR YOU

To learn more about your attachment style, watch the free video **How Your Attachment Style Impacts Your Relationship** by Michelle Mays. Visit michellemays.com/attachment-style-video to watch.

> Terror increases the
> need for attachment,
> even if the source of comfort
> is also the source of the terror.
>
> — BESSEL A. VAN DER KOLK

CHAPTER FOUR

I LOVE YOU, I LOVE YOU NOT:

The Dilemma of Attachment Ambivalence

Dictionary.com describes *ambivalence* as "the coexistence within an individual of positive and negative feelings toward the same person, object or action, simultaneously drawing him or her in opposite directions."

For me, as with most betrayed partners, the betrayal I experienced put me at war with myself. The hurt and pain caused by the betrayal now lay side-by-side battling with my feelings of love and connection. Being betrayed by the person I loved and trusted more than anyone else put me on an emotional rack and pulled my heart in opposite directions until I was begging for mercy.

Part of me felt anger, fear, disgust, and loathing for my cheating spouse. That part of me wanted nothing to do with him. I wanted him to go away and get fixed and only come back if and when he could be a decent partner. I wanted him to feel the same kind of pain he was causing me, to know what it felt like to be on the receiving end of his behaviors. I hated him, felt like I didn't know him, couldn't trust him, and didn't understand him.

But then, damn it, there was the other part of me that still loved my spouse; most days I even liked him. This part of me was invested in building a life with him. I had good memories with him. I had plans and hopes and dreams with him. Despite all that had happened, he was the person I counted on for companionship, support, comfort, and help.

This created an enormous dilemma. The person who caused the problem and pain was also the person that I most wanted and needed to hear me when I talked, hold me when I cried, and validate my feelings. These two powerful parts of me, living within the same heart and body, made me feel at war with myself.

THE ORIGINS OF THE DILEMMA

Bowlby identified human attachment as a motivational system, meaning that our need to connect is primal and instinctual. This motivational system drives us to seek connection with our attachment figure(s) when we experience threat or distress.

This is why when something stressful happens during our day, we will often call or text our partner. Our attachment system activates in response to the stress and prompts us to reach out for the comfort of connection.

Our attachment systems drive us to operate according to the primal rule: live together, die alone. Our most basic coping skill as humans is our ability to bond with other humans to ensure our (and their) survival. In modern culture, we do not live in communal villages or even large families anymore. Instead, our emotional, physical, and psychological survival has come to rest primarily on one singular attachment: our romantic partner. We have other friends and family, but our romantic partner is our true significant other, providing us with the safe base we need to enter the world with confidence and feel protected from danger. Our primary partner is the person we are most likely to turn to in times of stress, threat, or discomfort.

What happens then, when our romantic partner, our primary attachment figure, the one person we rely on most, betrays us?

Any disconnection from our primary attachment figure creates distress for us. Think about a time when you were talking to your partner, and you felt missed by them. Perhaps they didn't understand what you were saying, or they didn't pay attention and respond in the way you needed. Maybe you left the conversation and felt uneasy or tense. Or maybe the conversation turned into a conflict as you struggled to get your partner to respond to you.

The conflict we feel in such situations is the result of our attachment system reacting to the momentary loss of secure connection with our safe base. Often, our sense of well-being is only restored when we can resolve the conflict or close the distance and reestablish a sense of safe connection with one another.

If regular everyday disconnections threaten our attachment systems and send us into stress and tension, then imagine the conundrum that unfolds when our significant other cheats, lies, and hides evidence to cover up their betrayal.

When faced with this level of danger from our significant other, our attachment system fires hard and fast, and the response inside us is primitive. We do not have a rational, reasoned, gracefully equipped response. We have a screaming banshee caveperson reaction. We lose our minds. Completely and totally. We are under threat, and we might not survive. Our safe base has just tried to kill us—that is how it feels to the body, and our body reacts from a primal self-preserving instinct that says, "Restore safety now, by any means and at any cost!"

Attachment ambivalence arises out of our core need for relational safety and security from the very person who has erased it. Ambivalence enters the picture when a second motivational system, our threat response system, activates. Like our attachment system, our threat response system is primal and instinctual; its sole focus is on our survival, whether physically or emotionally. Once activated, it prompts us to fight or move away from danger and to safety.

Do you begin to see the dilemma here? Typically, as Bowlby writes, "The fear behavioral system and the attachment behavioral system in humans are generally well aligned: from infancy, we wish to escape to our attachment figures."[1] However, when we experience betrayal, these two systems come into conflict with one another.

Our attachment system says, "You are distressed, reach for your significant other. Connection will make you feel better." At the exact same time, our threat response system says, "You are under threat, fight or run away so you can be safe." Instead of protecting us from the tiger as promised, our partner has become the tiger and mauled us. Instead of having our back, our partner turned and plunged the knife in to the hilt. Our threat response system demands that we fight or move away and distance ourselves from the danger our partner represents.

Because our significant other now represents both our primary attachment figure and the source of danger, our two primal safety-seeking systems begin to war with each other.

This is the attachment ambivalence created by betrayal. The dilemma can make our emotions and behavior unpredictable, chaotic, and confusing, even to ourselves. While we are spitting mad and crying our eyes out, we also want our partner to say something to soothe our pain and ease our distress. While we want them to move out of the house, we also want them to hold us while we cry. While we know they are lying, we also desperately want to believe they are telling the truth. While we never want them to touch us again, we also want the comfort and connection of making love.

THE CYCLE OF AMBIVALENCE

Most betrayed partners caught in the throes of attachment ambivalence experience this emotional tug-of-war as a cyclical dynamic that they rotate through during the initial weeks and months after the discovery of betrayal. This cycle can happen multiple times in one day. It can also be experienced as smaller cycles happening within larger cycles.

Here is what the cycle looks like:

You wake up in the morning, lying in bed next to your spouse, who you recently discovered cheated on you. You are warm, sleepy, and cuddled up next to one another. For a few moments, you enjoy the sensation of comfort, safety, and connection that coming out of sleep next to your loved one provides.

Suddenly, though, you realize a feeling of dread lurking in your body. A sensation that something is terribly wrong, if only you could remember what. Seconds later, memory slams into you as you recall that your spouse cheated on you and has recently been diagnosed with sex addiction. You don't know all the details yet, but you know enough to have your world torn apart.

You roll away from your spouse as your body becomes rigid and filled with fear and anger, and your mind begins to race with thoughts and questions about *what* he did, *why* he did it, and what it means.

You ask yourself, "How could he? What was he thinking? How do I survive this?"

You get up out of bed; get the kids up; start the routine of helping them out the door to school. You are a shell, your body showing up to shove breakfast at them and gather backpacks and homework while your mind is far away, furiously trying to wrap itself around this new reality.

Your spouse wakes and showers and gets ready for work. You do not speak to him. You do not look at him. Your body radiates anger, shock, pain, and confusion. Your energy accuses him at every turn, communicating as loudly as a scream your distress about losing your lover, who you thought you knew, to this stranger who just crawled out of your bed.

Your spouse tries to talk to you, to ask if you are okay, if there is anything he can do. He tells you for the umpteenth time how sorry he is. You say nothing, waiting for him to leave before you completely lose control and smack him across his familiar face.

Your spouse leaves for work, and you spend the day just trying to get through. You receive several texts from him with more checking in, more apologies. You ignore all of them, steeling yourself against his pleas. You spend some time crying. You watch TV without seeing it. You try to clean the kitchen and think about the fact that you really should do some work because even though you work from home you still have deadlines. Instead of working, however, you have long, ranting, angry conversations with your spouse in your head, and finally you pick up the phone and have the fight for real.

The fight only makes you feel worse. Nothing got resolved, nothing got clarified, the pain and fear are still overwhelming, and your frustration at your spouse's inability to bring you any relief makes you want to howl. So, you climb under the covers and for a blessed few minutes you fall asleep from the sheer exhaustion of grief.

When you wake up, you feel like the life force has been drained out of you. You are shut down, numb. Once again, your body goes on autopilot as the kids come home from school and you start to get dinner on the table. About an hour later, your spouse walks in the door, looking exhausted and clearly unsure of the welcome he will receive.

You sit down to have dinner together and, as you both interact with the kids about their days, the air between you begins to thaw. Within the familiarity of a hundred other family dinners together, you begin to feel the numbness recede. When dinner is over, you both handle the evening routine of helping with homework, kicking the soccer ball around outside, playing a video game, etc. The fight slowly goes out of you as the evening unfolds; it has taken enormous energy to stay distant and protected all day, and you are exhausted and need relief.

You are no longer even angry by the time the kids are in bed and you and your spouse have retired to your room to lay on the bed and watch some TV. You are just sad and tired and sorely in need of comfort.

You roll toward your spouse, who immediately reaches out to tuck you into his side. You curl up against him and close your eyes while tears of relief and sadness roll down your cheeks. You let yourself be held and feel the comfort of being connected once again. You talk some, but not angry words. You both are careful to not say or do anything to ruin the moment of connection that you both need so desperately. Maybe you even make love, letting your bodies come together in a moment of intimate connection. Then you go to sleep, and you sleep the sleep of the relieved.

The next morning, you get up and talk with your spouse about the day. You kiss each other goodbye when you head off to work. You still don't feel like yourself, but you don't feel like you did yesterday either.

Throughout the morning you exchange a couple of texts and make plans for managing the kid's schedules that evening.

At lunchtime, you take a break from work, get something to eat, and plop yourself in front of the TV to watch your favorite show. But, uh oh. In this episode your favorite character, who is married to your next favorite character, finds out her husband has been cheating on her. Now you hate the husband. In fact, you hate him so much that you even hate the actor who plays him.

Suddenly you are back in the vortex. The pain and agony of betrayal sweep over you and the anger you feel takes your breath away. You text your spouse and tell him about the episode and what a lying, cheating asshole he is, just like the guy on the show. You let your anger fly, verbally pushing your spouse away from you as hard as you can as your need for protection from him comes rushing back.

That evening you are either fighting or not speaking and you go to bed, backs turned away from each other in an emotional standoff of pain.

The next morning you wake up and . . .

That is the cycle of ambivalence. The simultaneous need for distance to feel safe and connection to feel safe creates a push/pull dynamic for most betrayed partners.

UNDERSTANDING THE CYCLE

On the next page is a graphic showing the cyclical nature of attachment ambivalence and how it pulls you in and out of connection and disconnection as you search for a safe place to land after discovering betrayal. Understanding what is happening at each phase of the cycle is important, so we are going to take the time to fully unpack each phase.

Attachment Ambivalence Cycle

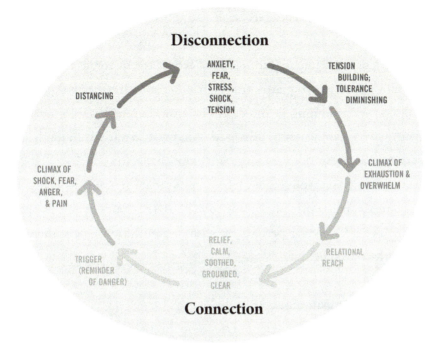

Disconnection

Let's start at the top of the cycle with disconnection. When faced with danger, our threat response systems tell us to fight or run away. Both impulses have one primary intent: to get us back to safety. However, in the case of betrayal trauma, the threat is coming from our primary attachment and source of security. To disconnect from the danger, we must sacrifice our connection to our significant other along with the benefits that this sense of connection brings.

Tension Building/Tolerance Diminishing

As a result, disconnection through distancing from our partner relieves us, but it also creates anxiety, fear, stress, and tension because we are farther away from our safe base. Most of us can only maintain this type of disconnection for short periods because it produces so much anxiety. As we enter the state of disconnection, we feel tension start to build and our tolerance for managing this tension starts to decrease.

The length of time we can tolerate being in the disconnection phase has much to do with our attachment style. Securely attached individuals will not stay too long in the disconnection, as it creates separation distress that is not easily tolerated. Anxiously attached individuals cannot stay distant for very long, as it is too anxiety-producing, so they will seek reconnection sooner. However, avoidant individuals may use disconnection as a primary coping tool. Thus, they can stay in this part of the cycle for longer periods because disconnection brings them a higher level of relief.

Climax of Exhaustion and Overwhelm

Regardless of our attachment style, most betrayed partners can stay distant from their significant other only for a limited period. Over time, the disconnection and the tension of the separation distress mounts. Often, this will end in a climax of exhaustion and overwhelm with the betrayed partner simply feeling unable to maintain the disconnection any longer. The need to feel the relief and comfort that being connected provides kicks in.

Relational Reach

At this point, the betrayed partner moves back toward the unfaithful partner, seeking to reestablish some type of emotional connection with their primary attachment figure. This can look like it did in our example above, where the partner collapsed into sadness and grief and turned toward her spouse for comfort. Or it can look like having a big fight that ends with connection. This may seem odd, but often fighting is a form of pursuing connection with our partner. The fight is about trying to get our partner to pay attention to us and give us what we need to feel safely connected to them again.

Connection

In our desire to alleviate the separation distress caused by disconnection, it is normal to reach for the behaviors that historically have reassured us that we are safe, and our relational connection is secure. Moving toward our partner, reaching out verbally, physically, emotionally, and sexually makes perfect sense. Reconnection is profoundly *relieving*. For a few moments, as we come back into emotional and physical proximity with our partner and feel the reassurance that our partner is there for us, our stress and activation are eased. Our body calms, our mind clears, our fear is assuaged, and we can breathe again. We can take a break and get relief from the onslaught of stress reactions and stress-related chemicals flooding through us. We need this connection and, unconsciously, without knowing why, we have reached for it.

Trigger/Reminder of Danger

For most partners, the period of reconnection and relief is ended by a reminder of the betrayal. This occurs through some type of triggering thought, memory, or event. This trigger is often a shock to our system, as we relaxed our defenses to reconnect with our spouse.

Climax of Shock and Fear

The reminder that our spouse has cheated and lied jars us from our state of relief and plunges us back into fear, anger, and pain. Often, these emotions are intense and erratic because they come in reaction to the recent moment of connection. While we were connected, we forgot for a while that our partner was also the source of our pain. Now the pain comes howling to the surface as the betrayal is again front and center and the reality of the threat coming from the cheating partner sets in.

Distancing

Betrayed partners now push away from the cheating partner, scrambling for safety. But this time we are not seeking the safety of connection; we are seeking the safety of distance. Whether through fighting, withdrawing into silence, or physically removing ourselves, we create distance, hoping that it will somehow translate into emotional safety, and we won't be hurt again.

THE PLUNGE INTO DISORGANIZATION

Mary Ainsworth identified the three attachment styles we looked at in Chapter Three through experiments she conducted with infants and toddlers in the late 1960s and early 1970s, called the Strange Situation Procedure. In these experiments, she identified the secure, anxious, and avoidant attachment styles that we have already explored. However, there is a fourth attachment style that we have not yet discussed, and it is significantly relevant to understanding partner betrayal trauma and the impact of attachment ambivalence.

In 1986, Mary Main and Judith Solomon proposed a fourth attachment style based on information gathered in replicated Strange Situation studies. As with Ainsworth, they found that securely attached children seek proximity and connection with their parent and receive it; anxiously attached children persist in pursuing their parent and their parent eventually responds; avoidant children repress their attachment needs and, as a result, do not consciously feel distress. For some children, however, none of these strategies work reliably, so they use all of them at different times to get their need for safe connection met and the distress of disconnection and separation relieved.[2] Main and Solomon called this fourth attachment style *disorganized* attachment.

It is easy to think that disorganized attachment means that the individual is behaving chaotically and randomly, but this is not how Main and Solomon intended this attachment style to be interpreted. Instead, they were highlighting how typical attachment strategies that children use to try to reestablish safe connection sometimes get disrupted due to the ambivalence created by being unable to trust their caregiver. Instead of using the strategies a secure, anxious, or avoidant child might use, disorganized children try all the strategies, sometimes starting to move toward connection with the parent only to abort the attempt in the middle and turn away. In this way, many of the same behaviors seen in the other attachment styles are used, but they may be alternating quickly or cut off in the middle as the child is caught in the dilemma of dealing with an unsafe parent.[3]

Below is a quote from Dan Brown and David Elliot from their well-researched tome *Attachment Disturbances in Adults*. As you read it, notice the similarity between what causes disorganized attachment in infants and the dilemma of attachment ambivalence for betrayed partners.

> Main and Hess theorized that the fundamental problem for the disorganized infant is that the same primary attachment figure was both a source of security and a source of fear. They called the resulting experience "fear without solution" (quote from Lyons-Ruth & Jacobvitz, 1999, p. 549). This impossible dilemma, over time, results in contradictory attachment behaviors, such as

moving toward and moving away from the primary attachment figure. In other words, children with disorganized attachment develop a contradictory pattern of using both deactivating and hyper-activating attachment strategies, either alternating or simultaneously.[4]

While this attachment style is called *disorganized* when talking about children, it is referred to as *anxious-avoidant* or *fearful-avoidant* when applied to adults.

The reason I introduce this fourth attachment style is that for many betrayed partners, particularly those who are insecurely attached (whether anxious or avoidant), the weeks and months after discovery of sexual betrayal can thrust us into a period where our emotional reactions and behaviors mimic an anxious-avoidant attachment style. This is normal and to be expected. This plunge into disorganized attachment is created by the unique dilemma at the heart of betrayal trauma: experiencing betrayal at the hands of our primary attachment figure.

THE IMPOSSIBLE CHOICE

Nobody says it better than author and researcher Sue Johnson: "(Cheating) Partners, like past attachment figures, are then simultaneously a source of safety and a source of threat and every interaction is a potentially impossible choice between isolation and dangerous connection."[5]

This "impossible choice" is what drives the cycle of ambivalence that betrayed partners are caught in and creates the push-pull that dominates so much of the relational interaction between the betrayed partner and the unfaithful partner in the days, weeks, and months following discovery.

The way in which these attachment-based responses play out can look vastly different for each person. But awareness of them, and the awareness that our attachment system is very much involved in how we respond to the trauma of betrayal, opens opportunities to cope in healthier ways that move us toward healing.

It is important to remember that these responses are largely unconscious. Our bodies' systems are firing off messages to connect and disconnect instinctually. Betrayed partners are often confounded by their own behavior as they swing wildly through the phases of connection, disconnection, protest, despair, and detachment. And if we are confused by ourselves, imagine how unclear things look for the cheating partner who may be trying to be responsive but with absolutely no idea what is needed from one moment to the next.

I cannot say enough that this process is NORMAL. Attachment ambivalence is not a problem to be solved or a sign of dysfunction. It is the normal biological response to partner betrayal. The explanation I provide here is meant to help you understand yourself and what is happening to you in the aftermath of betrayal. Countless betrayed partners have talked to me about the relief they experienced when introduced to the concept of attachment ambivalence. As researcher and author Dan Siegel has said, we name it to tame it, meaning that when we have language to describe what is happening to us, it immediately helps to decrease our feeling of being out-of-control and to ground us in understanding.

My hope is that you will use the graphic of the attachment ambivalence cycle to help locate yourself at any given time. Being able to identify where you are in the process can invite new ways of managing the moment in which you find yourself. It moves you out of unconscious reaction into conscious awareness, and it is in awareness that your power to choose your response lies. Once you know where you are and what is happening, you can use your voice to ask for what you need (whether that is more space and protection or more closeness and connection) rather than acting out your needs in ways that may not ultimately serve you.

Now that we understand the phenomenon of attachment ambivalence, we are going to look at a complicating factor that amplifies and exacerbates this dynamic significantly: the element of shame.

Shame is a liar
and a story-stealer.

BRENÉ BROWN

CHAPTER FIVE

SHAMED IF YOU DO, SHAMED IF YOU DON'T:

Understanding the Shame Bind Created by Betrayal

"What does it say about me?"

This is one of the most common and revealing questions I hear from betrayed partners. "What does it say about me that I was cheated on?" they ask. "What does it say about me that I still love the person who cheated on me? What does it say about me that I want to try to save my relationship? What does it say about me that I've been cheated on before? What does it say about me that I want to leave the relationship? Is something wrong with me? Am I sick? Codependent? Weak?" Many questions hide in one.

At the heart of these questions is a feeling of shame. This shame latches on to how we feel about *ourselves*. Shame attaches to our hearts and taints our most significant relational longings, desires, needs, hopes, and wants with self-doubt, critical judgment, and insecurity. This shame haunts us, dogging our steps and making us question our decisions about ourselves and our relationship over and over again.

I call this *attachment shame* because it is a very specific type of shame felt by betrayed partners. It is shame about our experience of connection and disconnection with the person who hurt us and violated our trust. Attachment shame is woven throughout the experience of attachment ambivalence, unconsciously driving the betrayed partner's emotions and behaviors.

SHAME IS RELATIONAL

In her book *Understanding and Treating Chronic Shame*, Patricia DeYoung describes shame as a phenomenon that occurs when we experience relational disconnection in a moment of need. DeYoung says, "Shame is the experience of self-in-relation when 'in-relation' is ruptured or disconnected."[1]

As a result, shame is not an individual phenomenon. It is a relational dynamic that occurs between two people. DeYoung states, "[S]hame is seen not as an individual's response to a painful stimulus sequence, but as what happens in the interaction between one person's affective relational need and another person's response to the need. In short, shame is essentially a two-person experience."[2]

If we understand that shame is fundamentally a relational dynamic, then we next need to define shame. While we all instinctively know what shame is because we have all felt shame at one point or another, it is still helpful to define it.

DeYoung defines shame as "an experience of one's felt sense of self disintegrating in relation to a dysregulating other."³ By talking about a 'felt sense of self disintegrating,' DeYoung is describing the internal collapse, fragmentation, and disorganization that the *body* experiences when relational disconnection and the resulting shame occur. This definition focuses on the fact that shame starts in the body with pre-verbal and unconscious bodily-based responses that happen *before* our feelings are recognized and given the name or meaning of shame by our rational mind.

This is important because sometimes we experience shame and are unaware of it. The body experiences the disintegration of self, but our mind does not bring this experience into conscious awareness. When this happens, shame can drive our reactions and behaviors without us knowing or understanding its role.

SHAME IS DISORGANIZING

The second part of DeYoung's definition focuses on the relational dynamic: the self is disintegrating in relation to a dysregulating other. According to DeYoung, "A dysregulating other is a person who fails to provide the emotional connection, responsiveness, and understanding that another person needs in order to be well and whole."⁴

DeYoung's description of emotional connection, responsiveness, and understanding dovetails with Sue Johnson's research defining what a safe attachment figure provides: accessibility, responsiveness, and engagement.⁵ DeYoung and Johnson are helping us to understand that shame is what we experience in our bodies when we turn to our significant other for safe connection but are met with withdrawal, unresponsiveness, or disengagement. This relational disconnection automatically creates emotional dysregulation and shame.

Here is DeYoung's description of what it is like to experience secure connection with a "regulating other" versus what happens when we encounter a "dysregulating other" and enter disconnection:

> [A] regulating other is a person on whom I rely to respond to my emotions in ways that help me not to be overwhelmed by them, but rather to contain, accept, and integrate them into an emotional "me" I can feel comfortable being. A dysregulating other is also a person I *want* to trust—and should be able to trust—to help me manage my affect or emotion. But this person's response to me, or lack of response to me, does exactly the opposite: it does not help me contain, accept, or integrate.

Young goes on to say:

> Instead of feeling connected to someone strong and calm, I feel alone. Instead of feeling contained, I feel out of control. Instead of feeling energetically focused, I feel overwhelmed. Instead of feeling that I'll be okay, I feel like I'm falling apart.[6]

Betrayed partners experience the disintegration that DeYoung describes when they discover their significant other has cheated on them and then lied about it, manipulating their reality to keep the secret hidden. The cheating partner becomes the very definition of a "dysregulating other" as they transform into a source of danger, pain, and confusion. This severe breach in safety plunges the betrayed partner into the bodily-based disintegration of the shame experience as their prior understanding of themselves, their relationship, and their importance to their partner all come into question. DeYoung says that this feeling of shame, at the core, "also feels like disorganization and panic—or like a profoundly incompetent self."[7]

Note DeYoung's use of the word *disorganized* here. In her definition of the felt experience of shame, we see the role that shame plays in moving betrayed partners into a state of high distress where their attachment behaviors become disorganized. Betrayed partners whose behaviors mimic an anxious-avoidant attachment style in the aftermath of betrayal are often dealing with an attachment system mired in shame.

THE ATTACHMENT SHAME BIND

When the confusion and ambivalence of both wanting to be connected and wanting distance from the cheating partner are experienced, shame rears its ugly head and attaches to both desires.

Relational disconnection automatically begets shame. Moving toward connection with the person who has hurt you also creates shame. Betrayed partners find themselves caught in an intense shame bind where they encounter shame no matter which direction they move. We are going to look at both sides of this acute dilemma, starting with the shame that is felt when relational disconnection occurs.

Attachment Shame and Disconnection

Betrayal automatically creates a rupture in relationship. The sense of safety that enables vulnerable interdependency is erased and the bond between partners is damaged as the premise of the entire relational connection (trust) is eliminated.

For betrayed partners, the rupture created by the sexual betrayal and systematic lying instantly creates distance and alienation and just as instantly sparks shame, self-doubt, and insecurity. Betrayal causes us to doubt our importance, value, lovability, and acceptableness to our partner. The disconnection and relational loss stir uncertainty deep in our hearts—we fear that perhaps, at the end of the day, we are not worthy of fidelity, faithfulness, and honesty. Perhaps we do not deserve safety, intimacy, and the joy of being known. Perhaps we are flawed or defective and therefore incapable of ever experiencing the safe and secure bond we desire.

This profound form of attachment shame haunts betrayed partners, who nearly always find themselves questioning their worth and value to the cheating partner post-discovery. In addition, this shame is not a singular event. It repeatedly returns as new revelations about the degree and depth of betrayal are revealed, stretching the relational bond thinner and thinner.

Attachment Shame and Connection

Relational connection also brings shame; it is the other side of the shame bind created by betrayal.

When we find ourselves reaching for relational connection with the cheating partner, shame often begins to whisper in our ear. As we draw closer and maybe even experience kind or loving feelings, a hit of accompanying shame arises, asking, "What are you doing? This person is dangerous. They have treated you horribly! Where is your self-respect? Where is your dignity? Why are you being nice to them? Why are you staying with them? What is wrong with you?"

Shame, when we emotionally reach for our partner, is about our longing for connection and our continued dependency on our partner even though our partner has deeply wounded us. We feel shame about our desire for our partner, shame about our need for our partner, shame about making ourselves vulnerable again to someone who has been untrustworthy.

I received an email a few months ago from one of my blog readers. Here's how she described her experience of relational shame: "Recently I've been feeling calmer, and he's been proving himself consistent in his recovery and rebuilding some trust, so I've been in reconnect mode. But now I feel guilty for having sex with my own husband. And then I feel crazy for feeling guilty. Ugh!"

When this reader allowed herself to trust her spouse's recovery and move toward him sexually, guilt (and I'm guessing shame) hit her immediately for moving close to and trusting the person who had hurt her. Her "Ugh" at the end of her email is the perfect utterance for summing up the stomach-turning feelings of shame that betrayed partners so often experience when they reach for relational connection with the cheating partner.

This is the shame bind created by sexual betrayal. Relational disconnection brings shame related to self-worth and mattering. Relational connection brings shame about dignity and self-respect. This shame bind leaves betrayed partners with no direction to turn within the relationship that does not trigger more shame.

ATTACHMENT AMBIVALENCE AND SHAME

In the last chapter, we defined attachment ambivalence as the relational dilemma that occurs when our fear and attachment systems fire simultaneously in response to the threat of betrayal but with opposing imperatives: one telling us to move toward the cheating partner to reconnect and one telling us to move away and get safety through distance. Now I want to introduce you to the pivotal role shame plays in this cyclical dynamic. Below is a graphic to help you see how shame animates and amplifies the cycle of attachment ambivalence.

Attachment Ambivalence and Shame

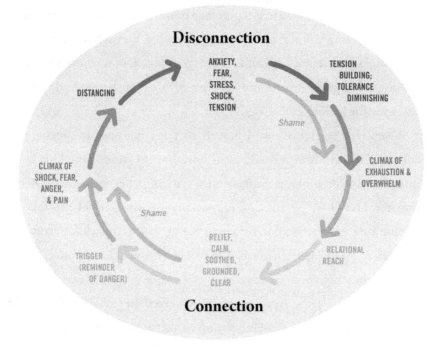

The Shame of Disconnection

Let's start at the top of the cycle. Each time we move away from the cheating partner, seeking safety through distancing behaviors, attachment shame is triggered as the relational distance reinforces self-doubt and insecurity about our worthiness. After all, the cheating partner chose someone else or something else over us and the relationship. Shame about whether we are valued by our partner can follow us like a shadow on a sunny day, inescapable and powerful in its ability to create doubt about our worthiness to be a loved and cherished mate.

The feeling of shame and doubt about our worthiness heightens the anxiety, fear, and tension that relational disconnection brings, moving us more quickly into exhaustion and overwhelm. This shame is part of what drives us out of disconnection and prompts us to reach out for our partner to try to reestablish some sort of relational touchpoint.

The Shame of Connection

When we move back into emotional connection with our cheating partner, it temporarily alleviates the feelings of shame about our worthiness through the reassurance that feeling connected brings. However, as we experience a moment, day, or week of relative peace and harmony with our partner—the quiet at the eye of the storm—here comes shame again.

This time the shame is about our dignity and self-respect. Why are we cuddled up to the tiger? Why are we being gracious, patient, caring, kind, or loving with someone who has betrayed our trust and hurt us so intensely? Have we no pride? Shame once again rushes in and causes us to doubt ourselves and to feel self-contempt or loathing toward our desire to be relationally joined with the person who harmed us.

This shame about allowing ourselves to connect with the cheating partner causes us to switch directions, pushing away to create safety through distance and to relieve the shame we feel about allowing ourselves to draw close. This distance alleviates the shame temporarily, as we feel like we are at least protecting ourselves from more harm. But as we stay in this space, the shame of disconnection swells yet again, and around and around we go as our efforts to avoid shame push us into and out of both sides of the cycle.

ATTACHMENT SHAME AND LEAVING

Attachment shame is not just felt by partners who are staying in their relationship. It is also experienced by partners who have made the choice to leave. Often, for partners who are leaving there is not as much push/pull relationally with the cheating partner (though for some individuals there can be). Instead, the attachment shame is about the failure of the relationship.

These betrayed partners are asking the exact same question: "What does it say about me?" but with the focus being on the ending of their relationship. They are asking, "What does it say about me that I stayed so long with someone who was cheating and lying to me? What does it say about me that my relationship has failed? What does it say about me that my partner cheated on me? What does it say about me that this is not my first relationship with an addict or a cheater?" These betrayed partners are wondering if they tried hard enough, if doing X, Y, and Z would have made a difference, if they have made the right decision for their children, if they have done the right thing for themselves. These and many other questions haunt partners who have chosen to leave their relationship.

SHAME INTENSIFIERS

The experience of attachment shame all by itself is enough for betrayed partners to deal with. However, there are dynamics within our cultural context that intensify this shame, adding fuel to an already blazing inferno. Below we are going to look at the following two key shame intensifiers that impact betrayed partners: 1) overwhelming cultural shame around infidelity and relationships and 2) the phenomenon of carried shame.

Overwhelming Cultural Shame

As a culture, how we live within our relationships and what we believe about our relationships is incongruent with how our bodily-based attachment systems function. We treat our attachments as much more "optional" than they really are at the level of our basic biology.

Our current cultural belief is that if your relationship isn't working for you and isn't healthy for you, you should leave it. Whether that is a relationship with your parents, best friend, family, or partner, we treat our attachments cavalierly; we do not respect the deep intertwining in our connection to significant people in our lives. We act as though leaving is much easier and much less costly than it is. But as anyone who has gone through a divorce can tell you, it's a bit like losing a limb. It feels like being emotionally and relationally torn in two, and it takes serious time and work to heal.

Part of the attachment shame that betrayed partners experience comes from living within a culture that denies the significance of their attachments and the level of negative impact that results from severing them. Partners who leave their relationships are encouraged by friends and family to "get out there" and start looking for a new partner before they have even filed divorce papers. Space to process what has happened, to grieve and mourn the loss of someone you have lived, loved, dreamed, and perhaps parented with, is not provided or even acknowledged as something you might need. Instead, we have the idea that we get over the loss of our attachments by replacing them. Betrayed partners are pushed toward a new relationship before they can absorb or understand what the loss of their current relationship means.

It is fascinating to me that at a time when we know and understand more about the importance of our attachment systems and the negative implications of ruptured attachments than ever before, our ability to sustain our attachments is decreasing alarmingly. Moreover, the value we place on our attachments in our thinking and beliefs is also diminishing.

Betrayed partners are caught in this confusion. Betrayed partners need support that validates the importance of their relationships and validates their desire to maintain their connection and rebuild a new life with the person they love. They need education about how their attachment system functions and understanding about the challenges inherent in deciding to stay in or end a long-term relationship. They need help grieving, whether that is grieving the relationship they thought they had or grieving the loss of that relationship as it ends. Either way, partners need permission, time, and space to be brokenhearted and to process their loss, pain, and sadness.

Most of all, betrayed partners need support that validates how important their significant other really is. This type of supportive understanding from therapists, friends, spiritual leaders, and family members can go a long way toward alleviating the attachment shame they so frequently feel.

Carried Shame

It is important to differentiate shame from guilt. We feel guilt when we have violated our own value system and our conscience pricks at us. We "feel guilty" and regret what we have done. This guilt is helpful because it lets us know when we are hurting ourselves or someone else. It helps us live in a manner congruent with our value systems.

Shame, on the other hand, is toxic. Toxic shame, rather than attaching itself to our behaviors and helping us to correct ourselves, attaches itself to our sense of worth and value. "I did something that I regret" becomes "I regret who I am." "I did something bad" becomes "I am bad." Toxic shame, over time, starts to define our self-perception and leads us into feelings of worthlessness and unlovability. It can define the narrative or story we tell ourselves about who we are.

Shame and guilt operate within relationships in diametrically opposed ways. DeYoung, talking about studies regarding the difference between guilt and shame, sums it up perfectly: "Shame emerges from their studies as an emotion and cognition that has destructive implications for interpersonal relationships, whereas the capacity for guilt is a relational strength."[8] Guilt is necessary for facilitating healthy behavior and repair, amends, and healing in relationships. Toxic shame destroys relationships by creating relational walls and power imbalances, not to mention the unhealthy behaviors that are often used to cope with and medicate the shame feelings.

When people are being shameless, they are not in touch with the healthy guilt that would make them stop and consider their behavior and perhaps choose a different course. As a result, shame attaches to the victim of the behavior as toxic carried shame.

Let me say it again because this is very important to understand. When someone is being shameless—behaving in an offensive or violating manner (by, say, cheating)—they are not connected to the healthy guilt that might prevent them from becoming offensive in their relationship. This disconnect turns into toxic shame and spills over onto the offended party (the betrayed partner); the betrayed partner then ends up carrying the shame of what happened.

For betrayed partners, carried shame is when the shame that belongs to the cheating partner bleeds onto you and you begin to carry it around with you, eventually letting it attach to your perception of yourself. "My significant other did something wrong" becomes "Something must be wrong with me."

Most betrayed partners experience this transfer of shame, but they usually don't realize it has happened, or they don't realize that it is carried shame that truly belongs to the cheating partner. In addition, carried shame can attach to so many different parts of the self that often it affects many different things at one time. Here is a list of ways betrayed partners can experience carried shame:

- Physical beauty and sexual desirability: Carried shame causes the partner to feel deficient, flawed, or "not enough".
- Sexuality: Carried shame causes the partner to feel deficient about sexual desires, sexual behavior, sexual expression, etc.
- Trust: Carried shame causes the partner to feel like a fool for having trusted the cheating partner and ashamed for not knowing about what was happening in the relationship.
- Lovability and inherent worth: Carried shame robs partners of their sense of value, creating deep insecurity about who they are and whether they are lovable, acceptable, and worthy.

This phenomenon of carried shame is why betrayed partners immediately feel the sense of a disintegrating self when sexual betrayal is discovered. The nanosecond that it takes for shame to attach itself to the betrayed partner is followed by a wave of shame-based emotion. Rejection, insecurity, worthlessness, self-doubt, and self-loathing rush in. These mingle with outrage, anger, pain, and indignation to create a cocktail of high-octane emotional overwhelm.

GIVING BACK CARRIED SHAME

When I was in my counseling Residency, my supervisor, Lou Argow, and I were discussing carried shame, and she said something I have never forgotten. She said, "You cannot heal carried shame because it does not belong to you. The only thing you can do with carried shame is to give it back."

Carried shame is about the shamelessness of the person who committed the betrayal, or the shamelessness of a cultural belief. It is not about you. Carried shame cannot be healed by working on it within yourself. The way that you heal from carried shame is to release it back to the person or culture that it belongs to.

We do not do this by shaming the other person in return. When we shame someone else, we are being shameless ourselves and simply moving from a power-under position into a power-over position, which keeps the toxicity alive in our relationships. Instead, we give shame back by releasing ourselves from the burden of carrying it and by expecting our partners to become accountable for their actions and behaviors.

To do this, we first must stare shame in the face. Remember, shame is one of the hardest human emotions to tolerate and, as a result, we often try to avoid or repress our shame. No one wants to feel the bodily-based sense of self disintegrating. However, we must bring shame out of our unconscious mind into our conscious awareness before we can choose how to respond.

One way to do this is to make a list of the ways you are carrying the shame for your partner around the sexual betrayal. Take some time to think about the ways you have allowed the cheating partner's behaviors to affect how you think and feel about yourself. This is what carried shame is—the change in your self-perception that results from someone else's behavior. Here are some examples:

- I carry shame around my partner's lying and gaslighting behaviors by believing I am a fool for trusting them.
- I carry shame around my spouse choosing to have sex with the affair partner by believing I am not beautiful or sexy enough for my partner to remain faithful to me.

- I carry shame around my partner's addiction by believing there is something wrong with me that caused me to marry an addict.
- I carry shame around my partner's cheating by feeling embarrassed about my sexual preferences and expression.
- I carry shame from a culture that tells me that if my partner cheated on me, it is because something is wrong with our relationship.

Once you have a list of the ways you are carrying shame from your partner (and you may want a list about the ways you are carrying cultural shame as well), it is time to write a letter to give the shame back. This is not a letter you will actually read to your partner, as this exercise is not about your partner. Your partner does not have to accept responsibility for you to stop carrying shame about their behavior. It is your choice and your choice alone whether you continue to carry or release the shame of betrayal.

This letter is intended to set you free and help you discharge the burden of carrying shame. It is intended to release you from the limiting beliefs and lies betrayal has told you about yourself. So, get yourself a cup of tea, coffee, or chai and find a comfortable place to sit. Take some time to do this piece of work around carried shame—creating a list of ways you are carrying shame and then writing a letter releasing shame or giving it back. Take as much time as you need, as this list and letter often require more than one sitting. Be as specific as you can. Be willing to face and feel the shame. And then, gently, with great love, lay it down and let it go.

> The urge to settle the score
> corresponds to the intensity
> of the shame that eats us up.
> And the deepest shame
> is that we were stupid enough
> to trust all along.
>
> ESTHER PEREL

CHAPTER SIX

ATTACHMENT-FOCUSED TRAUMA SYMPTOMS

For most betrayed partners, the days and weeks following discovery are full of turmoil. We find ourselves behaving in ways that shock and surprise us. We experience profound dysregulation that drives us outside our window of tolerance and activates our attachment system. We swing wildly through cycles of connection and disconnection as our attachment ambivalence and shame soar. We ask ourselves, *who is this distraught and angry person, and what happened to the self I knew and could rely on?*

During this devastating period, betrayed partners engage in three common coping strategies that emerge out of the attachment injury at the heart of betrayal: battling for empathy, repudiating shame, and declawing the tiger. In this chapter we will explore each of these strategies and in the next we will look at healthy coping practices to put into action instead.

BATTLING FOR EMPATHY

Battling for empathy occurs when we tirelessly and creatively try to engage our cheating partner's empathy so we can feel safe.

Battling for empathy can include the following behaviors:

- **Talking, questioning, and reviewing:** Most partners have at least one, and often many, stories of being up until the wee hours of the morning with their cheating partner talking, questioning, and reviewing the betrayal until they are both in a state of exhaustion.
- **Expressions of rage and anger:** Along with the endless talking come eruptions of rage about the cheating and lying. These behaviors occur when we feel the loss of ourselves acutely. Fueled by a cocktail of pain and anger, we say and do things we have never done before and would never deem appropriate at another time. This creates shame for us and confusion about who we are.
- **Acts of revenge and provocation:** This behavior flows from our rage and anger, but also includes the potent punch of jealousy and shame. Out of this flammable mixture, we find ourselves taking revenge on our cheating partner or their affair/acting out partner(s).
- **Manifesting the pain:** Sometimes, words are not enough, and we instead need to show our pain in other ways. This can look like sleeping all day, not showering, engaging in limited self-care, threats of suicide or suicide attempts, cutting, and other self-destructive behaviors.

The Relational Need

On the surface, battling for empathy behaviors look unhelpful and even destructive. This is where the early diagnosis of betrayed partner's behaviors as signs of codependence or co-addiction came from. And let's be honest, these behaviors are not pretty. In fact, they can be downright dark and ugly. As a result, it can be hard for the uninformed outsider to imagine how such raw clinging neediness or white-hot anger could be an attempt to reconnect with our partner and restore safety.

Battling for empathy is a form of relational protest rooted in our distressed attachment systems. As betrayed partners, we battle endlessly with the cheating partner in an attempt to communicate our level of distress as viscerally and clearly as possible. The relational attachment-based need that drives battling for empathy behaviors can be expressed this way:

- If you truly understand how badly you hurt me, you won't do it again, and then I will feel safe.
- The only way for you to truly understand is to feel the same type and amount of pain that I am feeling.
- I will make you feel and understand my pain so you will not hurt me again and I can begin to feel safe with you once more.

The underlying relational need driving our behaviors is the need for empathetic connection or reconnection. Our thinking goes something like this: "If the cheating partner connects to and feels my pain, then they will understand how devastating their behavior is and they will stop it and never do it again." The cheating partner's empathy, presence, and remorse are what could create the possibility of safety again in the relationship. But if the cheating partner dismisses our pain, stays separate and disconnected, responds with defensiveness, or continues the cheating and lying, then our pain, sense of danger, and mistrust will increase rather than decrease.

Negative Repercussions

The relational need at the heart of battling for empathy is real and acute. We need the danger and threat to end and safe connection with our partner to be restored. However, the battling for empathy behaviors we reach for to deal with this attachment-based need often backfire, heightening trauma symptoms and increasing our sense of relational rupture.

When we review the details of the betrayal again and again as we battle, we reactivate our pain and trauma, which moves us further and further outside our window of tolerance. Trauma symptoms such as intrusive thoughts and images, along with emotional pain and anxiety, increase and endure. And each time we present our cheating partner with our pain by thrusting it in front of them so they will "get it," each time we rage or take revenge, we fail to help them understand our pain. Instead, we push them toward their own pain.

REPUDIATING SHAME

The second common pattern that betrayed partners develop to cope with their attachment injury is repudiating shame. Repudiating shame occurs when we unconsciously try to rid ourselves of the carried shame of sexual betrayal. As discussed in Chapter Five, carried shame happens when someone is being shameless by behaving in a manner outside their value system (perhaps by cheating or lying). The healthy guilt that they repress turns into shame and spills over onto the offended party (i.e., the betrayed partner), who ends up carrying it. Repudiating shame can include the following behaviors.

- **Your problem, not mine.** As betrayed partners, we can refuse to seek help or tell anyone what has happened. We tell our cheating partner they are the one with the problem and they are the one that needs help. We think, *I didn't do anything wrong, so why would I go to therapy?* In this way we unconsciously try to distance ourselves from the carried shame we feel. We may also be afraid that if we go to therapy or a twelve-step meeting, someone will say something that makes us feel blamed and validates our worst fear: that maybe it is some lack in us that has caused the cheating. Unfortunately, this fear keeps countless betrayed partners from getting the help they need.
- **Grabbing a bullhorn.** This is when we tell anyone who will listen the gory details of the cheating partner's behaviors. This is an attempt to offload the carried shame by publicly shaming the cheating partner and making sure everyone knows who the "bad partner" is in the relationship.
- **Amping up and tamping down the sexy.** As betrayed partners, we feel carried shame acutely around our bodies and sexuality. Because the betrayal is sexual, it aggressively attacks this part of our identity and self-perception. Sometimes, to combat this carried shame, we will amp up the sexy by losing weight, changing our look, dressing differently, flirting with others, and becoming hypersexual with the cheating partner. On the other end of the spectrum is tamping down the sexy. With this, we manage our carried sexual shame by deciding to not even try. We move away from and avoid sexuality altogether.
- **Scrambling for dignity.** Betrayed partners, especially if we are attempting to stay with our cheating partner and repair our relationship, fear that staying means we are weak and have no

dignity. To repudiate our shame about staying with a cheating partner, we shower them with contempt and shame. This provides us with a sense that we are not letting the cheating partner get away with cheating; instead, we are making them pay for what they have done. We shore up our dignity by lashing out because it helps us feel that at least we have the self-respect to fight back and demand the justice of time spent in the relational doghouse.

The Relational Need

Shame is always relational. The attachment-focused need that drives our repudiating shame behaviors can be expressed this way:

- I feel enormous shame about being cheated on.
- My mind knows it's not my fault, but I still *feel* shame.
- I need to prove that the shame belongs to you and not me. I need you to own your choices and for others to understand that this is your fault, not mine.

Negative Repercussions

The shame from sexual betrayal comes from all directions: our culture, ourselves, our cheating partner (if they are blaming us), our religion, and maybe even friends and family. Shame is such a difficult emotion to feel that the urge to push it away and disconnect from it can be overwhelming.

All emotions contain an action tendency that they move us toward. Shame's primary action tendency motivates us to hide. When we allow shame to shape our reactions, it pushes us toward isolation or withdrawal. This can leave us afraid to share the details of what is happening with those who could potentially support us.

ATTACHMENT-FOCUSED TRAUMA SYMPTOMS

I have worked with countless betrayed partners who have come into my therapy office and told me that I am the first person they have told about the cheating. The shame they feel has kept them silent and removed from support. They have been coping with emotional overwhelm and dysregulation on their own, and because of this, they tend to be much more symptomatic than those who reach out for help and support.

For other betrayed partners, shame keeps them from pursuing even confidential help and support. These partners are even more isolated, and the severity of their trauma symptoms nearly always reflects the challenges that are created when we try to deal with severe dysregulation on our own.

DECLAWING THE TIGER

The final coping pattern betrayed partners use to manage the attachment injury created by betrayal is declawing the tiger. Declawing the tiger is about the power dynamics within our relationship and the power imbalance created by cheating.

When our cheating partner breaks our relationship agreements, they take a *power-over* position within the relationship. They have a secret. This is a power imbalance—knowledge about the state of our relationship that we don't have—and this unilaterally changes our sexual and relational agreements. Our partner hides important information from us, creating distance and confusion. Our relationship changes without our consent or awareness.

One of the most significant wounds we experience as betrayed partners is this loss of choice and personal agency within our relationship. Many of us describe this as dehumanizing.

When we discover sexual betrayal and come face to face with our powerlessness regarding the decisions that were made without our agreement or consent, we react. The typical reaction to an experience of *power-under* is to try to win back a sense of power—i.e., to gain *power-over*.

Declawing the tiger is how we do this. We shame the cheating partner, consign them to the emotional doghouse, treat them as second-class citizens, and try to control them to limit their power to hurt us.

We do this because it feels like when they were operating within their full power and freedom, they became dangerous. Our compelling need for safe connection causes us to assume that we can only find safety if we take power away from the cheating partner because when they had power, they abused it. As a result, we assert power-over within the relationship in whatever way we can. Shaming, criticizing, and controlling our cheating partner are ways we try to limit their power and "cut them down to size."

The Relational Need

The attachment-based need that drives declawing-the-tiger behaviors can be expressed this way:

- You did not use your power to protect me, our relationship, and our family. Instead, you used your power to hurt us.
- I need to reduce or take away your power so you are less threatening and less dangerous.
- If I declaw you and make you smaller, it will be safe for me to get close to you again.

ATTACHMENT-FOCUSED TRAUMA SYMPTOMS

Negative Repercussions

Declawing the tiger can be one of the hardest trauma symptoms to look at because what we do feels bad to us. When we shame our significant other, we are operating outside of our value system, and, as a result, we feel guilt, remorse, and our own shame. We also do not want to admit that we are taking a power-over position within the relationship because it violates who we believe ourselves to be. Because of this, it can be hard to be honest about our declawing-the-tiger behaviors. We don't want to be the person we become in these moments.

In addition to shame and feeling out of control, declawing-the-tiger behaviors rob us of our ability to feel respect for and attraction to our partner. Think about when you first met your partner and what attracted you. The qualities and characteristics of your partner that drew you in and made you fall in love might now be the very things that scare you to death. Most of us fall in love with our partners when they are operating in the fullness of their power as a person. They are being who they uniquely are, and that is what captivates us.

Declawing-the-tiger behaviors are always constricting. They are about using shame or control to make our partner less threatening. To do that, we inevitably reduce our partner. Maybe our partner has given up hobbies and other activities to be home where we can keep an eye on them. We feel safer because before when they said they were going to play basketball, they sometimes went to massage parlors instead. But now they have given up something (basketball) that makes them feel alive, interested, and engaged with life.

Often, our partners believe this is the least they can do, and if it helps us feel safe, it's worth it. But in reality, the smaller their worlds get, the smaller they become and the less we are drawn to them. To help us feel safe again, they often give up the parts of themselves that we were attracted to.

Many couples settle into a state of reduced being in exchange for the pseudo-safety it provides. When this happens, both partners reduce themselves in different ways. The betrayed partner settles for control rather than trust and a diminished partner rather than a robustly alive relationship. The cheating partner settles for a reduced self to maintain the relationship and attempt to meet needs for safety. This type of relationship is a ticking time bomb, and the lack of energy, aliveness, and joy within these relationships is always a heartbreak to witness.

YOU ARE NORMAL

If you have found yourself engaging in any or all of these behavior patterns (and most betrayed partners do), I want to remind you once again that you are normal. This is how we react when our attachment systems are in distress, we are mired in carried shame, and we can't find safety anywhere.

Unfortunately, our threat response system is not particularly smart in the ways of relationships. It works great for avoiding the lions on the Serengeti, but it is a blunt instrument when it comes to helping us navigate relational distress well.

We need tools to help us replace these reactive coping strategies with more helpful responses that move us toward regulation and stability. We focus on this in the next chapter.

> The plot of our lives is
> largely out of our control.
> We decide only the response
> of the main character.
>
> — GLENNON DOYLE

CHAPTER SEVEN

HEALTHY COPING STRATEGIES THAT SUPPORT OUR ATTACHMENT SYSTEMS

Instead of battling for empathy, repudiating shame, and declawing the tiger, we must turn toward new coping skills that calm our nervous systems. We must create other forms of safe connection—connection that can provide us with the support we need during this time of uncertainty. We must find healthy ways to cope with the power imbalance created by betrayal and we must develop new skills that move us out of powerlessness into empowerment. In this chapter we explore seven helpful coping strategies:

1. Focus on calming our bodies
2. Build an alternative safe base
3. Name shame to tame shame
4. Create space for our anger
5. Eliminate the doghouse

6. Take our power back
7. Set and maintain effective boundaries

FOCUS ON CALMING OUR BODIES

Unhelpful coping behaviors are driven by dysregulation in our bodies combined with our attachment-based need for empathy and safety. To move away from unhelpful behaviors, we need to calm our nervous system so we can move toward our window of tolerance.

In the initial days and weeks following discovery, we want to focus as much of our attention as possible on calming and soothing ourselves. This can be challenging when we are emotionally revving. But our bodies will respond to our efforts, and then momentum will grow and move us toward regulation. Remember, our bodies want to be in a regulated state, so they are on our side as we struggle to come back to ourselves.

The best way to calm and soothe ourselves is different for each of us. Often, we must try different things to see what we best respond to.

Here are just a few strategies to consider:

- **Deep breathing:** We can bring our focus to our breath by breathing in through the nose and out through the mouth.
- **Guided meditation:** There are apps galore that provide us with guided meditations to help us calm our minds and bodies.
- **Yoga, Tai Chi, stretching:** Gentle forms of exercise bring us into intentional connection with our bodies.
- **Walking, biking, jogging:** Exercise that moves our bodies vigorously help our emotions release and move through.
- **Warm baths:** The warm water of a bath provides a sensory hug

for the body that is soothing.
- **Weighted blankets:** Snuggling up under a weighted blanket helps our bodies feel held and soothed.

Whatever practices we choose, calming ourselves must be our number one priority. Our ability to access our mental and emotional resources rests upon calming our activated brain and body. If our nervous system stays chronically overstimulated, it is much more difficult to heal and to make wise decisions about how to care for ourselves. Doing everything within our power to calm and soothe our activated body/brain/mind is our essential first step.

For some betrayed partners, the nervous system is repeatedly activated by conflict with the cheating partner, particularly if the cheating partner is still engaging in or lying about the cheating. For these betrayed partners, separating from the cheating partner may be needed to provide enough space for the nervous system to be able to calm down.

One of my clients recently rented an Airbnb for a month because she discovered that her spouse had brought his affair partner into their house. Being in the house was keeping her so chronically activated that she could not think clearly enough to heal and make decisions. When she took action to help herself and support her nervous system, it made all the difference. She was able to calm and soothe her body, and she began to use her energy to help herself heal. She was eventually able to return home and decide with her partner to sell the house and move elsewhere as they worked to repair their relationship.

BUILD AN ALTERNATIVE SAFE BASE

Our best and most elegant regulatory tool is our attachment system. In fact, this is our attachment system's primary job: to help us regulate ourselves through safe connections with others. When our panicked and disorganized nervous system encounters a calm, grounded nervous system, it helps us move toward regulation. When we allow shame to drive us toward isolation, we rob ourselves of the most helpful healing process at our disposal: connection with others.

One of the most important functions of our primary attachment figure is to provide us with a safe base from which we can emotionally operate. Following betrayal, however, our cheating partner's ability to be a safe base for us is compromised. It may not be completely gone, but it has definitely been damaged.

During this time, we desperately need additional supports that shore up our sense of safe connection and grounding. No one outside person can completely replace the loss of safety and connection with our significant other. But when key relationships and communities of support are accessed, it makes an enormous difference in our healing trajectory. This is true regardless of whether we are staying in or leaving our relationship.

When we allow our attachment system to access relationships with others, that system works exactly as it is meant to work. Relational connection calms our bodies, regulates our nervous systems, helps us access our resourcefulness, and returns us to ourselves. Four key supports that can shore up our sense of safe base after betrayal are outlined below.

- **Connect to expert support.** A therapist trained in treating partner betrayal can be an invaluable source of connection and support.

HEALTHY COPING STRATEGIES THAT SUPPORT OUR ATTACHMENT SYSTEMS

Sue Johnson PhD, founder of Emotionally Focused Therapy for Couples (EFT), describes an effective relationship between a therapist and a client as a "safe haven therapeutic alliance."[1] In this relationship, the therapist becomes part of the partner's safe base, providing a felt sense of consistent connection, acceptance, and guidance during a turbulent and disorienting storm. The therapist becomes a co-regulating presence during therapy sessions. Partners can bring their dysregulating and overwhelming emotions and experiences into the relationship with the therapist. The therapist, in turn, operates as a stabilizing presence, creating a safe container in which partners are guided and resourced to access and process their emotional experience. As therapy unfolds, partners are helped to restructure their sense of themselves and their relationships so they can move toward healing and wholeness.

- **Recovery Groups:** Group therapy and twelve-step recovery groups can also play a vital role in creating a safe base for betrayed partners. Therapy groups where members understand one another's experiences and offer empathy, insight, and encouragement are essential to recovery for many partners. I have run groups for betrayed partners for over twenty years and have watched countless lifelong friendships develop as members bond and align with one another to navigate their healing. The same thing happens in twelve-step recovery groups.

- **Sponsor:** Betrayed partners who access twelve-step recovery programs often develop a relationship with a sponsor to who they speak regularly throughout the week. Nearly alw partners benefit enormously from this source of su Sponsors are often the one person they feel they can time, day or night. And knowing they have access to someone who will provide experience, strength, and hope whenever needed creates an additional layer of safe base support. Other twelve-step group members operate similarly, providing needed touchpoints that help partners feel supported and stabilized.

- **Safe Family, Friends, and Faith Communities:** As we consider connecting with others and getting help, we must remember that when it comes to nervous systems colliding, the strongest nervous system wins. This means that we want to think carefully about who we confide in and which friends and family members we choose as support. If we have a friend who is anxious and dysregulated on a regular basis, we may want to pass on that person and choose someone who is more grounded. We want to choose people who can help move our nervous system in the right direction, back toward our window of tolerance and connection with ourselves.

In my book, *When It All Breaks Bad*, I outlined a list of things to look for to help betrayed partners identify safe friends and family to invite into their inner circle. Here is that list again.

Safe friends and family are those who:

- Respect and maintain our boundaries and do not gossip or share information they have been entrusted with.
- Do not jump to conclusions about what we should do regarding our relationship; instead, they support our need to answer that question for ourselves.
- Do not immediately turn against or judge our significant other; instead, they give us the space and sounding board we need to work through our feelings.

- Understand that we are in a process that takes time and are willing to be in that process with us, rather than rushing us toward "being done and moving on."
- Do not collude with us in pretending things are better than they are or deciding things are hopeless; instead, they hold a middle ground attitude and simply hear our feelings as we bounce through the different emotions and reactions that follow betrayal.
- Do not stoke our fear by telling us horror stories about things that have happened to other people or by joining us in imagining worst-case scenarios.
- Have wisdom to share, and offer sound, thoughtful responses to the questions we ask.
- Are available and responsive when we need support.

NAME SHAME TO TAME SHAME

Once we have the right team in place, we want to name shame to tame shame. This means talking about the parts of our betrayal story that are tender and sore and that we wish we could hide away forever. When we take a risk and share the parts of our story that shame has attached itself to, shame begins to lose its grip.

Shame creates a strange paradox because the antidote to shame lies in doing the very thing that shame tells us not to do. Shame tells us to hide, keep secrets, avoid, and withdraw. But when we share our shame, when we open ourselves to be seen, when we tell the secrets and allow others to draw close, shame evaporates in the light of acceptance and understanding.

CREATE SPACE FOR YOUR ANGER

Unexpressed anger fuels unhelpful coping behaviors. And powerlessness is one of the most enraging things human beings can feel. As betrayed partners, most of us have deep reservoirs of unexpressed anger about our helplessness.

At the same time, we may feel shame or guilt when we express our anger. This is especially likely if we are female. Culturally, women have been taught that being angry makes us a bitch, a shrew, hysterical, or a drama queen.

When I was trained by Pia Mellody in her developmental trauma model, she spoke of the way that denied feelings create episodes of exploding emotions. As betrayed partners, we often look dangerous and unhinged when we have an episode of exploding rage. And then, after the dust settles (literally and figuratively), the shame we feel about our behavior causes us to crate our anger back up and tuck it away again. This works only until the next time.

The reality is that we have a right to our anger. Betrayal is a deep injustice, and our dignity as human beings responds to injustice with anger. If we are not able to express this anger, it eventually erupts out of us in rage, shame, and other contemptuous declawing-the-tiger behaviors.

The paradoxical antidote to rage erupting is to validate and feel our anger in the moment.

Pia taught a simple but powerful mantra for anger: "I am angry, and I have a right to be angry." Seems too easy, right? This mantra is powerful because it acknowledges and validates our anger, which is part of our dignity. I have had betrayed partners stand in my office and repeat this mantra until they're able to do it with power in their voice that connects them to their anger. Eventually, they are shouting, "I am angry, and I have a right to be angry," as the anger moves through them to be released.

This is not a one-and-done exercise. This is a mantra to be used anytime we feel anger welling up. Validating our anger and voicing our anger help the anger move through us and out, rather than building up and pushing us into declawing-the-tiger behaviors.

ELIMINATE THE DOGHOUSE

Early after discovery, cheating partners, if they are hoping to repair the relationship, will often give up parts of their autonomy to try to rebuild trust. They may give up privacy by making all their devices transparent. They may give up sleeping in their bed or living in their home. They may give up their sexual relationship with the betrayed partner. They may give up some independence, agreeing to check in more regularly. They may limit travel, social events, and social situations.

Each of these things can be part of the temporary boundaries we need to feel safe, and often they are essential to rebuilding trust. Where these helpful relational guardrails go awry is when they are implemented from a power-over position.

Many betrayed partners insist that their cheating partner lost all relationship rights when they cheated and lied. I understand this sentiment and the enormous sense of helplessness and powerlessness that drives it. However, the belief that one person's misuse of power means they should lose all access to both individual and shared power is a relational death sentence.

The path to relational recovery does not involve putting our cheating partners in the doghouse by taking away their power. Instead, we must set boundaries around what we need within the relationship in light of the betrayal. And we must do this without moving into a one-up stance or expecting our cheating partner to adopt a one-down stance.

This. Is. Hard.

To do this, we must resist the threat center's all-consuming drive toward safety at any cost, even the cost of our and our partner's dignity. Instead, we must come back into contact with our deepest attachment needs and longings. After all, most of us do not want a long-term relationship where trust is dependent on monitoring our partner or reducing them to a shadow self.

TAKE YOUR POWER BACK

The paradox in power-over and power-under positions is that they are both forms of abdicating our true power. Power-over and power-under are reactive positions. When we allow another person's thinking or behaviors to dictate how we think or behave, we lose our personal power. The center of our personal power lies in the fact that *we always get to choose who we are going to be in any circumstance or situation.*

Shortly after I separated from my spouse and got good therapy support, I had an enormous lightbulb moment. I realized I was allowing my spouse's behavior, thinking, and beliefs, all of which were enormously distorted by his sexual addiction, to determine how I operated in the relationship. I was giving my power away to my partner, and it left me sick, confused, and fragmented.

Once I got this concept, I stuck my landing. My ability to choose who I would be and my ability to come back into connection with my core self changed almost overnight. That realization turned the page for me, and my recovery looked completely different from that moment forward. I reclaimed my sense of personal power by recognizing that

HEALTHY COPING STRATEGIES THAT SUPPORT OUR ATTACHMENT SYSTEMS

my power resided in my ability to choose my responses based on who I am and who I want to be in my life and relationships.

SET AND MAINTAIN EFFECTIVE BOUNDARIES

Most people know about boundaries and instinctively understand they are important. However, what a boundary is, how to set a boundary, and how to effectively maintain a boundary is often misunderstood. For betrayed partners, learning to create healthy boundaries is critical to moving away from declawing-the-tiger behaviors and toward our personal power.

Here are some key things to understand about boundaries:

- **Boundaries facilitate relationships.** One of the many misconceptions about boundaries is that they are a way of keeping people out rather than a way of allowing people safely in. We often put up a relational wall and call it a boundary. Boundaries balance protection with vulnerability, allowing us to move to an appropriate degree of closeness while also staying safe.
- **Boundaries are about our own behavior.** Boundaries are always about our own behavior and not about other people's behavior.

Often, we try to use boundaries as a tool to control another person's actions. For example, one of my clients whose partner had a two-year affair and continued to lie about the details said to me, "I set a boundary that my partner has to be honest with me from now on because I won't tolerate any more lying."

Can you see the issue with that attempted boundary? My client wanted and needed her partner to stop lying and tried to control her partner's behavior in this regard by setting a boundary. But my client has no control over her partner's choice to be honest or lie. A more effective boundary would have been something like, "I cannot tolerate any more lying or secrets about the affair. It is creating more hurt and mistrust and damaging any potential for healing our relationship. I need you to stop lying to me and to do whatever work you need to do with your therapist to be honest and rebuild trust. (*This is the need she has and the request she is making. Now she sets her boundary.*) If you continue to lie to me, I am going to pull back from our relationship until you can be honest. I will either limit contact with you or ask you to move out of the house for a while. But in some way, I will need to have more distance from you if you keep lying to me."

Notice that now the boundary is about what my client will do to keep herself safe from further harm if her partner does not stop lying. Also notice that she leaves herself room to sort out what will be best for her. Rather than drawing a hard line in the sand by saying, "If you lie again, I will separate from you," she has given herself options to exercise depending on how the situation unfolds and what she needs in the moment. That is what healthy boundaries are all about.

A LOT TO TAKE IN

Are you still with me? We have covered significant ground in exploring the attachment injury at the heart of betrayal. We have looked at our attachment styles and how betrayal trauma catapults our attachment systems into disorganization. We identified attachment ambivalence and the relational bind created when we are betrayed by our primary attachment figure. We discussed the shame that accompanies this relational bind and animates the cycle of connection and disconnection. Finally, we examined the three common behavior patterns that emerge for betrayed partners out of the attachment injury created by betrayal.

It is time for a break! Go take a walk, take a nap, stretch it out, get some coffee or a big glass of water. This book is not a sprint; it is a marathon. Taking breaks to absorb what you have read and unpack what it means for you are necessary. So, no rush. Take the time you need, and when you return, we will dive into Part Two, where we investigate the emotional and psychological injury at the heart of betrayal.

PART TWO

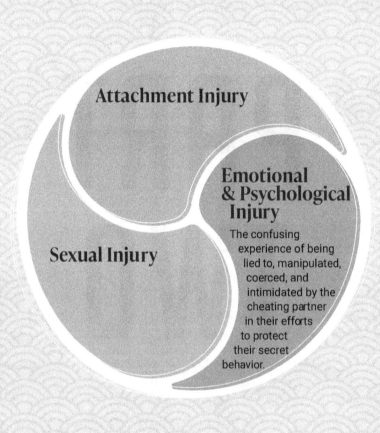

INTRODUCTION

THE EMOTIONAL AND PSYCHOLOGICAL INJURY AT THE HEART OF BETRAYAL

The second injury created by sexual betrayal is the emotional and psychological injury. This chronic and systematic dishonesty is a form of emotional and psychological abuse. As betrayed partners, we have been robbed of our reality. We have been left to question our five senses, our instincts, our memory, our perception, and our judgment.

If, as M. Scott Peck so eloquently said, "Mental health is an ongoing process of dedication to reality at all costs,"[1] then to be stripped of our ability to know reality is to put our mental health in jeopardy. Thus, we experience a cheating partner's chronic lying and reality manipulation as emotional and psychological trauma.

In Part Two, we identify the four types of gaslighting experienced by betrayed partners. We look at the dilemma that is created when the need for full disclosure about the betrayal runs up against the cheating partner's unwillingness to be fully honest. Then we explore the coping strategy of *betrayal blindness*, which happens when partners hold information outside their awareness. Last, we dive into the impacts of fear, shame, and powerlessness.

> The language you speak
> is made up of words
> that are killing you.
>
> — MONIQUE WITTIG

CHAPTER EIGHT

LIAR, LIAR, PANTS ON FIRE:

The Four Types of Gaslighting

Betrayal grows in the fertile soil of dishonesty. It can be very difficult for betrayed partners to wrap our minds around the comprehensiveness and sincerity with which our cheating partners can lie. One of my clients put it this way: "This was hard for me to accept. I always felt my spouse had a good heart, didn't lie, and was just awkward when it came to expressing himself. It was hard for me to recognize that he was and had been lying to me so convincingly for so long!"

For most betrayed partners, this lying is at least as painful as the sexual behaviors—often more so. While the sex is a huge breach of trust, the lying feels like an even deeper betrayal. When our partner lies to us, it creates a sense that we cannot know what reality is. We cannot believe what our partner says is true. As a result, secure bonding and trust are lost.

THE DISTORTED WORLD OF SELF-MANIPULATION

Unfortunately, cheating partners can look us in the eye, cry crocodile tears, and knowingly lie the whole time. Most start out lying to hide their sexual behaviors and end up lying for the sake of lying. This is because dishonesty is like an insidious weed that starts to take up space in places it was never intended to be.

Before unfaithful partners lie to their spouse, friends, family, and others, they must first lie to themselves. Cheating partners may:

- Lie to themselves about the nature of their behaviors, telling themselves they don't have a problem and can stop whenever they want.
- Lie to themselves about their marriage, picking fights with their spouse so they can tell themselves they are dissatisfied in their relationship. They then use this unhappiness to justify cheating.
- Tell themselves their use of porn and sexting is not the same as real sex, so it doesn't count as betrayal.
- Lie to themselves about getting caught, believing no one will ever know and no one will ever get hurt.
- Lie to themselves about their motivations, pretending that it's only this one time.

These and similar lies are not separate from a cheating partner's sexual behaviors. Instead, these lies are an integral part of the problem. To maintain the sexual behaviors while also maintaining a primary relationship and external life, the unfaithful partner must develop an inner story that justifies and rationalizes why the infidelity is acceptable or at the very least justified.

For many unfaithful individuals, sexual infidelity is at odds with their self-concept. Their sexual behavior may violate their relationship agreements, the boundaries of people around them, boundaries at their place of employment, and their personal values system. To override the discomfort created by acting against their boundaries and self-identity, they create and use self-manipulation defenses.

Self-manipulation defenses keep unfaithful partners from feeling shame about being out of control, crossing lines they never thought they would cross, and betraying the person who is most important to them. Without these defenses, their sexual behavior would be difficult to sustain, as they would have to honestly face what they are doing, who they've become, and the consequences of their actions. They need these defenses to sustain their double life and to live with themselves while betraying their significant other.

When unfaithful partners lie to themselves (and others) long enough, they cease to think clearly. Eventually, the line between reality and fiction blurs as they begin to believe their own lies. Their thinking process becomes unclear, unpredictable, and illogical. As a result, they begin to speak and act based on thought distortions and delusions. This is the "stinking thinking" that is talked about in twelve-step recovery programs.

When I work with unfaithful partners, we spend as much time intervening on impaired thinking as we do on arresting problematic behaviors. This is because recovery begins with confronting lies and dishonesty. The distorted thinking that supports destructive behaviors must be identified and brought into awareness so the cheating partner can consciously make different choices.

As unfaithful partners get more familiar with how their protective defenses operate, they can intervene on their thinking and replace lies with truth. This takes power away from the cheating and opens the door to a new way of living—a way of living based on honesty, integrity, and authenticity.

Without this intervention, the problematic behavior continues.

For most betrayed partners, the secrets, lying, and destruction of trust are the most painful parts of betrayal. It feels like each lie is a deliberate choice the cheating partner has made with premeditated intention. It is only when betrayed partners understand how dishonesty is embedded within the cheating that it becomes clear how habitual, chronic, and out of control the lying has become.

This in no way excuses the cheating partner. Cheating partners are responsible for each secret, lie, and manipulation. This does, however, help betrayed partners understand why it takes time for the dishonesty to stop, and how much hard work and focus is required for cheating partners to become honest with themselves so they can then be honest with others.

THE CRAZY-MAKING EXPERIENCE OF BEING GASLIGHTED

Sadly, unfaithful partners' chronic dishonesty means most betrayed partners have been lied to and lied to and then lied to some more.

Somewhere in your healing process you may have heard the term *gaslighting*. This word is used to describe the emotional and psychological trauma that results when a person is chronically lied to or manipulated by a loved one.

This term originates from a movie released in 1944 called *Gaslight*. In this movie, a woman, Paula, is seduced by and marries a seemingly charming man who deliberately and systematically tries to drive her insane as part of his scheme to find and steal hidden family jewels. His goal is to have her institutionalized so he can discover and escape with the jewels without her being in the way.

As he nears his goal and Paula becomes more and more convinced of her own mental illness, an investigator who meets the couple by chance and witnesses some of the husband's manipulation begins to look into things. He eventually comes to the house to meet with Paula, and he helps her discover the truth.

Guess how Paula is restored to sanity? The investigator validates her reality by affirming that the footsteps in the attic that she hears are real and the house's gaslights are indeed dimming. These and many other things were being done by her spouse and then denied, causing her to doubt her reality and feel crazy. When she would see the lights dim, her husband would tell her that it wasn't happening and that it was all in her imagination. Sound familiar?

If you have been betrayed, it's likely that you have experienced one or more of the following types of gaslighting: the straight up lie, reality manipulation, scapegoating and coercion.

THE STRAIGHT-UP LIE

The straight-up lie is the least damaging form of gaslighting, though still harmful. This tactic is aimed at hiding secret behaviors. Cheating partners may glibly lie about where they were, what they were doing, who they were with, how much time they spent doing something, and where the money went. Betrayed partners are often stunned at the ease with which their loved one has repeatedly lied to them. This type of lying creates a deep sense of mistrust in the relationship. It also creates a double whammy of betrayal for partners because they feel betrayed by their spouse and betrayed by themselves for believing their partner's lies.

REALITY MANIPULATION

Reality manipulation makes betrayed partners feel like they are slowly and inexorably losing their grip on sanity. This is because their ability to perceive what is real and to trust their memory and judgment is being attacked and undermined.

Let me give you an example. You and your husband have gone out to eat at a lovely restaurant. Your husband, who compulsively uses flirtation and seduction as a part of his problematic behavior, flirts openly with the waitress throughout the meal. When you mention your discomfort with this, your husband denies it. Moreover, he turns it around on you. He tells you that you are a prude and making a big deal out of something that is minor. He tells you that you have become paranoid and are seeing things that don't exist. He tells you that he is worried about your self-esteem because you seem to be so insecure, and maybe some therapy would be helpful.

In this type of gaslighting, unfaithful partners attack the betrayed partner's sense of reality. They create uncertainty, doubt, and confusion about what the betrayed partner is observing or experiencing. Rather than lie about their own behavior, they attack their partner's perception of reality. This type of reality manipulation is incredibly damaging because it violates the betrayed partner's sense of self and erodes their mental equilibrium, self-confidence, and self-esteem.

SCAPEGOATING

The word *scapegoating* is defined by dictionary.com as "the act or practice of assigning blame or failure to another, as to deflect attention or responsibility away from oneself." Cheating partners frequently use scapegoating to covertly scoop blame onto their significant other so they can justify their sexual acting out.

For example, cheating partners might pick a fight with their spouse and get indignant and self-righteous in the argument. They then tell themselves that their spouse is a nag or unavailable or not empathetic. From there, it is a short leap to telling themselves it is okay to cheat, and, in fact, it is their spouse's fault that they are unfaithful.

With this type of gaslighting, cheating partners emphasize and exaggerate their partner's character defects as a rationale for infidelity. This can look like complaints about the partner not being sexual enough or not sexual in the way the cheating partner wants. It can look like criticism about how the partner looks, how the partner dresses, the partner's personality traits, or how the partner interacts relationally. It can also look like accusations about unmet relational and emotional needs.

For betrayed partners, scapegoating can be particularly lethal, especially as they try to sort out what is and is not their responsibility in the relationship. There is no question that we all bring significant imperfections and character flaws to our relationships. That said, one person's character flaw is not another person's excuse to violate the relationship agreements.

Scapegoating, by distorting and exaggerating what is true, takes advantage of a betrayed partner's desire to be open to receiving and responding to feedback from the unfaithful partner. This distortion is confusing. Betrayed partners can find themselves taking responsibility for things that are not actually problems or that, at the very least, are not problems that validate the cheating behaviors.

COERCION

Coercive behavior ranges along a continuum from the charm offensive on one end to intimidation or violence on the other. In between, there is pressure and manipulation.

The Charm Offensive

Betrayed partners often experience full-force charm offensives. Cheating partners can be persuasive and distracting. This charm can be packaged in endless shapes and forms, such as wit and humor, but the end goal is always the same: to distract the betrayed partner from the infidelity.

Charm offensives can look like solicitous caretaking, sexual seduction, playful flirtation, or teary-eyed attempts to glean pity. They can include gifts of jewelry, flowers, or a fun trip. Again, these behaviors are aimed at distracting the betrayed partner from evidence that might lead to discovery or convincing the betrayed partner that all is well in the relationship.

Betrayed partners who have been longing for their significant other to pay attention to them, to show empathy, and to invest in the relationship can be vulnerable to this type of manipulation. They can easily mistake such seduction for caring and connection, and find themselves being taken advantage of once more as a pawn in the chess game of betrayal.

Pressure and Manipulation

In this type of coercive behavior, the unfaithful partner pressures the betrayed partner through verbal manipulation, emotional manipulation, or a combination of the two.

For example, one of my clients told me that her spouse had talked to her repeatedly about his belief that her sex drive was too low. He bought her books and asked her to go see a doctor, which she did. He bought sex toys and lingerie and found Internet research to convince her of her problem.

When this couple entered recovery, her spouse acknowledged that he was sexually addicted. He had been using his sexual relationship with her to act out his compulsive behavior. For the betrayed partner, this was both relieving and infuriating, as she had spent years fearing that her sexual desire was deficient in some way.

For other betrayed partners, pressure and manipulation are not related to sex. They are focused instead on allowing the unfaithful individual to continue behaviors that enable cheating. There can be pressure to accept things like:

- An inconsistent schedule.
- Not returning phone calls.
- Coming home late.
- A "friendship" with someone that feels too close.
- Spending time drinking and in bars.
- Flirtatious behavior.

This type of gaslighting aims to convince the betrayed partner that the cheating partner's behaviors are harmless and acceptable, invalidating the betrayed partner's concerns.

Intimidation or Violence

This type of coercion moves into full-on boundary violations, such as yelling, physical intimidation, threats of abandonment or physical harm, rigid control of finances or other family resources, forcing unwanted sexual contact, having sexual contact when the other person is not able to give consent (such as when the other person is sleeping), and more.

Such coercive behavior layers interpersonal violence over infidelity and creates profound harm and mistrust in the relationship. Many cheating partners who have used violating or bullying behaviors were unaware of how damaging this was to their spouse. They were caught up in accessing their "drug of choice" and protecting their secrets. In their driven, compulsive state, they deceived themselves about how far across the line their behaviors traveled.

THE IMPACT OF GASLIGHTING

In her book, *The Gaslight Effect*, Dr. Robin Stern lays out a four-stage process that individuals who are being gaslighted (she refers to these folks as gaslightees) often go through.

Disbelief

When being gaslighted, the first response is shock and disbelief. We wonder if we heard what was said correctly or if we misunderstood. We wonder if our partner really meant what they said. We can't believe our partner would deliberately lie and manipulate us, so we are stunned into disbelief.

For example, let's say you find two condoms tucked into the side pocket of your partner's briefcase after he returns from a trip. He tells you he has no idea how they got there. He is upset with you because you are upset and accusing him. How can you not trust him, he asks? You look at the condoms and listen to what he is saying, and you know it does not add up. However, the idea that he would betray you (as the condoms seem to indicate) and then lie to you on top of it is too painful to believe. You are filled with shock and disbelief as you try to wrap your mind around the tangled web of misinformation your partner is busy weaving.

Defense

The second stage is defense. During this part of the process, we begin to marshal facts, evidence, and arguments to try to prove the truth and to counter the gaslighting. We don't want to believe our partner would lie to us this way. At the same time, we know what we have found, seen, heard, etc., so we argue with our partner, countering their lies and manipulations with our evidence and suspicions.

If we continue our example from above, in this stage you begin to ask questions. Lots of questions. "How could two condoms end up in your briefcase without you knowing about them? Why are you lying? Do you think I believe what you are saying? Can't you just come clean and tell the truth?"

During this defense stage, the gaslighter will usually double down on the lying by spinning a tale to distract from or cover up the secrets. Now the condoms were put in the briefcase by a prankster co-worker, or they were left over from a vacation the two of you took last year, or maybe you put them there to entrap your partner. Round and round the two of you go with you drilling for the truth and your cheating partner evading.

Depression

After trying to find the truth, after defending against the lying but getting nowhere, depression sets in. This depression is a form of exhaustion and resignation. No matter how clear the evidence is or how much you demand, plead, and beg for the truth, your partner continues to gaslight you. You have not been able to get any resolution and your sense of safety has been even more gravely eroded by your partner's lies and manipulations.

During this stage, you come to an impasse. You know you are not getting the truth. At the same time, you desperately want one or more of the stories your partner has told to be true and to explain the condoms in a way that leaves your relationship unharmed. The alternative creates panic and terror inside your chest. As the tension mounts, you become exhausted and overwhelmed. You feel powerless to change what is happening and you're afraid to assume the worst without confirmation.

Discard Reality

Defeated (for now), you move to stage four of the process. You abandon your efforts to try to figure out why the condoms were there. You either give up and accept one of the tales your partner has spun, or you abandon your efforts to find the truth because it is exhausting, disruptive, and your partner will not budge. You move on with your relationship, sweeping the incident under the proverbial rug. The only alternatives are to keep fighting in an exhausting, damaging loop where you feel crazier and crazier or to stand your ground and live in unbearable, unresolved tension with your partner.

HOW TO HELP YOURSELF WITH GASLIGHTING

Most betrayed partners experience all four types of gaslighting from their cheating partner: lying, reality manipulation, scapegoating, and coercion. Most also loop through the cycle of gaslighting from disbelief to discarding reality multiple times before the final discovery blows the lid off their partner's secrets for good. For betrayed partners who have experienced this type of emotional manipulation and brainwashing, it can be quite some time before they're able to think clearly and to trust themselves to know once again what is real and true.

Below are some steps to help you begin to unwind the gaslighting and reclaim your ability to hold on to your reality.

Identify Your Hooks

We are often clear about our partner's gaslighting behaviors, and we want them to stop. We are usually less clear about being the gaslightee—what causes us to get hooked by our partner's lies? How does this happen?

We look at this issue in more detail in Chapter Eleven. For now, one of the most important things you can do is to identify where in the gaslighting cycle you tend to discard your reality and get pulled in.

For example, is there a point where conflict with your partner gets scary and then, to keep it from escalating, you abandon your reality? Does fear of disconnection create so much anxiety that when your partner becomes defensive you let go of what you know to keep connection intact? Do old beliefs from childhood tell you that you aren't enough or aren't lovable or desirable?

These fears are often the hooks that pull you toward abandoning yourself and believing the lies and manipulations of your partner. Identifying what hooks you and why is the first step toward exiting the gaslighting dance.

Find and Listen to Your Gut

Betrayed partners who come to see me almost always ask within the first session or two, "How will I ever trust my cheating spouse again?"

My answer is that this is not the best question to be asking right now.

The better question is, "How will I rebuild trust with myself? How will I learn to trust my gut and know what I know?" Until you can trust yourself, you will never trust your partner. Trust in your partner is based on trust in yourself and your ability to correctly perceive what is happening in the relationship.

A key step in healing is to begin to believe the inner voice that resides deep in your gut and watches out for your best interests, trying to warn you, protect you, and help you to notice and see the things that are important. This is not always easy. As one of my clients so eloquently put it, "First I had to find my gut, then I had to figure out how to listen to my gut, and only then could I finally start to trust my gut."

Our gut is our bodily-based response to danger or threat. Our bodies always know when we are in danger, even when our mind has not yet become aware of and named the danger. Every betrayed partner I have ever worked with has been able to look back after discovery and see signs and incidents that made them uneasy or created momentary fear but that they brushed past. Everything else at the time seemed fine or there wasn't enough evidence to support the emotional discomfort they were feeling. These moments of unease are our bodily-based responses to threat. We need to learn to listen to ourselves when our body signals that we are in danger or that what is happening is important and we should pay attention.

Learning to listen to ourselves is challenging when our threat center is chronically activated. This throws off our gut instincts because instead of the threat center activating occasionally when the situation calls for it, the gas pedal is always on the floor and the threat center is HEE-HAWING constantly about danger here and danger there. Because we have been walloped by rounds of betrayal and lies, our threat center decides it is just better to assume danger than to wait to respond.

As a result, when we try to listen to what our body is telling us, we can be misled in the weeks and months following betrayal. We can think there is danger when there isn't, and we may tend to assign negative meaning to almost everything happening between us and our partner. We do this because if we assume our partner is lying or continuing to cheat, we will at least not be blindsided again, and that seems like the safest course of action.

This creates yet another dilemma for betrayed partners. We are learning to trust ourselves and hold onto reality while dealing with a dishonest partner and a chronically activated threat system. This is where a trained therapist, a twelve-step group, a therapy group, and other forms of support are invaluable. We need trusted others to help us sort through our emotional experience so that we can determine what is protective, fear-based thinking and what is grounded, intuitive knowing.

Learn to Hold onto Your Reality
Another important step in healing is to learn how to hold onto your own reality even when your reality and your significant other's version of reality do not align.

Let's take our earlier example about finding two condoms in your partner's briefcase and his denial about how they came to be there. If your partner were to keep on denying and not take ownership, you might have to decide that you are going to hold onto your reality anyway.

In this case, you might tell yourself something like the following: "I don't believe that those condoms got there by accident, and I think there is probably something happening with my spouse that is very scary and threatening for me. I can't get him to tell me the truth about this right now, but I believe something is wrong, and I am going to hold onto that belief until I receive evidence that confirms there is a problem or there is not a problem."

This is an intentional choice to not discard your reality in the face of gaslighting, but to instead hold on to it even though it creates discomfort.

Develop the Skill of Wait and See

This leads us to the next skill you need to deal with gaslighting (and please don't throw a shoe at me when I tell you this one because it does really stink, and I know it stinks, and I wish it were otherwise, but it isn't): You need to be able to wait and see. I know. It's terrible. But it's the truth, so here we are.

What this means is that when you choose to hold onto your reality, you may have to enter a period where you wait for the truth to surface—for information that confirms there is or there isn't a problem. In the case of the condoms in the briefcase, you might have to wait and watch to see if you notice other signs and indications of cheating.

The hardest part about this is that it creates a rift in your relationship because, by holding onto your reality and waiting to identify what is true, you enter a place of mistrust. When you don't trust, you can't relax. You are left living in the tension of a big, scary, unresolved issue. This is why *waiting to see* is so very hard and why it can be so tempting to discard your reality instead.

Get Skilled Help

Lastly, you need support. If you believe that you are being lied to and gaslighted by your significant other, you need support to deal with it in a healthy manner. You need a skilled therapist to help you hold onto your reality and confront the dishonesty in appropriate ways. You need other betrayed partners to give you advice about how they have dealt with similar issues. You need to know you are not alone.

Typically, one of the hardest parts of healing from betrayal is uncovering and dealing with repeated lies and manipulation. You must recognize how pervasive the lies and manipulation have become and identify the ways you can become emotionally hooked by your significant other into believing the dishonesty. Becoming more aware of the lies and manipulation helps you regain your sense of trust in your gut (your intuition or inner voice of wisdom) and increases your ability to trust your perceptions and hold onto reality.

As you engage in this difficult work, be aware that facing the ways in which you have been gaslighted can bring up anger and pain. You will benefit from talking with safe friends, working through your feelings in therapy, journaling, and doing lots of calming, soothing self-care.

Now that we understand what gaslighting is and how we get hooked into being a gaslightee, let's explore the dynamics that unfold when betrayed partners need full disclosure about the scope and depth of the betrayal and yet the cheating partner is not ready to be honest.

> Trust is the assured reliance on another's integrity.
>
> — DAVID RICHO

CHAPTER NINE

A HORSE AND WATER:

When You Can't Make Someone Tell the Truth

After learning about infidelity, most betrayed partners feel an intense need to know the scope and depth of what has happened. The discovery of being lied to, sometimes for years or even decades, and the resulting sense of reality fragmentation leaves them shocked, destabilized, and overwhelmed. It can feel like the only way to escape the insanity is to discover the whole truth about what has happened. Then reality might seem knowable again. Piecing together the truth feels like the only way to piece themselves back together.

This process of searching for the whole truth is about trying to find the edges of the betrayal. When betrayed partners learn that they have been cheated on, they typically find out only a piece of the story at first. Then, over the ensuing days and weeks, more dribbles out or is uncovered. During this time, the cheating partner often lies about or hides parts of the story, desperate to keep the whole truth from coming out.

As a betrayed partner, this stokes your fear. The betrayal feels uncontained until the whole picture of betrayal is pieced together. Fear of what you might learn causes you to imagine a panoply of possible horrors to be discovered, each one worse than the last. You need to define the edges of the betrayal so you can contain your experience. You need to know exactly what happened, so you know where the betrayal begins and ends.

This need is about safety. You cannot feel safe if you don't know what your reality is. Imagine being blindfolded on a platform 100 feet off the ground. You don't know where the edges are or how close to the edge you may be. Any movement could bring you closer to safety or closer to danger, but you have no way of knowing which. Freezing in place seems safest, but you can't stay still forever. At some point, you must move in one direction or the other.

This is what discovering betrayal feels like. The search for information is about unfreezing from the initial shock and beginning to search for the edges of the platform; until you know where the edges are and where the danger lies, you cannot know how to protect yourself from further harm and how to move toward safety.

Getting containment around the betrayal by knowing the scope and depth of the behavior is one of the most important steps in the healing process. The shadowy threat of undiscovered details must be eliminated. Also, this is not merely a need you have—it is also *your right* as a betrayed partner. When your partner breaches the agreements regarding fidelity and faithfulness, it changes the nature of your relationship. When this breaking of the relationship agreements is kept secret, it violates your right to know that you are now in an altered relationship, and that your partner is operating according to "rules" that you did not agree to and that, in fact, you don't even know about.

I sat with a couple recently who were dealing with this issue and the betrayed partner said to her husband, "You have made me feel like I'm less of a person, like I'm not fully human and don't deserve to be treated like a full person with rights." She was putting words to the experience of finding herself in a relationship where the agreements had been violated and actions kept secret so she could not have a say about whether she wanted to continue in the relationship in its current, unilaterally altered state. By lying to her and hiding his behaviors, her husband robbed her of this choice. He took away her right to choose the type of relationship she wants to be in.

This dynamic also puts the cheating partner in a "one-up" power-over position; the relationship is no longer operating from an emotionally level playing field. As the only one who knows the whole truth about the relationship and the one who is keeping this information secret, the cheating partner disempowers the betrayed partner and then internalizes that power, taking a "one-up" position.

We all have a right to choose the type of relationship we want to be in. As a betrayed partner, you have a right to know how your significant other has broken your relationship agreements, lied to you, and betrayed your trust. You have a right to know how long that has been going on, in what ways the agreements have been broken, and with whom. To level the playing field in the relationship and restore your relational rights, you need full disclosure regarding what has happened.

Disclosure is the term used to describe a therapeutically facilitated process where the cheating partner writes up a full accounting of their cheating behaviors and deception to share with the betrayed partner to establish a foundation of truth and honesty. The information shared in disclosure allows betrayed partners to make informed decisions about whether they want to continue in the relationship, how they want to continue, and what they need from their partner and the relationship to take care of themselves moving forward.

Now, if only things were this simple.

Where your need for and right to information becomes an issue is when it runs into your partner's discomfort with disclosing the truth.

I have seen articles posted on various websites for betrayed partners where the author is adamantly advocating for the betrayed partner to know the full truth of what has happened in the relationship. These writers talk about the right of the betrayed to know, and the duty of therapists to facilitate the process of full disclosure. I agree with them. However, what is often left out of these discussions is the dicey issue of two people, the betrayer and the betrayed, who are usually in very different places after discovery.

This raises a key question: *What happens when the rights and needs of the betrayed partner collide with the cheating partner's reluctance or refusal to disclose the entire truth?*

THE CHEATING PARTNER'S DILEMMA

Several years ago, through some world-class sleuthing, my client Marissa discovered that her spouse, Mark, had been having anonymous sex with strangers he met online or picked up in bars. Once Mark's behaviors were discovered, he confessed to having anonymous sex during their relationship, but he was unclear with details. In the hours of discussion that followed, Marissa desperately tried to learn the complete truth about Mark's infidelity. The conversation alternated between bouts of angry yelling and painful tears cried together.

The next morning, Marissa called and made therapy appointments for herself and Mark, and they entered treatment. Marissa came to her appointment stuck in a nightmare of fear and pain, feeling she knew only part of the story from what Mark had confessed, but not everything. She felt like there was more. She was also having a hard time holding on to and making sense of what she did know because she was in a state of shock and emotional overwhelm.

Still, she wanted the full truth. She had questions about when, where, who, how many, how often, etc. And it felt imperative to her that she get honest and complete answers to these questions as soon as possible so she could ground herself in the facts and stop the swirling chaos of being lied to.

Mark, on the other hand, came into treatment knowing his relationship was on the line. He knew he had to do something, or he was going to lose Marissa and his family, and that terrified him. He felt terrible about the pain he had caused Marissa and was shocked at the level of hurt and damage he had created. He wanted to stop the pain and somehow put the genie back into the bottle. He did not, however, want to disclose any more about his infidelities. It paralyzed him to think of what might happen if the full truth were known.

Mark was caught in a very common dilemma that cheating partners experience when their behaviors are discovered. The dilemma goes like this: "I don't want to hurt my partner and I'm terribly upset that she is in pain and our relationship is in jeopardy. I don't want to lose my relationship. However, I am not ready to give up my affair or sexual behaviors or to tell the full truth about what I have been doing." Typically, the cheating partner's dilemma occurs because they have competing attachments. They are attached to two things: their partner and their sexual behaviors. These two things are now in conflict, and the cheating partner is being presented with a choice.

Even if the unfaithful partner is willing to enter therapy or has stopped the affair or other cheating behaviors, the dilemma is still active. The desire to keep the truth about secret behaviors hidden is incredibly powerful. The fear of negative repercussions is overwhelming.

Mark's solution was to do what most cheating partners do when caught: to keep both attachments intact. At this stage of newfound crisis, almost all cheating partners attempt to keep both their relationship and their sexual behavior (or, if they give up the infidelity, they attempt to keep secrets about what they did).

In this dynamic, the cheating partner usually tries to minimize the damage caused. To do this, they make heroic efforts to try to calm and ease their partner's fears while simultaneously protecting and hiding their past (and sometimes ongoing) sexual behaviors. Usually, this involves telling some portion of the truth while maintaining a stash of lies about the full extent and scope of the cheating behaviors. This partial truth is almost always presented as the full truth, with swearing on the family Bible and copious tears of remorse intended to convince the betrayed partner that now they know all there is to know.

Cheating partners often believe that the way to minimize damage and prevent the loss of their relationship is to continue lying and withholding information. They do this because they are terrified of losing the relationship; they see the amount of pain and damage they have caused, and they have great fear about increasing the level of anguish by revealing more. As a result, they keep secrets and tell lies, hoping the whole story will never be discovered.

In addition, cheating partners often have enormous shame about their secret behaviors. To expose the full extent of the double life they have been leading is to expose themselves to intolerable feelings of shame and worthlessness.

Cheating partners often convince themselves that telling the truth is the most dangerous and damaging thing they could possibly do, and that lying and hiding is the safest path.

This is the exact opposite of what is true. Over and over at our counseling center, my team and I work with unfaithful individuals who are convinced that telling the truth will end their relationship. We spend a great deal of time helping them see that it is not the truth but *their behaviors*, including their continued dishonesty, that will end the relationship. Telling the truth is not what ends relationships; it is the lying and the keeping of secrets that make a relationship unsustainable for betrayed partners.

Most relationships terminate because of ongoing secrets, manipulation, and deception. Betrayed partners cannot find any safe emotional ground if they are still being lied to, so eventually they give up and end the relationship.

THE TOXIC DANCE OF STAGGERED DISCOVERY

This is the awful dynamic that couples dealing with betrayal frequently get stuck in. In our example with Marissa and Mark, Marissa wants and needs to know what has been happening in their relationship. She has been blindsided and tumbled about, and for her it feels like the only way to return to solid ground is to know the entire truth about the betrayal.

Meanwhile, Mark is terrified he will lose Marissa and feel intolerable shame if he tells the whole truth. He will also have to confront his addiction and face the arduous process of becoming sexually sober and learning to live life without self-medicating. It feels to him like telling the truth is the surest way to lose his relationship. He believes that if Marissa knows the full truth, she will stop loving him, lose respect for him, and leave him.

So, Mark and Marissa entered the toxic dance of staggered discovery. Staggered discovery is when information about the cheating and betrayal trickles out in dribs and drabs. Each time new information is provided there are assurances that the whole truth has been revealed and no more lies will be told. But that in itself is a lie. There are still plenty of secrets, and many lies will be told to cover them up.

Here is what staggered discovery looked like for Marissa and Mark:

Marissa started off asking questions, imploring Mark to tell her the whole truth and impressing upon him how critical this was for her. As they talked, she started to hear slightly different versions of the information he had shared previously. She noticed that some details changed, so she drilled down on those details, calling Mark's attention to the discrepancies in what he had told her and demanding an explanation. Mark, realizing he had tripped up by disclosing a detail he had previously kept hidden, provided a little bit more information but not the entire truth.

For example, Mark had previously made it sound like his cheating started after they had their first child. But then, in a later conversation, he mentioned that he had cheated in previous relationships, too. This caused Marissa to ask when the infidelity in their relationship really started. Did he cheat on her from the beginning of the marriage? Eventually, Mark said yes, it did start at the beginning of the marriage. The reality, however, is that he was sleeping around when they met and began dating and he never stopped. But he did not tell her that. Instead, he answered the specific question she asked about the beginning of the marriage and hoped to keep the rest hidden.

This new information sent Marissa into a spiral of new betrayal and pain as she tried to wrap her mind around the idea that she had been cheated on during the entire relationship. For a few days, she and Mark fought, cried, talked, and fought some more as she tried to process this new information. Mark, for his part, assured her that she now knew everything there was to know. And he cried his own tears of pain and sorrow about what he had done to her and their family.

Eventually, things settled down in the relationship and they began to move forward. Until Marissa found a notebook where Mark had been doing some of his therapy homework. In this notebook, Marissa read that Mark had dozens and dozens of partners over the course of their marriage—sometimes while traveling, sometimes locally. Mark had previously told her that he had only hooked up for sex when traveling one or two times per year. Now she found out he had many more sexual encounters than he'd led her to believe, and that it wasn't just when he was traveling. It was also happening in their hometown.

Marissa was once again swept back into the vortex of betrayal. For her, the new information was a fresh betrayal that she had to wrap her mind around while simultaneously dealing with the betrayal of being lied to again. Mark had sworn he was telling the entire truth and seemed sincerely apologetic, even comforting and reassuring her in her pain. To learn that he was lying the whole time felt even more unbearable than the new information she had learned.

When cheating partners are still lying and feigning sincerity, even using therapy and recovery language or behavior to hide their secrets, there is untold damage to the relationship. Betrayed partners can no longer trust anything their cheating partner tells them. They can no longer trust that therapy, recovery language, and new behaviors are indicative of true change. When cheating partners use these tools to continue to lie, they rob themselves of the very tools they need if they hope to rebuild relationship trust. They set their betrayed partner up to mistrust their words and new behaviors. And because of this, neither the betrayed partner nor the relationship can move forward in the process of healing.

For betrayed partners, this is death by papercut. It is the damaging cycle of repeated rounds of betrayal as the partial truth trickles out over time. It deepens mistrust, heightens trauma symptoms, and worst of all, at the end of all the drama, the betrayed partner still doesn't have the whole truth.

The alternative to the toxic process of staggered discovery I'm describing here is a full therapeutic disclosure. Discovery is shocking, unplanned, overwhelming, and usually only a portion of the betrayal is revealed. Disclosure is the exact opposite. In disclosure, the cheating partner voluntarily tells the betrayed partner the full scope and depth of the cheating. Discovery is part of the betrayal. Disclosure is part of the healing.

When done in a thoughtful, contained, directed manner (don't try this at home), disclosure can be a significant turning point for couples dealing with betrayal. For couples who get therapeutic help with this process and do it well, disclosure lays a foundation upon which the relationship can begin to be rebuilt. The betrayed partner now has the whole story, the lies and secrets have been disclosed, and the betrayal can slowly but steadily be processed and healed.

The incredibly challenging dilemma at the heart of this issue is that despite your right as a betrayed partner to know the full truth about what has happened in your relationship, despite your emotional and psychological need to receive full disclosure about the betrayal, despite the reality that honesty, truthfulness, and restored integrity are the only possible way forward in the relationship, you cannot make your cheating partner tell you the truth.

MOVING OUT OF STAGGERED DISCOVERY

So, what is the solution? What is the way out of this dilemma?

The way out of the toxic dance of staggered discovery is to rescue yourself from the damage of ongoing lies and half-truths by making the empowered decision that you are going to protect your own heart by stepping out of your part of the dance. There are two steps in this process.

Step 1: Become Willing to Wait

Become willing to wait for your significant other to find the willingness to tell you the entire truth about the cheating and dishonesty. Decide to wait for your cheating partner to prepare and present a full disclosure.

And yes, I know that at this stage of the game the absolute last thing you want to hear is that you are going to have to wait to get the whole story. In fact, the idea that after being lied to, cheated on, manipulated, shamed, and heartbroken, you must wait on the full truth until your lying, cheating partner is ready to tell it probably makes you want to pound your fists against the wall in fury.

If you're like most betrayed partners, the idea that you, the injured party, should have to wait for your cheating partner to become willing to tell you the entire truth is such an abomination to your sense of justice that it is almost impossible to accept. The only thing likely to bring you to a willingness to consider this option is the recognition that the alternative—staggered discovery, death by papercut, repeated rounds of betrayal—is even worse.

It may also help to understand why it takes time for cheating partners to get to where they are willing and able to tell the whole truth about their sexual behaviors.

I asked one of my sexually addicted clients how many sexual partners he had outside of his primary relationship. He told me four. The next week he came back to therapy and told me that he had gone through his social media and chat history to see if what he told me was correct. He was shocked to realize he'd had over twenty-five partners since getting married five years earlier. "Last week when I told you four, I truly believed that was the number," he told me. "I cannot believe that I was able to forget these encounters so thoroughly that I fooled myself into thinking that I only cheated occasionally."

==It takes time for unfaithful partners to come to a place where they can provide complete and honest disclosure because they must dismantle the psychological structure they have built to protect themselves from the truth about their behaviors. They must become willing to know the whole story themselves—they must permit themselves to remember the events they have tried to forget—and then they must excavate the past, confront their behavior, and accept the truth.==

This is not a process that can be done alone. The ability to deceive the self is too embedded and the need to protect the self from discovery is too strong. It takes a skilled therapist, trained in helping clients to break through their denial, and identify and then move their lies and self-manipulations out of the way.

This does not happen in one therapy session or even in a day-long intensive. It has taken many years to build up the internal defenses protecting the secrets, and it takes both time and intentional effort to dismantle those defenses and integrate the secrets into full conscious awareness. Usually, this is a process that takes several weeks of intense and focused work and effort with a skilled therapist guiding, challenging, encouraging, and pushing for accountability.

Many betrayed partners have been told that they can't have disclosure yet because the cheating partner is not ready. This is maddening for betrayed partners if they do not understand the strength of the defenses guarding the secrets and feel like the cheating partner is simply choosing to continue to lie and can make a choice at any moment to tell them the whole truth.

Understanding the dynamics underlying the chronic lying and dishonesty helps betrayed partners move out of the feelings of helplessness and powerlessness they have experienced throughout rounds of staggered discovery. Then they can move into an empowered stance where they make a choice to protect their own mental health and hearts as they wait for their cheating partner to do the hard work of preparing to give them full disclosure.

Most betrayed partners go through a process of staggered discovery very similar to Marissa's. Each new piece of information is a fresh betrayal, shocking their system all over again and deepening the original traumatic impact. Round after round of this painful process drains them, stripping them down to a place of raw, broken wounding. It exhausts their resources, uses energy needed for self-care and wise decision-making, and keeps them in a constant state of stress and anxiety.

For most partners, it is only after they have gone through several rounds of staggered discovery, feeling more beat up, traumatized, suspicious, mistrustful, and angry each time, that the idea of waiting to hear the full truth in one sitting starts to make sense.

Coming into acceptance that you cannot make your cheating partner tell you the truth is a very hard thing to do. Coming into acceptance that even if your cheating partner is willing to disclose the entire truth, you are going to have to wait to hear it while the cheating partner gets support and sorts through internal distortions, self-manipulation, fear, reluctance, and denial? This is not an easy choice to make. However, most betrayed partners find, at some point, that they must step out of the dance of staggered discovery and start taking care of themselves more proactively.

Step 2: Set a Bottom Line Around Receiving Disclosure
For you to feel like you can take a step back and wait for your significant other to break through their internal denial and prepare a full disclosure, you need to know your need for the whole truth and your right to the whole truth will be honored. To do this, you can set a bottom line by letting your cheating partner know you need a full therapeutic disclosure by a certain date.

To do this, I encourage you to consult with your therapist and your partner's therapist about what to reasonably expect in terms of a date for completing disclosure. Two weeks is not reasonable. Remember, it takes time to dismantle the psychological defenses that your cheating partner has built up around the addiction and infidelity. Two weeks is going to get you more staggered discovery, and nobody wants that. You need to give it ten to twelve weeks to get the job done adequately. And for some cheating partners, it takes even longer depending on how much work their therapist must do with them around lowering their defenses. Setting this date in conversation with your therapist and your partner's therapist will help you understand where your partner is in the process of telling the truth and what you can expect as a timeline.

The second part of a bottom line for disclosure is determining what you will need to do to take care of yourself if your partner fails to provide full disclosure in a timely fashion. The purpose of this boundary is not to pressure or threaten the cheating partner; it is to hold yourself accountable to your needs and to not fall prey to any more deception or manipulation.

This boundary does not need to be held rigidly. If your partner gets the flu and is out of work for two weeks and misses therapy as well, it can be adjusted. However, if your partner cancels therapy appointments for no reason or simply drags the process out, then you may need to enforce your boundary to honor your need and right to full disclosure.

You will need to do some thinking about what you need in terms of a boundary, as this is different for everyone. You want to ask yourself, "What will it mean for me if I don't receive full disclosure in a timely manner?"

For most betrayed partners, this question is about the level of safety they are able to feel in the relationship when they don't yet know where the edges of the betrayal fall. If disclosure is not provided within the timeframe requested, some individuals will need to ask for a separation until they receive full disclosure. Others will need to ask for their partner to move out of the bedroom, or to put couple's therapy on hold, or for their partner to increase therapy sessions to twice a week until disclosure is provided.

Again, this is a very individual issue, so you need to connect with your inner wisdom and ask yourself what you will need to feel safe until disclosure is received.

Interestingly, when you do accept the need to wait, your stress and anxiety levels are likely to decrease. Your desire to know everything will not go away, nor will your stress and anxiety completely disappear. But knowing that you're eventually going to hear it all, and all at once, frees you from the ongoing, cumulative, papercut pain of staggered discovery.

A good friend once said to me that she believes most suffering comes from a refusal to accept reality. She believes that when we balk and fight against what is true and what is happening in our reality, that is what creates mental anguish and suffering.

I think this truth applies here. If you, as a betrayed partner, can wrap your mind and heart around the idea that you need and have a right to the whole truth, but to protect your heart from further trauma you must wait for your significant other to sort things out to the point of being willing and able to give you that truth, you can avoid a significant amount of pain and suffering. If you can accept this reality as it is, holding all these principles together at once, you give yourself a huge gift. You preserve your dignity, protect your fragile and precious heart, and create a possibility and a pathway for your healing and perhaps that of your relationship.

Now that we have identified the four types of gaslighting and looked at several key issues around receiving disclosure, in the next chapter we are going to explore an attachment-based phenomenon that complicates and heightens the emotional and psychological injury: betrayal blindness.

Note:
Disclosure is a complex process that requires skill and training to properly facilitate. It is beyond the scope of this book to give a full description of how a well-done disclosure proceeds. If you would like information (either as a therapist/coach facilitating disclosures or as a betrayed partner who is preparing for disclosure) that thoroughly describes the disclosure process, please visit https://michellemays.com/programs/disclosure-prep-for-couples/.

> **Denial is the
> worst form of the truth.**
>
> ELLA THE WISE AND POWERFUL

CHAPTER TEN

SEE NO EVIL, HEAR NO EVIL:

Understanding Betrayal Blindness

Joe lost his job for viewing pornography at work. His wife, Sandy, believes him when he says he was looking at an email someone sent him, it was only that one time, and how crazy and unjust is it that his company fired him? Joe and Sandy tell everyone that he was fired unfairly and are thinking about suing the company.

Keith notices that his partner Jill flirts seductively with his male friends and family members. Lately, she has been late from work or not available at times when he reaches out by phone and text. When he asks her about it, she tells him that nothing is going on and that he is being possessive, jealous, and controlling. She is just having fun when she flirts, it's harmless. Keith doesn't want to be "that guy" and chastises himself for being paranoid. He decides to try to loosen up and not be such a downer.

Bob and Jack have been married for five years and have agreed to be monogamous. Jack has a long history of cheating in his previous relationships. Bob notices that Jack is sexting and has been out clubbing and involved with other partners. When he confronts Jack about this and suggests that perhaps he has a problem regarding compulsivity around sexuality given his long history of cheating, Jack denies that there is a problem. He apologizes profusely and promises to stop and stay stopped. Bob breathes a sigh of relief and believes Jack's promise.

In the past, we would look at these individuals and label their behavior denial. The concept of denial originated with Freud, who considered it a defense mechanism. Over time, denial entered the addiction treatment field as a term used to describe the way addicted individuals block out awareness of their problem and the negative consequences being created for themselves and those they love. As addiction treatment expanded to include the entire family system, denial was applied as a form of codependence to partners and family members of addicts.

This is another area where we now know better and can do better.

When betrayed partners block out information and enter the state of "knowing but not knowing" that is so common, they are dealing with a complex attachment-based phenomenon called betrayal blindness. This term was first coined by Jennifer Freyd PhD, the founder of Betrayal Trauma Theory.

Freyd says it this way: "In this situation, it is more adaptive to not know about the trauma that is occurring. Therefore, the theory proposes, people become blind to betrayal to the extent that being aware of it would threaten a relationship in which they are dependent."[1]

We know from our exploration of attachment in Chapter Three that our adult romantic partners are our primary attachment figures and any rupture in our secure bond with them is experienced as a survival-level threat. Betrayal blindness is an adaptive coping strategy that mitigates against threat to our relationship by blinding us to danger.

Betrayal blindness is an elegant solution to danger because it brings our threat system (fight or flee danger) into alignment with our attachment system (reach for connection in the face of danger). We preserve our attachment to our partner by holding dangerous information that could threaten our relationship outside our awareness.

As a result, betrayal blindness creates the pretense that our world is the way we want it to be, rather than how it really is. Betrayal blindness takes a thousand different forms, but its function is always the same—to protect us from a reality that feels too big and too difficult to handle.

For most betrayed partners, betrayal blindness is a part of our experience whether we are attempting to stay and repair the relationship with the cheating partner or we have chosen to leave the relationship.

THE BIND THAT CREATES THE BLIND

Betrayal blindness brings us right back to the key relational bind at the heart of betrayal trauma: the person who we depend upon the most and turn to in times of trouble is now the source of our distress. Going blind to what is happening is how we attempt to deal with the no-win bind that betrayal creates.

Freyd's research originated with the study of children dealing with betrayal traumas perpetrated by a parent or primary caregiver. Betrayal trauma theory homes in on the specific dilemmas and impacts created when abuse or neglect are perpetrated by the person one is attached to and dependent upon. Because these types of betrayals are relational and happen in the context of bonded attachment, their impact is different from non-relational trauma (like a car accident) or trauma experienced at the hands of a stranger.

Because as children we are dependent upon our caregivers, we must preserve our attachment to them even if we do not receive the attention, nurture, and protection we need. As a result, children will often assume neglect or abuse are a result of something bad or wrong with themselves. This allows them to maintain their attachment to their caregivers by placing the blame for abuse or neglect with themselves.

This transfer of responsibility is where childhood shame begins. The belief that gets encoded in the child's nervous system, often before speech is even possible, is, "I am deficient or defective in some way and that is why I am unworthy of care and can't get my needs met." This transfer of shame and blame rescues the child from the overwhelm of being attached to someone who is absent, painful, or dangerous by blocking awareness. The more important a relationship is to us, the more critical it is for us to maintain our attachment and the more vulnerable we are to betrayal blindness.

BUT I'M A GROWN-UP

It is perhaps easy for us to see the bind children are in. However, it may be more challenging for us to understand how these same dynamics can play out in relationships between adults who have physical, cognitive, and emotional resources at their disposal and are therefore able to be independent and autonomous and survive.

Maintaining our relationship with our partner protects us from stress and danger. As a result, any adult, no matter how self-sufficient we believe ourselves to be, can become susceptible to betrayal blindness when faced with the threat created by being cheated on and then chronically gaslighted.

Betrayal injures the safe connection at the heart of secure bonding. This attachment injury is felt as a primary danger, threatening our sense of survival. The more threatened we feel, the more we will take steps to try to preserve our attachment and therefore our survival. One effective way to preserve our sense of safe connection is to not know what we know and not see what we see, particularly if what we were to know and see would threaten our relationship.

That said, we will be even *more* susceptible to betrayal blindness if we have a history of childhood trauma. In her research, Freyd talks about the human survival strategy of "cheater detectors," meaning the ability to tell if someone is trustworthy and safe to attach to. Those who experience childhood betrayal traumas can have difficulty accessing their cheater detectors, and therefore have a harder time identifying dishonesty or a lack of trustworthiness in adult relationships.[2]

If, as children, we adopted the coping strategy of dissociating and holding information outside of our awareness, we can be more vulnerable to betrayal blindness as adults. As a result, betrayal blindness occurs on a continuum, with some partners experiencing milder forms of it and others (often those with a history of childhood trauma) experiencing more severe forms.

WHEN BETRAYAL BLINDNESS AND GASLIGHTING COLLIDE

While betrayal blindness is an attachment-driven survival behavior, it creates a potent cocktail of crazy-making confusion when it collides with the cheating partner's gaslighting.

Freyd says, "Betrayers often help those they betray to remain unaware of the betrayal. For instance, rather than making explicit demands for silence, perpetrators often groom their victims for unawareness and denial. Some perpetrators may do this without even realizing it. Such perpetrators may even remain partly blind themselves, and this blindness may help account for the lack of awareness of others around them."[3]

Because cheating partners must lie to themselves before they lie to those they love, it creates a form of blindness. They hold the consequences of their behaviors outside of their awareness. For most cheating partners, if they were to let themselves know about the level of hurt and destruction their cheating would create, it would deter them. Instead, awareness of violating their value system and hurting those they most love gets blocked off by a mental scaffolding that justifies, minimizes, or rationalizes their behavior.

Cheating partners then gaslight the betrayed partner, who is vulnerable to the gaslighting because of the typical trust that most people have in their partner and the normal fear of relational disconnection that is always present in long-term relationships. Trust combined with fear of relational loss creates a significant investment in wanting and needing to believe the excuses, distractions, reassurances, and outright lies and manipulations the cheating partner offers. Gaslighting and betrayal blindness merge into a compelling dynamic that keeps the betrayed partner in the dark.

Freyd was also the first person to identify DARVO, a gaslighting strategy that is highly emotionally abusive. DARVO stands for:

- **D**eny the behavior,
- **A**ttack the individual who is confronting,
- **R**everse the roles of **V**ictim and **O**ffender.[4]

DARVO is scapegoating and reality manipulation combined. Freyd has said, "Not only does DARVO likely cause psychological harm, but we suspect it also often leads to retraction or silence."[5] This is because DARVO is much more than a simple lie. Instead, DARVO attacks, blames, and threatens with relational disconnection and abandonment all at once.

One of my clients told me recently that she discovered her spouse's sexual behavior through contracting an STI. When she confronted her spouse, he became incredibly angry and indignant (denied the behavior) and accused *her* of having an affair (attacked the partner who was confronting). He gave an Oscar-worthy performance as he cried tears of anger and rage about his perceived betrayal (reversing the roles of victim and offender). He stuck by this story so adamantly and for so long that my client began to wonder if she had some form of mental illness that caused her to lose her memory of the supposed affair.

When gaslighting and betrayal blindness fuse in this manner, they form a crucible for the betrayed partner, who is confronted with two terrible choices: either acknowledge their significant other is manipulating and emotionally abusing them or abandon reality to preserve relational connection. It is just too much. To create protection, body and mind go blind and retreat.

HOW WE GO BLIND

When we experience danger, our threat response systems fire up and activate our core coping strategies of fight, flight, and freeze. Freyd has argued that betrayal blindness is an adaptive strategy that is part of the freeze response. "If we are strong enough and in a good enough situation, we confront (fight) the betrayal to correct the situation. If we cannot do that, we withdraw from the person or the situation (flight) to avoid future harm. If that option is too dangerous—for instance, because we are dependent on the betrayer—our next best defense is to block out awareness of the betrayal; in other words, a kind of mental freeze (betrayal blindness) is our next best option."[6]

There are three primary ways that the freeze response of betrayal blindness can manifest for betrayed partners: through dissociation, loss of connection to emotions, and shame.

Dissociation

Betrayal blindness as a freeze response moves us into a hypo-aroused state where we are numb, stuck in avoidance, and often dissociated. When we are dependent on another person, we are profoundly vulnerable. This vulnerability is only possible because we trust the other person to be there for us in a reliable manner.

When betrayal occurs, it destroys trust while our vulnerability often remains. The lack of trust while we remain vulnerable to our partner is the unbearable dilemma that creates dissociation.

The American Psychiatric Association defines dissociation as "a disruption and/or discontinuity in the normal integration of consciousness, memory, identity, emotion, perception, body representation, motor control, and behavior."[7] This definition covers an enormous amount of territory regarding the many ways we can separate information. Dissociation is what allows one part of us to know something while another part of us does not.

Freyd and other researchers have looked closely at the coping strategy of dissociation in response to betrayal, using a well-established psychological test called the Dissociative Experiences Scale (DES). Their findings are summarized in her book, *Blind to Betrayal*, where she states, "We and other researchers have found a relationship between DES scores and trauma exposure: the more exposure to trauma, particularly betrayal trauma, the higher the DES score is likely to be. We understand this in terms of betrayal trauma theory—that dissociation serves to support betrayal blindness, so people who have had considerable exposure to betrayal trauma develop stronger abilities to dissociate."[8]

This means that for betrayed partners, the longer the history of betrayal or the more rounds of betrayal we have been through, the more likely we are to have used dissociation as a coping strategy.

Loss of Connection to Emotions
In addition to holding events and information out of our cognitive awareness, dissociation can also create a loss of knowing about our emotions. When we regularly struggle to identify or express our emotions this is sometimes a result of what is called Alexithymia. Research into dissociation and betrayal trauma have examined the loss of connection to emotional experience as another form that betrayal blindness can take.[9]

For betrayed partners, holding emotions outside of awareness can be a profoundly adaptive strategy. If we allow ourselves to fully face the sexual betrayal, we run the risk of feeling loss around our deepest needs: the need to feel that we matter and that we belong. The loss of worth engendered by betrayal creates feelings of shame, rejection, despair, self-loathing, rage, desolation, and loneliness. Just writing that list of feelings gives me a pit in my stomach. Of course, we don't want to feel these emotions. They are too hot to touch. To dissociate from these emotions is a perfectly logical coping strategy and one many if not most betrayed partners engage in to some extent.

One way dissociation from emotion commonly plays out is in the way betrayed partners tell their betrayal story. Dozens of betrayed partners have sat in my office and told me truly horrendous details about the sexual betrayal they have endured. They have done this matter-of-factly, with little emotion. Some have even smiled or laughed as they walked me through the crime scene of their relationship. These partners are connected to the events and information of their experience, but they are blind to their emotions. They are protectively holding their grief, pain, and anger out of their awareness. Their dissociation from their emotions protects them from emotional overwhelm and protects their relationship from the repercussions of allowing themselves to feel.

Shame

As we discussed in Chapter Five, betrayed partners are vulnerable to carrying the shame of sexual betrayal and to feeling shame about their attachment to the cheating partner. One of the ways we can go blind to betrayal is by shifting the shame of betrayal onto ourselves rather than holding our cheating partner accountable.

When we carry the cheating partner's shame, we excuse, minimize, or rationalize their behavior into something more palatable that we can tolerate. After all, if we hadn't been busy with the children and work, if we hadn't gained those ten pounds, if we had been more sexually adventurous, if we had focused more on our partner's needs, then they wouldn't have cheated.

Our responsibility-taking allows us to know but not know about our partner's choices and the dynamics that propelled the cheating. In addition, if we are to blame, then we can fix it. We not only protect ourselves from fully knowing about the betrayal, we soothe ourselves with the illusion of control over the cheating partner's behaviors and choices. In this way, shame can play a role in betrayal blindness. We preserve our attachment to the cheating partner by carrying shame and blame for them.

Betrayal blindness also protects us from the shame we can feel about staying in our relationship with the cheating partner. One client who had chosen to stay with her sexually addicted spouse said to me, "I'm afraid to let myself know what my partner has done because I feel like if I know about it, I will lose my self-respect and feel humiliated that I've chosen to stay. I stay blind because I don't want to feel shame and humiliation." How brave and honest to identify this for herself! Putting her finger on what betrayal blindness was protecting her from (shame and humiliation) allowed her to move into awareness about her partner and acceptance about her decision to stay and repair the relationship.

BETRAYAL BLINDNESS AND ATTACHMENT AMBIVALENCE

When our attachment systems fire in the face of danger, they motivate us to move toward our primary attachment figure. If our attachment figure is the source of the danger, then we need a solution that allows us to still connect with them while protecting us from the danger they represent. Betrayal blindness allows us to do that.

On the following page is the graphic showing the cycle of connection and disconnection created by attachment ambivalence and shame. Now we've added betrayal blindness to help us see how the need to protect ourselves from information that threatens our relationship animates the cycle and drives us in and out of connection with the cheating partner.

THE BETRAYAL BIND

Attachment Ambivalence and Betrayal Blindness

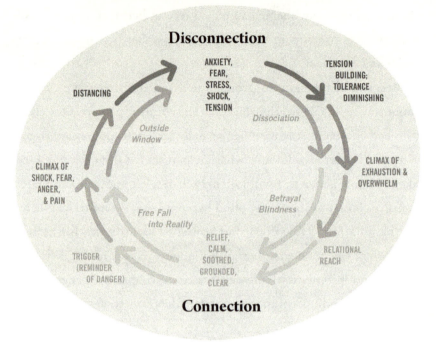

Betrayal Blindness and Connection

Let's start at the bottom of the cycle this time with the betrayal blindness that leads to connection. Sometimes, to feel the relief of being connected to our safe base again, we will move into betrayal blindness. We will hold out of our awareness the information that creates fear or danger. By going blind, we create a pathway that allows us to relax into connection with our partner. Sometimes this form of blindness-based connection can last for a day; sometimes it can last for months or years.

Free Fall into Reality

At some point, something will happen to remind us of the betrayal. There will be a new discovery or there will be a trigger that brings our pain and panic flooding back. This brings us into emotional contact with everything that our cheating partner did to hurt us and destroy our trust. Because we have been in a state of blindness, the process of coming back into awareness is not gentle. Instead, it often feels like being dropped off a cliff and landing flat on our back on the rocks of reality.

Climax of Shock, Fear, and Anger that Pushes Us Outside Our Window

Because we were floating in the pink cloud of non-awareness created by betrayal blindness, when we come back into contact with the lying and cheating, the pain and anger are shocking. We are jolted awake, and our trauma symptoms roar to life in response as we are pushed outside our window of tolerance.

Distancing

Now we push away from our partner. Our awareness of their behavior makes them seem dangerous, so we move away to protect ourselves from threat. We may fight or withdraw, but in some way, we create emotional or physical distance to defend against the engulfing pain and fear.

Disconnection

Ah, but disconnection is its own form of torture, torture that arises as our attachment system goes into distress from losing connection to our primary attachment figure. The longer we stay here, the more the stress, anxiety, and tension build up inside of us, crying out for relief.

Dissociation to the Rescue

Betrayal blindness beckons, and without even knowing it is happening, we dissociate from the pain and fear as we tuck information out of our awareness so we can move back toward our partner. We need to connect to bring our distress levels down and soothe our ragged attachment system. Betrayal blindness allows us to move danger out of the way so we can come back into the relief of relational connection.

PUTTING IT ALL TOGETHER

When we put it together, we can see how shame, betrayal blindness, and attachment ambivalence sync up to create the complex and chaotic relational dynamics that follow discovery.

Attachment Ambivalence, Shame, and Betrayal Blindness

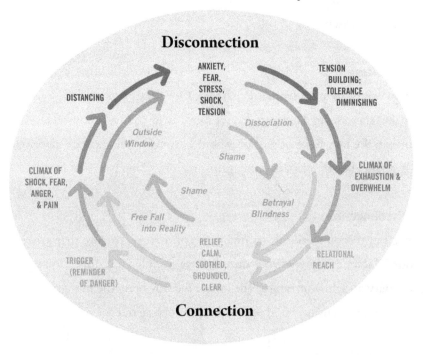

This is all normal. These dynamics are neurobiological (body/brain/mind); they are how humans respond to betrayal at the hands of their most trusted loved one. When we understand what is happening to us and why, there is less shame. When shame lifts, we are better able to make choices about how we respond, how we cope, and how we heal.

I also want to caution you to not pathologize connection to your partner. It can be easy to think something must be wrong with you that you keep moving back toward your cheating partner. This is not true. Not all connection with the cheating partner involves betrayal blindness, and it is important not to assume it does.

Still, you want to be aware of the role betrayal blindness can play and identify the ways you have gone blind so you can come back into full awareness and make healthy choices for yourself. Those healthy choices may include moments (hopefully growing moments) of safe connection with your partner. This may be the result of the two of you moving into a recovery and repair process together. Or it may be the result of choosing to leave the relationship and learning to collaborate with your partner around co-parenting or uncoupling.

Either way, it is vital that we remember we are relational creatures and a relational problem like betrayal requires a relational solution. Learning to be relationally connected in ways that are healthy and life-giving is the name of the game.

In the next chapter, we are going to continue our exploration of betrayal blindness by looking at coping strategies that can be deployed by betrayed partners who are caught in betrayal blindness.

ADDITIONAL RESOURCES FOR YOU

To learn more about betrayal blindness, watch the free video **How to Avoid Going Blind to Betrayal in Your Relationship** by Michelle Mays. Visit michellemays.com/betrayal-blindness-video to watch.

> Fear is a deeply ancient instinct,
> in other words,
> an evolutionarily vital one . . .
> but it ain't especially smart.
>
> — ELIZABETH GILBERT

CHAPTER ELEVEN

GOING BLIND:

Patterns of Betrayal Blindness

By the time partners discover betrayal, weeks, months, or years of lying and secret-keeping on the part of the cheating partner have gone by. Gaslighting compounds betrayal blindness as our desire to avoid fear and pain colludes with the cheating partner's goal of keeping the double-life hidden, creating a potent formula for not knowing and not seeing.

By the time there is enough discovery to convince us there is a real problem, betrayal blindness and the resulting dissociation may have become a chronic coping pattern. As a result, betrayed partners who seek help and enter treatment often come through the door with active betrayal blindness that has been ongoing for months and sometimes years. For this reason, working with an expert who understands the complex nature of betrayal blindness is essential.

Below I have outlined some of the coping strategies that betrayal blindness creates. This is not a complete list; it is simply a starting point for understanding common patterns and behaviors that reflect the presence of betrayal blindness and dissociation.

FANTASY ISLAND HONEYMOON

This is a stage many betrayed partners pass through after discovery of betrayal. During this time, most cheating partners are still hiding some of their secrets and may even still be actively cheating. However, they are also making heroic attempts to limit the damage their sexual betrayal has caused and to reassure their partner. At the same time, betrayed partners are reeling from pain and disbelief and have enormous fear about what the cheating means for their relationship. This high-octane relational moment is the perfect petri dish for growing betrayal blindness.

Many partners will believe what the cheating partner is telling them during this phase. It is too painful to consider that after being caught cheating and seeing the terrible pain and anguish it has caused, our significant other could continue the hurtful behaviors and extravagant lying. Instead, we want to believe that what we have discovered is the whole story. We buy into the idea that our partner's promise that they have stopped and will never do it again is possible, and they can willpower their way out of the situation. We will agree that we don't need therapy, we need to focus on our relationship, spend more time together, amp up the sexy, and all will be well.

Part of the cheating partner's attempts to keep secret behaviors hidden can include becoming highly attentive and relationally available to the betrayed partner. Betrayed partners, who have been starved for attention and connection while the cheating partner's focus has been elsewhere, will respond to these overtures, believing the relationship is turning around and things are going to get better.

This is an attachment-based phenomenon that is powerfully compelling. Both partners saw the edge of the cliff when the cheating was discovered and felt the possibility of losing one another for good. Both individuals' attachment systems went into distress over this potential loss. To manage their fear and anxiety, both partners use coping strategies that allow them to reassert their attachment bond with one another. The cheating partner is lying, hiding, and wooing, and the betrayed partner has entered into betrayal blindness, holding the larger scope and depth of the problem outside of their conscious awareness.

This phase can last days, weeks, or months. What usually brings it to an end is more discovery. The ongoing betrayal is revealed, the cheating partner is caught in more lies, or more consequences are discovered (STIs, missing money, an affair partner's pregnancy). This new round of betrayal punches through the betrayal blindness and brings betrayed partners into the reality that all is not okay, there is a significant problem, and much more is going to have to be done to deal with it. This is the point when expert help is critical for betrayed partners, as they need support to tolerate staying in awareness about something profoundly scary, uncertain, and dysregulating.

NOT CONNECTING THE DOTS

Another common way betrayal blindness manifests is in a compromised ability to track information. This again combines with the cycle of attachment ambivalence and can depend on where partners are regarding their level of connection or disconnection with the cheating partner. When in a phase of relational connection, they may forget details about the cheating, or they may block key information from their awareness. For example, they may have sex with their partner while blocking from memory that they or their partner are waiting on the results of an STI test.

Betrayal blindness can prevent betrayed partners from connecting dots that seem obvious to everyone else. My client Susan spent months telling me that the child of her husband's affair partner was not his biological child. She held this belief despite the financial support the husband had provided to the child since birth and the close resemblance of the child to her spouse. Knowing that her spouse had a child with another woman was simply too unbearable, so she did not let herself connect the dots around that experience. It took months of slow stabilizing work for her to begin to allow herself to see and know about this child and to grieve the losses this represented.

Betrayed partners who avoid therapy or do not want to receive a full therapeutic disclosure are sometimes stuck in betrayal blindness. Unconsciously, they may be terrified of the emotional impact of finding out more information. Instead, they avoid therapy, telling the cheating partner to go get fixed because, after all, the cheating partner is the one with the problem. Or they decide they do not want disclosure because they don't want to know more.

Sometimes the decision not to pursue more information can be a healthy protection from further pain and damage. Other times it is a form of betrayal blindness designed to avoid information that may threaten relational connection. When it is the latter, it can create deeper problems as relationships built on secrets and avoidance cannot function well or provide a sense of secure bonding.

HYPER-FOCUSING ON WHAT YOU DON'T KNOW TO AVOID WHAT YOU DO KNOW

This pattern can be subtle and tricky to spot. Most betrayed partners are highly activated by details of the betrayal and are on the hunt to find any hidden information. At the same time, however, there is another part of them that is stuck in the freeze state of betrayal blindness. This part is actively avoiding the emotional load that the details of the betrayal present.

One of the ways partners avoid encountering the devastating emotions associated with betrayal is to ignore the information they do have and to instead focus on what else might still be unknown. For example, Stacy and her long-term boyfriend entered recovery a year ago. They dug into the work and her boyfriend completed a solid therapeutic disclosure and passed a polygraph test.

Despite the positive disclosure process, high engagement in recovery activities, and a lack of evidence, Stacy was sure there was more information to be discovered. The possibility that there was more she did not know became her primary focus, and she talked about it in therapy incessantly, fought about it with her boyfriend regularly, and became stuck in obsessive thought loops.

As Stacy and I worked together, I began to be curious about how her focus on the unknown might be protecting her in some way. As we peeled back the layers, it became clear that by hyper-focusing her mind, emotions, and energy on the possibility of some unknown nugget of information, Stacy was able to dissociate from her emotional experience around the disclosure and betrayal.

Her focus on what she didn't know protected her from the emotional impact of what she did know. Over time, she was able to inch closer to these painful emotions and begin to process and integrate them into her experience. As she did this, her belief that there were more hidden secrets diminished. Eventually, this became a non-issue, especially as her boyfriend continued to demonstrate solid recovery.

Another way to hold information and emotional impact outside of awareness is to rerun the details of the betrayal over and over again. This is counter-intuitive because it seems like the person is immersing themselves in the pain of the betrayal by retelling details repeatedly. However, this too is often a protective strategy to avoid pain and loss.

My client Jill provides a great example of this coping strategy in action. Jill had accidentally found her husband's first step document. In it, he had written in detail about his thirty-year history of acting out with sex workers, including secretly spending a significant amount of their retirement funds. Jill copied this document and reread it multiple times every week for months.

She told me she did this because she didn't want to forget what he had done. However, as we explored this behavior over time, she was able to see that rereading this document kept her so dysregulated that she was unable to process her emotional experience of the betrayal. Instead, she stayed hyper-aroused, angry, and overwhelmed.

Rereading the document kept her outside her window of tolerance. It allowed her to avoid the painful process of connecting with the core emotions that needed to be processed for her to heal. When she put the document down and created space for us to start to explore her emotional responses to the betrayal, she was able to begin healing.

CREATING CHAOS AND INTENSITY

This pattern is a favorite of mine. In fact, I overachieved on this one in my own betrayal blindness. Chaos and intensity allowed me to stay busy, distracted, and mentally preoccupied so I could not and did not have space to connect to my emotional experience. The intelligence that my emotions were trying to communicate and the guidance and clarity that could have resulted were buried under a towering pile of activity.

For betrayed partners, behavior patterns that divide attention and create intensity can be easy coping strategies to turn to. We may stay preoccupied with parenting, careers, caretaking a parent or family member, volunteering for projects, coaching a team, exercising or training, hobbies, etc. Nothing on this list is problematic in and of itself. However, each of these can morph from healthy life-giving activity to a maladaptive coping strategy under the wrong circumstances. And sexual betrayal is definitely a wrong circumstance.

In addition, we can divide our attention by creating intensity with the cheating partner. Fighting, battling for empathy, repudiating shame, and declawing the tiger can all create high levels of emotional intensity in our relationship. This intensity is made up of defensive and protective emotions. While we are angry, in pain, anxious, and panic-stricken as we fight and talk and fight some more, we can be doing all of this as a way of dividing our attention and staying occupied while we avoid our deeper, more tender emotions like sadness and loneliness.

Patterns of chaos and intensity help us go blind. We are too busy to let the niggling sense something is not right rise to the surface. We are too overwhelmed with rage and pain to let ourselves feel the deep grief and loss that might push us toward a decision we don't want to make. We are too focused on managing the madness of our hectic schedule to make time for therapy and recovery activities. As a result, we learn to live with constant pain as the background music of our lives. Our divided attention saves us from facing difficult emotions and potential relational loss, but it also blinds us to our reality and creates needless suffering.

MOVING OUT OF BETRAYAL BLINDNESS

Because betrayal blindness is a protective attachment-based coping strategy, it is important to honor its role and function. Moving out of betrayal blindness is gentle, step-by-step work and must be done with the right care and support.

Group Support

One of the best ways to support betrayed partners with betrayal blindness is to work on it in a group setting. I have done this in small group-therapy settings and in our larger online group-based coaching program. Group learning and support is one of the most effective ways to help partners build the internal strength and emotional resilience needed to move from unawareness into awareness—where their emotional reality can be processed.

Working on betrayal blindness within a group provides support and community. As new information is allowed into awareness, it is held not just by the individual but by the group. The knowledge that each person within the group knows and understands the experience being processed provides a healing balm. This emotional buttress enables the betrayed partner to draw not just on their own resources but the resources of the entire group to help them hold the information and begin to digest the emotional and relational ramifications it brings.

In addition, the stories and information shared by other group members help move information out of dissociation and into awareness. Betrayed partners often talk about the aha moments they experience while listening to other partners do their healing work. These aha moments are flashes of clarity and insight that connect dots or help vague and fuzzy information become clear.

In her research, Freyd discusses shareability theory and says,

"Shareability theory proposes that through the sharing of information—that is, through communication—internal knowledge is reorganized into more consciously available, categorical, and discrete forms of knowing. This means that information we have never shared with others is organized differently than information we have shared. So, disclosure affects the *way* we know our own experiences internally."[1]

Individual and Couple Support

In addition, working with an individual therapist who is trained in treating betrayal blindness and understands the many ways it manifests in the lives and relationships of betrayed partners is essential. Without clarity about how betrayal blindness factors into the cycle of attachment ambivalence and impacts couple dynamics, therapists can go in misguided directions regarding individual and relationship healing. Couples' therapists can mistake betrayal blindness for a betrayed partner's willingness to repair or forgive and go down the road of trying to heal the relationship before the betrayed partner has come fully into awareness and emotional connection with their own experience around the betrayal.

Individual work that supports the betrayed partner in fully accessing their experience and building the internal resilience needed to do so is essential prior to couples work that focuses on repair of the relationship. Betrayed partners cannot make informed choices about their relationships while stuck in active betrayal blindness. Instead, therapists need to recognize the orderly progression of healing that is essential and prioritize work around betrayal blindness for betrayed partners.

Another pitfall to be aware of is the fear of pushing activated betrayed partners toward more emotional overwhelm. Therapists confronted with a highly activated betrayed partner can at times avoid nudging the partner toward more painful material. They fear that bringing the betrayed partner into more awareness of their emotional experience will only create more dysregulation. This may be true at the beginning. But a skilled therapist will be able to slowly walk the client toward awareness and help them connect to and process their emotions in a way that will eventually relieve the chronic activation. Avoiding this process leaves the client stranded in the dysregulation that accompanies dissociation with no path back to awareness and self-regulation.

For betrayed partners, the path to healing lies in growing awareness and confidence in our ability to handle painful situations without collapsing into fear, powerlessness, or shame. When we move out of betrayal blindness and grow our capacity to deal with difficult situations and big emotions, we grow our sense of self and our belief that we are capable, resourceful, and can trust ourselves.

In the next chapter, we look at the emotional states of fear, shame, and powerlessness and how these emotions can keep betrayed partners stuck and prevent healing.

It is when the
fear of losing themselves
is greater than the
fear of abandonment
that [betrayed partners]
are most apt to begin
their own recovery process.

CLAUDIA BLACK, PhD

CHAPTER TWELVE

GETTING STUCK:

Fear, Shame, and Powerlessness

Thus far, we have identified three attachment-driven relational binds created by sexual betrayal: attachment ambivalence, attachment shame, and betrayal blindness. These relational binds are driven by three primary emotional states: fear, shame, and powerlessness. In this chapter, we will explore these three powerful emotions that drive partner behaviors, animate the relational binds, trap partners in their trauma symptoms, and block progress in treatment.

THE KINGPIN: FEAR OF LOSS

When sexual betrayal is discovered, it creates a cascade of losses. The loss of relational safety, sexual safety, and emotional wholeness. The loss of the past you thought you had, the present you believed you were living, and the future you dreamed of. There is the loss of self, the loss of who you thought your partner was, the loss of your ability to function, the loss of respect, and the loss of time, energy, and money. These losses plunge betrayed partners into an experience of acute grief. The human heart and mind have difficulty absorbing so many losses at once. As a result, betrayed partners are set adrift on a sea of heartbreak.

Our dilemma is this: to heal, we must risk experiencing *more* loss.

Emerging from betrayal blindness and moving toward healing brings us face to face with the possibility of more relational loss. For example, if we become wise to the gaslighting tactics of the cheating partner, we must then stare straight into their eyes as they lie to us and shock our hearts. If we ask for what we need, we risk the disappointment of our need going unmet. If we risk setting boundaries, we face the possibility that our partner will refuse to stop the affair or addiction and may either leave us or force us to leave them.

These are reality-based moments that are acutely painful and perilously risky.

When healing requires the possibility of more loss, is it any wonder that coping strategies to help us avoid loss are put into action? As a result, *fear of loss is one of the central motivators shaping partner behaviors and responses after betrayal.*

Fear of Loss and Therapy

This fear of experiencing more relational loss is the most significant sticking point that blocks forward progress for betrayed partners. To heal, we must learn to set and maintain boundaries, use our voice effectively, ask for what we need, and take protective action on our own behalf.

These are the skills that trained therapists often introduce and begin to cultivate when betrayed partners enter treatment. However, each of these skills contains risks of experiencing more loss as we gamble with the uncertainty of the cheating partner's response. What if we try to set a boundary and our request is ignored? What if we ask for what we need and our partner says no? What if they keep cheating? What if they keep lying?

We are already reeling from the losses that piled up as we learned about the betrayal. Now, we have sought help and we are being asked to do what? Risk more potential loss? Risk more grief, pain, and panic? Our nervous system is going to look our therapist straight in the eye and say, "Please. You must be joking."

Most of the time, our fear of loss is unconscious. We may listen attentively to the therapist, take our workbook home, and do our homework diligently. However, underneath our efforts to help ourselves heal, a part of us is working diligently to protect ourselves from more loss. This part does not want to feel what neuroscientist Jaak Panksepp calls primal panic—our body/brain/mind reaction to relational disconnection. This part is trying to help us survive by getting us back to safety in whatever way possible.

As a result, the boundaries that we worked so hard on aren't maintained, or the decision to separate gets reversed, or the movement toward disclosure gets sabotaged. The list of ways that we avoid risk of loss due to fear is innovative and endless.

When we do this, we are not being resistant, unwilling, or difficult. Instead, we are responding unconsciously to the bodily-based imperatives of our attachment systems. We fear that we will not emotionally survive more loss and we cannot tolerate the level of risk the healing process requires. As a result, forward movement around the important skills of recovery can be repeatedly blocked or avoided.

I want to reiterate that this is largely unconscious behavior. Partners can talk a big game. We may say we are going to leave the cheating partner if they don't go to treatment, or we are going to call the lawyer if they don't take a polygraph. In the moment, we mean what we say. However, we can lose sight of the gap between what our mind is telling us to do (our cognition) and what our bodily-based attachment system is telling us to do (seek safety through connection). We believe our minds while our bodies go right on avoiding loss through undermining our moves and intentions.

The degree to which this fear of loss keeps us stuck in betrayal blindness and other unhealthy coping strategies depends on our backgrounds. Our sensitivity to relational loss as adults is molded by the moments of disconnection we experienced as children and the way in which those losses were processed and absorbed. If, as children, we experienced relational loss and disconnection that created a pattern of insecure attachment, we are going to have a harder time coping with the losses inherent in adult sexual betrayal. We are going to struggle to find the internal resources needed to risk more potential loss by using the skills of recovery.

SHAME

For betrayed partners, fear and avoidance of relational loss are also about avoiding the discomfort of shame. When we experience loss of connection with our partner, even temporarily, it creates shame by threatening our belief that we are lovable, acceptable, and worthy. Shame produces the bodily-based sense that some lack in us is the reason we are experiencing loss.

The shame that relational disconnection brings falls along a continuum. If we experienced abuse and neglect as a child, we learned to transfer responsibility for that onto ourselves, encoding shame into our nervous systems and core beliefs about ourselves. This transfer of responsibility allowed us to maintain attachment to our caregivers—a necessity for our survival. Unfortunately, this childhood experience of shame follows us into our adult relationships, making us susceptible to acute shame whenever relational loss is experienced.

If the experience of loss so easily generates shame, it is no wonder we find ourselves unconsciously avoiding more loss by avoiding risky (albeit healthy) behaviors that make us vulnerable to further relational disconnection and therefore to the intolerable feelings of shame.

POWERLESSNESS

This brings us to the issue of powerlessness. Part of the stunning pain of betrayal is the sheer powerlessness to stop it. We did not choose to be cheated on and lied to. We did not choose the STI we were given. We did not choose the financial wreckage, the impact on the children, the public humiliation, the loss of our relationship, the loss of safety in our home, etc. The shitstorm of pain that flows out of cheating comes whether we want it to or not.

The loss of control over our bodies adds to our despair. We can't stop shaking; we vomit; we twitch, scream, cry, and rage. We lose hair, suffer panic attacks; we are sleepless.

Powerlessness can be one of the most dangerous emotions for humans to feel. History has shown us that prolonged powerlessness cannot be sustained. Revolt, revolution, protest, and war are often born out of people's waning ability to tolerate situations in which they feel powerless.

Powerlessness makes humans desperate, and desperate people do desperate things. Betrayed partners' rage, attempts to control, threats, demands, hyper-vigilance, and violence are all rooted in the powerlessness we feel. Behavior that violates everything we believe and hold dear can suddenly spew out of us. These behaviors are often self-destructive, harmful to the relationship, and unhelpful to those who love us. But like the wolf caught in the trap, we will chew our own paw off if it means gaining some sense of control and relief from the unremitting powerlessness of being betrayed.

For these reasons, betrayal trauma treatment focuses on helping us move out of powerlessness into a state of personal empowerment. Learning to set boundaries, manage our trauma symptoms, shift our mindset and core beliefs, find and use our voice, and ask for what we need are all part of effective treatment.

However, as discussed above, the fear of potential loss that learning new skills creates is a significant barrier for betrayed partners. The very skills and behaviors that can resolve the torturous feeling of powerlessness are the same skills that may create more loss, shame, and, yes, more powerlessness.

Operating from our personal power center, where we make choices for ourselves that are good for us and move us toward the life we want, also brings us face-to-face with our powerlessness over our cheating partner. We cannot make our partner do what we want them to do or want the same things that we want.

This is yet another relational bind that betrayed partners face on the path to healing. To move out of powerlessness into empowerment, we must first be able to tolerate our powerlessness over our partner's choices and behaviors.

STAYING IN POWERLESSNESS TO AVOID LOSS

Powerlessness is a paradoxical issue for betrayed partners. While it is entrapping, feels awful, and creates desperation, it is also a highly effective way to avoid further potential loss and shame.

We can stay busy with reading, talking, therapy, groups, online resources, etc., all while engaging in powerless behavior patterns that keep us stuck yet also let us avoid further loss. *Until we have the resilience to handle the risk of more loss and the ability to separate from the shame that loss triggers, we run the risk of staying mired in powerless behaviors.* Identifying and naming patterns of powerlessness is essential for breaking the betrayal binds and helping us move through our fear of potential loss so we can operate from a place of empowered choice.

Below are several ways patterns of powerlessness can manifest for betrayed partners. This is not an exhaustive list, and helping professionals will want to develop their skills in identifying the endless ways that powerlessness can become operationalized in the lives of betrayed partners to avoid loss and shame.

Conflict with the Cheating Partner

One of the powerless behavior patterns that betrayed partners get stuck in is engaging in rounds of endless conflict with the cheating partner. For example, we may have fight after fight with our partner about the fact that they won't go to treatment or won't seriously invest in recovery or won't do a disclosure. While these fights create tension in the relationship and we feel anger, frustration, and powerlessness about our partner's obstinance, the conflicts also protect us from and blind us to realities we find too difficult to face.

If we were to stop the fighting, nagging, threatening, and convincing to create space for our awareness to grow, we might recognize that if our partner won't do what we are asking of them, then we are not going to be able to rebuild trust. If we can't trust them again, we will not be able to feel safe in the relationship. Living in a relationship where we feel emotionally and physically unsafe is not a healthy long-term situation. Therefore, if our partner continues to refuse to do X, Y, or Z, we may have to terminate the relationship.

Here comes the primal panic! The potential loss of our relationship creates enormous dysregulation, pain, and terror. The possibility of losing our primary attachment figure can be so overwhelming and painful that we cannot go near it emotionally. To avoid these big hot emotions that threaten to overwhelm us, we instead cycle round and round in fight after fight with our partner.

This fighting is steeped in powerlessness. We are frantic for the cheating partner to respond to our needs but are unwilling to risk loss by getting clear in our communication and intentions, setting a boundary, or taking protective action.

Because the needs at the heart of these conflicts are very real, we can be unaware that we are engaging in a powerless behavior pattern. Therapists, too, can get distracted by the conflict and lose sight of the conflict's true purpose—to maintain connection (fighting is a form of connection) while avoiding the risk of more relational loss.

True healing involves identifying the purpose of the conflict and the fear of abandonment and loss that are driving the powerless pattern. Forward progress will not be achieved until the fear that is operating in the background and motivating the behaviors is identified, brought into conscious awareness, and worked through.

Raging

Jenny had been married for twenty years to her high school sweetheart. Four years ago, she discovered he was having an affair. By the time Jenny got to my office, she had spent four years raging at her husband, who continued his relationship with the affair partner while living at home with Jenny and their children. As Jenny and I worked together, we began to explore her rage. She was rightly incensed by his betrayal of her and his callousness in continuing to flaunt the affair while also saying he wanted to stay married. I validated her deep sense of injustice and pain around his behavior and the ongoing daily betrayal she was living with.

Once we identified and validated her anger and pain, we began to get curious about how her episodes of rage might be serving her. Her rage was protective, but she was so caught up in it that she did not know what she was protecting herself *from*. As we peeled back the layers, Jenny finally said to me, "I need him to know that how he is treating me is not okay and the only way I can show him that is by raging at him. I can't leave him, so that is all I know how to do."

I asked Jenny to close her eyes and connect to her body, and then I asked her to tell me what happens in her body when she thinks about leaving the relationship. Jenny's eyes popped wide open, and she looked at me in panic-stricken terror. "I feel like I will die, like I will be falling through black empty space forever."

Jenny's rage toward her spouse felt empowering. Her rage made her feel like she wasn't just "letting him get away with it." However, at the core, her rage was a very distracting exercise in powerlessness. It covered up her abandonment fear, which surfaced with a vengeance when she was finally able to connect to her inner world. Her rage let her feel like she was doing something while she stayed profoundly stuck in an unbearable situation.

Once Jenny connected to her terror around losing the relationship, our real work began. We looked at the origins of the fear, which, for her, were embedded in childhood experiences of neglect, loss, and abandonment. Her adult relationship was awakening the primal terror she had felt as a child and paralyzing her ability to act on her own behalf. As we worked on the original wounds and grew her adult resilience and resourcefulness, Jenny was able to stop raging and start making incremental steps toward setting boundaries and making decisions. Eventually, she was able to free herself from her toxic relationship.

Maintaining Motivation through Crisis
Another powerless behavior pattern is maintaining the cheating partner's motivation by staying in relational crisis. Underneath this pattern is the unconscious belief that if we heal—if our trauma symptoms abate and we move out of crisis—the cheating partner will stop their efforts to repair the relationship or will let their recovery lapse. This pattern is one that is particularly prevalent for betrayed partners who are staying in the relationship with a cheating partner who is working on repair.

Once again, the fear of potential loss motivates partners to opt for powerlessness rather than empowered choice. Our fear of finding out our cheating partner won't stay the course and do what is needed to heal the relationship prompts us to take on the role of motivating the unfaithful partner. We do this by staying in pain and crisis ourselves. We unconsciously believe that it is our pain, distress, and trauma symptoms that keep our cheating partner committed to recovery. We fear that if we let ourselves heal, our cheating partner will believe that everything is fine and things can go back to business as usual. We fear this will lead to a return to cheating or sexual acting out, and we cannot bear the thought of another round of pain and betrayal. As a result, we sacrifice our healing in service of motivating the cheating partner.

This fear creates a cyclical dynamic for betrayed partners. We begin to feel better. We are happy for a few hours, or we have several days in a row where we don't cry, or we have a whole afternoon where we don't even think about the betrayal. This is a welcome relief as we see glimmers of our old self returning. But this relief brings with it the fearful suspicion that if we feel better and are not in acute distress, our cheating partner will forget, become complacent, or go straight back to the cheating behaviors. Now, instead of the relief cueing safety, it cues danger. Primal panic raises its head again as we future trip about the potential loss and devastation we might experience if the cheating partner loses momentum. Like a wound that has begun to scab over and heal, we take our progress and rip it apart, rubbing the betrayal raw until we are once again emotionally bleeding. And then we hold our pain in front of the cheating partner, making sure they remember what they have done and all the damage it has caused.

Our fear of loss once again traps us in powerlessness. We cannot allow ourselves to heal for fear that the unfaithful partner will mistake our healing for acceptance of their behaviors or at least permission to relax their efforts at repair.

Any relationship that requires one or both partners to stay in pain for the relationship to feel safe is a dysfunctional relationship built on a false and fragile idea of emotional and relational safety. To move toward true robust safety within our relationships, we must risk allowing ourselves to heal, trusting that the cheating partner's motivation for relational connection, fidelity, and honesty will come from inside their own heart and mind.

To do this, we need skilled guidance from helpers who can assist us to identify the ways we hold ourselves hostage to our pain. We need support to build the inner resilience and resourcefulness needed to risk loss so we can gain true safety and secure bonding with our partner. We need to know, deep in our bones, that if, as we begin to heal, our partner returns to the cheating and lying or refuses to stop the cheating and lying, we will be able to make good decisions for ourselves and to emotionally tolerate the loss we will experience if the relationship must end.

Focusing on the Cheating Partner Rather than Ourselves

Another common way that betrayed partners stay stuck in powerlessness is by focusing on trying to get the cheating partner to do, say, think, and believe the things that will move the relationship back toward safety. Copious amounts of mental, emotional, and physical energy can be spent on this draining task.

One of my clients lives in a small town. He told me recently about being out to dinner when what he had been dreading finally happened. He and his girlfriend ran into one of her affair partners. They had discussed this possibility endlessly. My client had made clear how he would want his girlfriend to handle it, and she had promised to deal with any such situation in accordance with his wishes. And yet, when it did happen, she failed the test miserably. My client was apoplectic and wanted to know what he should do to get her to say and do the things they had so successfully planned together.

As I listened, what stood out to me was how trapped in powerlessness my client was. He was focused on getting his partner to behave a certain way and had left himself un-resourced and unprepared.

I asked him to tell me what plan he had put in place for himself in the event that they were to run into an affair partner. He looked at me blankly, and after a meaningful pause said, "I just told you; we practiced it. We even role-played what she would say and do." I gave him a meaningful pause back and said, "Yes, I understand that part. But I'm wondering what your plan was for *you*. How had you determined to take care of yourself and protect yourself in this situation?"

Because it was not my client's first rodeo with me, he got it this time. "Oh, my word, I did nothing! I had no plan for me!" I nodded and said to him, "Right. It is great to put together a plan for the two of you and to ask for her to handle things a certain way. I'm glad you did that. However, when that is all you did, you left yourself vulnerable to feeling profoundly powerless and unable to protect yourself in a critical and painful moment."

My client shook his head as he told me, "I was so focused on getting her to do what I needed her to do that I didn't even think about taking care of myself. And that interaction was so painful, and I felt so hurt and angry, and I was just stuck there with her and him and had no way to rescue myself out of that mess."

I gave him a wry smile as I said, "You needed a plan for you so that you wouldn't need to feel stuck in powerlessness in that excruciating interaction. I want you to have the ability to rescue yourself out of moments like that, so you feel empowered to take care of yourself regardless of the situation."

Our true source of empowerment lies in making choices for ourselves about what is best for us in any given moment and then using our resourcefulness on our own behalf. When we make choices that are good for us, and we use our energy and creativity to come to our own rescue, it is the most powerful thing we can do to move us toward safety. This is because it builds our trust in ourselves and creates a deep knowing inside ourselves that we will be okay and can handle whatever life brings as we go through the healing process. This is true whether we are staying and repairing our relationship or are leaving and grieving the ending of our relationship.

Avoiding the fear of loss by staying stuck in powerlessness is a profoundly pervasive pattern for betrayed partners. Once again, this pattern is completely normal. It is how attachment systems in distress operate. However, it is vital that betrayed partners are supported in identifying the fears about relational loss that underlie their patterns of powerlessness.

We must bring these fears into our conscious awareness so we can move closer to these difficult and scary emotions and slowly grow our resilience and resourcefulness. This allows us to tolerate the risk of loss and move out of powerlessness. Only by bringing our fear of loss into awareness, coming close to it, and holding space for it to be felt, processed, and moved through will fear lose its grip, allowing us to break our patterns of powerlessness.

SUMMARY

Once again, we have covered a lot of territory in exploring the emotional and psychological injury at the heart of betrayal. We have looked at the four types of gaslighting and how to help ourselves step out of the gaslighting dance. We defined disclosure and identified a pathway out of the tortuous suffering that staggered discovery creates. We named betrayal blindness and explored the way in which not seeing and not knowing is a protective coping strategy that while normal, does not serve our healing in the long term. Finally, we discussed how fear, shame, and powerlessness can drag betrayed partners down and keep them circling the drain rather than moving forward toward hope and healing.

GETTING STUCK

Each of the injuries created by partner betrayal is its own multilayered phenomenon. To heal, we must unpack and understand all the facets of the injury and the attachment-based dynamics that animate and activate not only the harm we have experienced but also our reactions and responses.

It is time for another book break! Take some space to digest what you have learned so far before jumping into the last and final injury in Part Three of the book: the sexual injury.

PART THREE

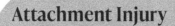

Attachment Injury

Emotional & Psychological Injury

Sexual Injury
The impact to the betrayed partner's sexuality resulting fom the cheating partner's betrayal of the sexual agreements within the relationship.

INTRODUCTION

THE SEXUAL INJURY AT THE HEART OF BETRAYAL

What is the least addressed topic when dealing with sexual betrayal? The topic that is often left completely out of couples therapy? The topic that gets almost no focus in addiction treatment? The topic that betrayed partners can hardly find a book or article about?

Sex.

Even though the betrayal is sexual in nature and cuts to the core of trust and intimacy, there are limited resources and little focus on the way betrayal impacts a couple's sexual relationship. And if those resources are scarce, it is even rarer to find information that addresses the impact of cheating on the sexuality of the betrayed partner specifically. This leaves betrayed partners without a clear path for healing the sexual wounds created by intimate betrayal.

Partners need experts and helpers who understand the common patterns and negative impacts that accompany infidelity and addiction, and who join with their clients in exploring and healing the sexual harm. This can only happen if those helpers are willing to listen to the stories that partners share about the abuses, traumas, and hurts they have sustained while dealing with secret sexual behavior and chronic lying in their relationships.

In this part of the book, we focus on the sexual injury. We are looking at the sexual injury last because it is highly impacted by the attachment injury and the emotional and psychological injury.

When our safe connection is broken, and thrusts us into attachment ambivalence, it impacts our sexual lives. The safety needed to engage freely in sex is damaged, and we see our need for connection and distance from the cheating partner play out as we struggle with whether to move toward our partner sexually or to move away.

In addition, betrayed partners report a high level of gaslighting in the sexual arena. Cheating partners engage in all four types of gaslighting, but the scapegoating is particularly high around sex. Betrayed partner's sexual preferences, libido, boundaries, bodies, and performance all become vulnerable to criticism and judgment as the cheating partner attempts to justify their extracurricular sexual behavior.

An examination of the sexual injury—close up, and in detail—is needed. Betrayed partners need the private traumas sustained in the bedroom brought into the light so the sources of those injuries can be held accountable and the betrayed can heal. With this, change is empowered.

As you read about the sexual injury, pace yourself. Read this section in small chunks and pay attention to what is happening in your body. Notice if your muscles tighten, your heart beats faster, your breathing changes. This is an indicator that the information is creating dysregulation in your nervous system. If so, it is time to put the book down, take a break, and do something comforting and soothing. Take a walk, meditate, listen to some music, call a friend. The book and its information will be here for you when you are ready to come back and digest another bite. Go easy and take care of yourself.

One last word of caution. Discussing sexual issues can easily arouse our fear and hyper-vigilance. This can create the urge to review every nuance of your sexual life, looking for signs of trouble. However, not everything we discuss in the following pages will apply to you and your relationship. As you read, be careful not to "borrow problems" that don't exist. Look for the things that resonate and that you can clearly identify as part of your experience. Think about the material that is not relevant for you as educational only.

Let's get started.

> When desire is
> bent by our sense
> that the world is one of scarcity,
> it devolves into devouring.
>
> CURT THOMPSON

CHAPTER THIRTEEN

SEX AND ATTACHMENT:

*Meeting Our Needs for
Belonging and Significance*

Have you ever wondered what makes sex so compelling and powerful? Throughout history, sex has been the animating force around which relationships, families, friendships, careers, organizations, religious bodies, political entities, and entire empires rise or fall. Sometimes sex creates powerful allegiances and unbreakable bonds of love. Other times, it is the hammer that destroys those same bonds. Why is this? What makes sex so potent and imperative for humans?

One answer to this question is its multifaceted nature. Sex is one of the most pleasurable activities we can experience. Sex also connects us to one another and can be part of our bonding process protecting us from loneliness. Sex is of course a primitive drive motivating us to procreate and it is also fun, meeting our needs for adult play and adventure.

However, these elements don't tell the whole story. Sex touches something primary inside of us, and when that happens, sexual pleasure rises to even greater heights, becoming even more alluring.

So, if it isn't pleasure, connection, or procreation that makes sex such a powerhouse, then what is it? What is this larger piece of the story? If you have been paying attention so far, you know where I'm going: to our attachment systems once again!

Our attachment systems (how we connect relationally) are driven by our attachment needs. These are the basic survival-level needs that we come into the world with and that motivate us to bond with our caregivers and others. I'm not talking about our needs for water, food, and shelter. I am talking about the needs attached to our sense of identity. These needs shape how we see ourselves, how we see others, and how we form the foundation for all our life experiences.

WHEN OUR CORE NEEDS GET MET

Our attachment-based needs fall into two categories: the need for belonging and the need for significance (the need to matter). To really understand how important these needs are, let's do an experiment together. I want you to read the following list of words and while you read them, pay attention to what you feel in your body.

- Desired
- Wanted
- Known
- Loved
- Understood
- Accepted
- Connected

- Seen
- Heard
- Noticed
- Validated
- Included
- Important

Did you feel a resonance inside yourself as you read those words? The sense of, "Yes, I want to feel all of this and more as often as I can!"

These words describe the desires and longings at the core of our needs for belonging and significance. When we feel wanted, heard, seen, and acknowledged, we feel safe. It is when our needs for belonging and significance are met consistently that we feel safe and secure in our relational bonds with others. When they are not met consistently, we are left not just with insecure attachment (which we have already talked about), but also to cope with the pain and distress of unmet needs and longings.

Take another look at the list of words above. Notice that each one of these words describes a feeling state. We know when we feel desired, important, seen, and understood. And each time we feel those things, we are filled with a sense of warmth and well-being. This is because these feeling states meet our core needs and fill our emotional tanks to the brim.

Now take one more look at the list. Notice that each of these words is also an identity. Each word describes something about us or who we are in any given moment. We are desired, which means we are desirable. That is an identity. We are accepted, which means we are acceptable. That is also an identity. We are important, noticed, seen, and heard, which means we are worthy and valued. All of these are identities. See how this works? These core needs, when met, create feeling states that profoundly validate our sense of self.

WHEN CORE NEEDS GO UNMET

Here is another list. Same instructions. Read through the list and pay attention to how you feel in your body as you do this.

- Undesired
- Unwanted
- Unknown
- Unloved
- Misunderstood
- Rejected
- Disconnected

- Unseen
- Unheard
- Ignored
- Unworthy
- Excluded
- Insignificant

I don't know about you, but this list makes me want to engage in some good old-fashioned escape behavior. I want nothing to do with these feeling states, and even less to do with how they make me feel about myself.

These words describe how we feel when our core needs go unmet. And here is the most important thing to notice: unmet core needs are not neutral. We do not land at, "I'm okay. I don't feel like I belong or am significant, but I'm still okay." There is no neutral ground with our core attachment-based needs.

How well our needs are met or unmet typically happens on a continuum, and we can go from feeling pretty good about ourselves to abject shittiness in a matter of moments. We never live in a space where our needs don't matter. We are either living in the sunshine of our needs being met or the darkness of our needs going unmet. And we are always living in the reality of how this makes us feel about ourselves and others.

COPING WITH UNMET NEEDS

As we know, our relationship to these vital attachment-based needs is shaped in infancy and early childhood through the bond we form with our caregivers. If we do not receive the consistent message that we are seen, heard, understood, important, and wanted, there is a devastating impact for us in terms of our self-perception and our beliefs about whether others are safe to be close to.

To live with unmet attachment-based needs is uncomfortable and distressing. As a result, from a very young age we develop ways to cope with chronic loss and longing. We do this by disconnecting from the pain of feeling unworthy and unlovable. We tuck our needs out of our awareness. It is too much for us to stay in conscious contact with those feelings, so we bury them and we layer coping strategies on top to make sure the pain stays underground.

Perhaps we become Type A overachievers or service-oriented people pleasers. Perhaps we become the jester who makes everyone laugh or the girl who brings the party wherever she goes. We become the rebel who is best of the bad or the business executive, politician, pastor, or educator who leapfrogs to leadership. Even a child who is acting out has determined that the best way to get their needs met is to create problems that demand focus and attention.

We are often unaware that our achievements are a way of trying to be seen, heard, and acknowledged. We miss the important fact that pleasing others is a way of gaining attention, praise, value, and connection. We know our escape behaviors and addictions are not good for us, but we mistake them for the problem when they are actually the symptoms—pointing to a heart full of loss, longing, and the desire for significance and belonging.

Author and clinician Curt Thompson describes this phenomenon in his book *The Soul of Desire*, saying, "We are formed by being known by others . . . we long to be so consummately known that we carry the reality of it with us in our interpersonal neurobiological experience wherever we go and in whatever endeavor we find ourselves."[1]

This is the essence of secure attachment—the felt sense of being truly known by those important to us, which transforms and supports our body/brain/mind as we move through our lives and relationships. Without this, we are left with unmet longings that sit in the cradle of our hearts and impact every relationship we have, including our relationship with ourselves.[2]

SEX, BELONGING, AND SIGNIFICANCE

What happens when sex enters the picture and converges with our core attachment needs? When we connect sexually, whether with another live person, someone in our imagination, or through the guided fantasy of porn or other forms of digital/virtual sex, we enter an experience that has the potential to reach in and touch our core attachment-based needs in a powerfully life-giving way.

The moment of sexual connection contains within it a powerful affirmation of our core needs. As we feel arousal heighten and as sexual play grows more intense, along with the physical pleasure there is a piercing sense that we are wanted and desired by our partner. In the sexual joining, there is often an extraordinary feeling of intense belonging that occurs. Our need to matter is met and satiated as we revel in a moment of desiring and being desired.

Sex is a powerful force because it can meet our deepest needs for belonging and significance, even if just momentarily. Cheating and betrayal are places where sex and our core needs intersect and play out in relational and sexual dramas that are often mistaken for something shallower and more trivial than what is at stake. The degree to which betrayal rocks our relationships and creates such enormous distress tips us off to the reality that cheating is about much more than what first appears. Cheating is about getting some of our core needs met outside of our primary relationship, and it is that reality that makes betrayal sting so painfully for the betrayed.

THE VULNERABILITY OF LONG-TERM RELATIONSHIPS

Sex in long-term relationships is inherently vulnerable and risky. We are being sexual with the person who knows our deepest strengths and gifts but also our most serious flaws and character defects. Sex with the person we not only laugh with, play with, and companion with, but that we also parent with, pay bills with, handle chores with, and fight with is very different from sex with a stranger or a new lover.

Because our partner is our primary attachment figure, they matter more to us than others. When we see joy, disappointment, admiration, or pain in their eyes, it impacts us more powerfully than any other relationship. As a result, we feel our most potent moments of mattering and belonging with our partner. But we also encounter our most troubling moments of feeling less-than, insignificant, unseen, or unworthy.

Learning how to stay engaged with our vulnerability as we are sexual with a partner who knows all of us (good and bad), who sometimes makes us feel wonderful and deeply loved but other times makes us feel angry, alone, or misunderstood, is challenging developmental work. Keeping sex alive, erotic, and engaging in this context requires significant vulnerability and risk.

Cheating, whether in a traditional affair or through compulsive sexual acting out, provides a taste of getting our deepest needs met while avoiding the vulnerability and risk inherent in long-term romantic partnerships.

Sex with anonymous partners, sex workers, or someone we've just met through an app is often about one or both people co-creating a fantasy that culminates in sexual activity. Because contact with the sexual partner is fleeting and fantasy-based, lower levels of vulnerability are required while a powerful (though momentary) hit of mattering and belonging can be felt.

Even ongoing affairs require less vulnerability than a long-term relationship. With new lovers, we can enjoy the vulnerability of sharing our hopes and dreams with each other. In longer-term affairs we typically show only our best selves to one another, and we create a fantasy based on this interaction between our best selves. In our primary relationships, however, where we are together in the relational foxhole 24/7, we must deal with a mix of our best and worst selves—all showing up and creating the ongoing drama of long-term relationships.

This is why cheating is so compelling. And it is why individuals who never imagined themselves cheating can get caught up in an affair or an addiction that blows their lives apart without understanding why they have done what they have done.

A long-term romantic relationship and the ability to maintain sexual agreements (whatever those look like) requires a high level of conscious awareness about our deep attachment needs, our ability or inability to get those needs met in healthy ways, and the susceptibility we all share to look for easy substitutions.

WHY SEXUAL BETRAYAL HURTS SO BAD

When cheating enters a relationship, it attacks our core attachment-based needs. Turn back a few pages to our two lists of words that describe our needs to belong and to matter. Now reread the second list of negative feeling states. These are the feeling states that betrayed partners are plunged into when cheating is discovered.

Sexual betrayal is a painful double whammy of loss around our core needs: we lose our sense of safety and security with our partner as our importance to them and our sense of belonging with them is severely undermined by the cheating. At the same time, we are aware that in some way the cheating is being used to satisfy some of our partner's core attachment needs. This deepens the sense of betrayal as we wonder why we are not enough and what they are getting from the sex, affair, porn, etc., that they aren't getting with us.

Often betrayed partners will reach for sex as a solution, mistakenly believing that amping up the sexy in the relationship will solve the issues and bring their partner back into connection. However, the reality is that cheating is often the sexualization of core attachment-based needs. Healing requires a deeper look into what is happening for the cheating partner around their primary needs, and the limitations they may be encountering in getting those needs met in healthy, life-affirming ways.

Below, we will look at some examples of how a cheating partner's behaviors often avoid the risks of intimate vulnerability while still temporarily meeting core attachment needs. This in no way eliminates the cheating partner's responsibility for their behavior. Instead, these examples can help us grow our understanding of what drives cheating, deepening our insight into why betrayal is so devastating.

Lloyd: Pornography Will Save Me

Lloyd grew up in a violent home with a father who was sexually abusing his sisters and physically abusing his mother. Lloyd was parented by TV—placed in front of it at an early age to keep him occupied and out of the way. This TV had open access to pornography due to his father's subscriptions, so from the time Lloyd was six years old he spent hours each day viewing porn. By the time he made it to my office, he was in his early thirties, utterly addicted to pornography, and about to lose his marriage to his husband of five years.

As we talked about what porn meant to him, Lloyd said, "I thought porn could save me. Actually, it did save me. When I entered the fantasy of porn there was touch that felt good, and pleasure that felt good, and I could imagine that the actors were looking at me and wanted and desired me. I left my crappy home and all its crazy pain and felt safe and wanted and cared for. It felt lifesaving then, and it feels lifesaving now."

Lloyd had turned to porn to feel safe and to feel as if he mattered and belonged. His normal human needs had been thoroughly ignored by his parents, leaving him searching for a way to create safety and security for himself. He was a functional adult when he came to see me, and that was largely due to his resilience and his ability to adaptively use porn in childhood and adolescence to get some of his needs met. But this also left him stranded in adulthood, with few skills and limited understanding about how to get his needs for safety, significance, and belonging met through real-world relational connection with others, especially his husband.

Cindy: I Want to Be Wanted

Cindy came to see me after being caught by her husband having sex with another man. This was only the most recent episode, as Cindy had been having sex with anonymous partners outside of her relationship for years. As we started to explore her behavior, I asked Cindy to help me picture what happened for her when she was getting ready to meet someone for sex.

Cindy described a separate wardrobe that she wore only when she was planning to hook up sexually. I asked her what she felt when putting on those clothes, boots, and makeup. She said, "I feel like a different person. I want to be noticed, and when I'm noticed I feel powerful, sexy, and desirable. I want to be wanted and I feel really good about myself because I know I can have any guy I want."

I asked Cindy to close her eyes and think about the most powerful moment for her during a sexual encounter. Cindy sat quietly for a few moments, then opened her eyes and said, "It's not during sex. It is when I know the person is hooked and we are going to have sex. It's the moment I know they want me so much that they are going to have sex with me even if they are married or it goes against their beliefs or is a bad decision."

We sat together and thought about her answer for a moment. Then I asked, "Why do you think that is such a powerful moment for you? Why is this a moment you seek over and over again, even though you risk your marriage and family?" Cindy's face changed from the exultant look that had been there when she was describing hooking a new partner to a look of sad uncertainty. "I crave the feeling of being wanted," she said. "I want to know that I am so important that I'm the only thing that matters in that moment. It is a high like no other, and it touches this place inside of me that nothing else touches. I'm afraid to give it up because what if I never get to feel that way again? What if this is the only way I'll ever get to feel that important or desired?"

Jim: No One Has Ever Known Me like This

Jim came to see me after receiving an ultimatum from his wife to end a two-year affair. Jim was struggling to end the affair even though he loved his wife and did not want to lose his marriage. As we talked about what the affair meant to him, he said, "I feel like she (the affair partner) gets me, and our relationship feels easy and unencumbered in a way that is relieving. It makes the sexual connection intense. I feel free to be myself in a way I don't in my marriage."

I asked Jim why he thought the relationship with the affair partner felt easier. "Because I feel accepted for who I am. There is no arguing about parenting or stress about the finances or disappointment about not connecting relationally—all things I deal with at home regularly. Instead, there is just sharing about our days or our dreams and having sex."

Kevin: The Focus Is on Me

Kevin runs a large company with enormous demands on his time and energy. He also has a wife and five children. He sought treatment after years of compulsively using massage parlors and sex workers. As we walked through a typical visit to a massage parlor, I asked him to revisit the scene and tell me what happens emotionally for him as he is being sexually serviced. He began to tear up as he responded. "I feel taken care of. The focus is entirely on me and making me feel good. No one needs anything from me or expects anything from me. It feels, for a moment, like I am free of all my burdens. And that is so incredibly relieving."

Kevin was using massage parlors and sex workers as a form of sexualized self-care. He did not know how to meet his emotional needs, set boundaries to protect his time and energy, and reach for significance and belonging with his wife relationally. So instead, he visited massage parlors where, for a few minutes, his needs to be nurtured and cared for were met through sex.

When we drill down underneath the surface of our sexual experiences, we will always find our core attachment-based needs. Sex touches these core needs in powerful and provocative ways. The goal is to get our needs for belonging and significance met through an array of relational, emotional, and sexual experiences. However, if we didn't learn how to do this in childhood, sexualizing our attachment needs and using sex to momentarily alleviate the distress of unmet needs can become a compelling option.

We have started our exploration of the sexual injury by identifying the ways in which sex, vulnerability, and our core attachment needs join and impact one another. We are beginning our exploration here because all the dynamics that are part of our sexual wounding happen within this larger context. No matter where we turn our attention in examining the sexual injuries, they all occur within the context of our need to feel that we matter and belong and the crushing heartbreak that follows when those needs are betrayed. As you read the chapters ahead, keep this larger context in mind.

> Sex, after all,
> is one of the great acts
> of communication.
>
> PATRICK CARNES, PhD

CHAPTER FOURTEEN

KILLING THE SEXY:

Common Patterns in Relationships with Hidden Cheating

When betrayed partners are asked about their sex lives, they share an astonishing array of sexual experiences as they sort through what has happened in their relationships. Each betrayed partner's story is unique. However, over time, as I have listened to thousands of betrayed partners talk about their sex lives, I have learned that there are common patterns that surface in relationships impacted by cheating. In this chapter we are going to explore four of these sexual patterns. They are: the normal sex life, no sex for you, objectified sex, and duty sex and the cycle of dread.

My hope is that by naming and discussing these common sexual patterns that appear in relationships damaged by betrayal, we can break the silence that often shrouds the sex lives of betrayed partners. As you read this chapter, please be aware that not all of it will apply to you. Your story is your own. Look for what helps you understand your experience better and let the information that is outside of your experience pass by.

THE "NORMAL" SEX LIFE

For some betrayed partners, the discovery of cheating is a total shock. Whether an isolated infidelity or a long-term porn or sexual addiction, the cheating has been so thoroughly hidden that they were unable to see warning signs or red flags indicating trouble. Many times, the sexual relationship has been alive and engaging despite the cheating.

As my client Nichole said, "We have a good sex life. I mean, we've had the normal ups and downs, but for the most part we have sex regularly and we both enjoy it—or at least I thought we did. I've never wondered if there was something else going on because he was always sexually interested and told me regularly how much he desired me."

Nichole paused and tears filled her eyes as she said, "I don't understand how he could cheat on me with those women for the past four years but still be showing up in our sexual relationship the way he was. I don't know how I will ever trust him again because he's able to make things seem so normal while lying to me."

Nichole was putting words to one of the common sexual patterns that occur for betrayed partners. The seemingly "normal" sexual relationship that doesn't indicate trouble and is carried on right beside the double-life of cheating.

In this pattern, the cheating partner thoroughly compartmentalizes each relationship. In one compartment there is the primary relationship. This is the front-facing life where the relationship moves forward as though the sexual agreements are intact. Jobs, parenting, friends and family, hobbies, and sex all continue without a hiccup. In the other compartment is the cheating. Whether affairs, pornography, or compulsive sexual acting out, cheating partners keep this part of their lives partitioned off so they can function "normally" within their primary front-facing life.

When the cheating is discovered, betrayed partners go into deep shock. The lack of indicators that something was amiss is too much to absorb. Trust is destroyed as they struggle with how to ever know what is true. They question their entire perception of reality because the cheating partner so competently hid the infidelity.

These relationships are difficult to repair because the betrayed partner cannot look for concrete behavior change as a sign of deeper emotional and relational healing. Because the unfaithful partner was present and engaged relationally and sexually while cheating, their continued or deepened ability to be present does not reassure the betrayed partner.

These betrayed partners also struggle to understand their relational and sexual place with the cheating partner. After all, their partner was telling them "I love you" and "I want you" while also wanting and perhaps loving someone else. Betrayed partners struggle with this duality and wonder how they can ever trust or believe the words of the unfaithful partner again. Often, the choice to leave the relationship can feel like the only route to safety.

NO SEX FOR YOU

The second sexual pattern common in relationships where secret cheating is present centers around no sex or a lack of sex within the relationship. This can be particularly confusing if the cheating partner is sexually addicted. I have had many clients say to me, "Oh no, they can't possibly be a sex addict, they're not interested in sex. It's been one of the biggest conflicts we've had because they have such a low libido and that creates so much frustration for me."

When these betrayed partners find out that there has been a secret history of sex outside of the relationship—either sex with others or sex-with-self through masturbation and pornography use—the shock leaves them stunned and confused.

Betrayed partners who experience this sexual pattern often struggle with a deep sense of personal rejection. Rather than being able to write off the lack of sexual interest as "low libido," it now feels like their partner just didn't want to have sex with *them*. This feels personal, deeply painful, and rejecting, and it directly attacks their need for significance and belonging.

The reality is almost always more complicated than this. Cheating partners who avoid sex within their primary relationship do so for a host of reasons, most of which have very little to do with the betrayed partner. Two common dynamics driving this pattern are avoiding the riskiness of real-world sex and avoiding sex out of guilt.

Avoiding the Riskiness of Real-World Sex

For some individuals, having sex with a real live person is intimidating. As a result, sex with a long-term partner (or any real-world partner) can become something they avoid. This pattern shows up most frequently with individuals who are addicted to pornography.

Often the compulsive use of pornography began in their early teens (or even earlier) and has continued into adult life. From the start, the use of pornography takes the place of real-life experiences. These real-life experiences are key to the developmental stages of adolescence and early adulthood and are where individuals learn to interact with romantic partners emotionally and sexually. As a result of porn use, developmental growth is stunted, and real-world relationships can start to feel intimidating and difficult to navigate.

As adults, these individuals continue to turn to pornography because it feels easier and safer than a real-world partner. The screen fantasy does not require anything from them, does not know them, does not have opinions, feelings, or thoughts. There is no risk of rejection, awkwardness, or failure.

Sex with a real-world partner is often high-risk, uncertain reward. What if they initiate sex and their partner says no thank you? What if they are feeling playful and flirty and their partner is feeling tired and sleepy? What if they (or their partner) cannot get aroused or reach orgasm? What if their partner is just not really into it? What if, what if, what if? Sex with a real-world partner requires vulnerability, while sex with a screen fantasy is predictable, safe, and contained.

Compulsive pornography use can also create sexual dysfunction—issues like erectile dysfunction, delayed orgasm, inability to reach orgasm, etc. These and similar issues make partnered sex more challenging and increase the draw to instead return to porn.

There are many opinions on whether the use of pornography constitutes cheating within a relationship. Each relationship is different in terms of the couple's views and values related to porn use. However, behaviors that are secretive, compulsive, or that wall off one partner's sexuality from the other's will create betrayal and destroy trust when discovered.

Betrayed partners whose cheating partners avoid sex while compulsively using pornography can feel despair about competing with the pornographic images their cheating partner is hooked on.

Partners can also be dismayed to discover the types of pornography their significant other is viewing. After all, a common issue with addiction is that it escalates over time. With porn, as the user becomes habituated to onscreen images, arousal lessens and the need for higher levels of kink or intensity to achieve the same experience of arousal occurs. When this is discovered, betrayed partners can feel unable, unwilling, or uneasy about trying to compete. They can be left feeling that they—in all their normal, real-world personhood—are not enough and cannot be enough for their partner sexually.

Avoiding Sex Out of Guilt

Some individuals who have a secret sexual life will avoid sex in their primary relationship out of guilt about the cheating. Sometimes this looks like avoiding sex altogether; other times, it looks like a sex life that runs hot and then goes cold for weeks or months at a time.

Often, when betrayal is discovered, it becomes clear that the cheating partner was avoiding sex with their significant other during periods when they were sexually acting out or actively involved in an affair. In these cases, sex in the primary relationship is avoided out of guilt or a sense of split loyalty between the significant other and the affair partner. Either way, it leaves the betrayed partner stuck in confusion about why the sexual relationship waxes and wanes.

Discovering your partner has cheated on you is a significant blow. Discovering your partner has been cheating with others while avoiding sex with you creates even deeper pain, uncertainty, and confusion. You may even feel shame about the lack of sex in your relationship, and this shame can keep you from talking about your experiences. If so, you need skilled helpers who gently open the door and create a safe space for you to speak about these tender and raw wounds.

OBJECTIFIED SEX INSIDE THE RELATIONSHIP

The third pattern common in relationships with hidden cheating centers around the pursuit of objectified sex within the relationship.

When we think about sexual betrayal, we usually focus on sexual behavior *outside* of the primary relationship. However, many betrayed partners experience objectified sex *inside* their relationship. Objectified sex is when one partner views the other partner as a means to the high, escape, or getting off that sex can provide and uses them to this end. Objectified sex is dehumanizing because it separates sex from personhood.

Objectified sex is challenging to discuss because it is also the place where violation and sex can meet, crossing over boundaries of consent. In this dynamic, one partner pursues, uses, and sometimes abuses the other partner to access sex.

Objectified sex inside the primary relationship can confound both betrayed partners and their helpers, especially when cheating (sex *outside* the relationship) is the focus of therapy. However, for those who have experienced being objectified and used by their significant other as a sexual outlet rather than a true sexual partner, the damage is enormous. Here are a few stories shared with me by my clients:

- *Joy endured years of sex with her spouse in which he laid pornography on the bed bedside her or on top of her while having sex, often never breaking eye contact with the pornography to acknowledge her presence.*
- *Stacy's husband insisted on having sex with her three days after the birth of their second child, causing her extreme physical and emotional pain.*
- *Amber's spouse required sex one to three times per day, every day, withdrawing in angry silence or erupting in rage and taking out his*

anger on the children when she wasn't willing to engage. The children would get to the point that they would beg her to "give Daddy what he needs so he'll be nice."
- *Callie discovered that her husband had been drugging her and then raping her while she slept.*

These are stories of bodies being used, physical pain being caused, and shame being experienced. Each of these clients told their story with sadness in their voice and confusion in their eyes as they tried to understand how the person who claimed to love them and spoke the language of wanting to *make love* was using their body the way a drug addict uses a drug.

In this dynamic, the emotional intimacy and connectivity that can be part of sex are replaced with onerous entitlement. Over time, sex becomes a central topic of conflict in the relationship, as the objectifying partner progressively becomes more sexually demanding and manipulative. When this happens, the hesitancy or outright objections of the betrayed partner are seen as obstacles to overcome. Betrayed partners express feeling dehumanized—used as a "receptacle" or "tool"—rather than being connected with and loved as a person.

Objectified sex inside a relationship damages the relational bond. Below are three different ways that the emotional and sexual dynamics can become distorted by this pattern.

1. **Sexual entitlement: the objectifying partner's sexuality becomes the organizing force in the relationship.**
   Because sex has become a central organizing experience for the objectifying individual, they can elevate the importance of their sexual needs and desires above the needs of their partner. They might play the gender card: "I'm a man and need more sex," or

"I'm a woman and I need to be romanced a certain way." They might also play the uniqueness card: "I have a high libido," or "I have special sexual needs that you need to take care of." Either way, the relationship begins to revolve around their sexuality. The betrayed partner's sexuality is diminished, existing only in service to the objectifying partner's sexuality, not as a separate entity worthy of attention, equality, and respect.

For women, this can be particularly challenging. Women are socialized to believe that they are responsible for pleasing and caring for men sexually. Women's sexuality—what they want, what they enjoy, who they are sexually—can be viewed as secondary or nonexistent.

2. **Manipulation and coercion are used to gain sexual cooperation.** Objectifying individuals can badger, cajole, nag, and guilt their partner into providing sex. Betrayed partners will often give in simply to stop the pressure and manipulation and to alleviate feelings of guilt. This type of coercion can look like:

- Pressuring you to provide sex more frequently than you desire.
- Manipulating you into sexual activity you are uncomfortable with.
- Criticizing your sexual preferences, sexual desires, or sexual expression.
- Forcing you to be sexual or being sexual when you are unaware and cannot consent.
- Pressuring you to accept behaviors that violate the sexual agreements.

3. **The betrayed partner is threatened with some form of abandonment.**

Some individuals will use the (sometimes unspoken) threat that if their partner doesn't cooperate sexually, they will abandon the partner in some way, either by walling off and distancing emotionally or by going outside of the relationship sexually. This dynamic keeps the objectifying partner in a one-up position in the relationship. The individual is asserting power and control by threatening the withdrawal of relationship connection or fidelity if their partner does not agree to sex on their terms.

This is one of the most common dynamics I hear from betrayed partners. They describe receiving the silent treatment for days, and fending off anger and irritability directed at them; their partner erects emotional barriers regularly and becomes uncooperative until sex is provided. This dynamic can cross over into a form of emotional manipulation and abuse that can impact the whole household, dragging children into the toxic dynamics.

These dynamics are often overlooked and go unnamed and untreated because they are difficult to confront. Betrayed partners have told me truly horrific stories of predatory abuse perpetrated by their significant others. These significant others are often known to me as well. They are good, upstanding, engaging individuals who I like very much. However, their sexuality has a secret entitled side, and therapists and helpers must be able to fearlessly wade into the darkness, name the behaviors, and explore the impact of those behaviors without shaming the individual or losing sight of their dignity.

Emotionally Caretaking the Objectifying Partner

One of the dynamics that betrayed partners who are being objectified can fall prey to is using sex to emotionally caretake or manage the objectifying partner. Betrayed partners can become vulnerable to providing sex to avoid their partner's anger, emotional withdrawal, nagging, or coercion.

One client who was working on reclaiming her sexual self said to me, "I know that if I will just have sex with my husband, the rest of the weekend will be lovely. He will pay attention to me; he will be patient and engaged with our children. Everything will be better for the next couple of days."

This individual was working on finding her voice and power sexually within the relationship. The temptation to go back to using sex to manage her spouse's emotions was strong. Choosing a new pattern of behavior meant living with the anxiety and uncertainty of leaving her spouse to manage his own inner world.

My client sighed and said to me, "I can't do it anymore. I can't have sex from that place. It sets me back and it makes me angry because I feel like a sexual object instead of a person. It makes me want to avoid sex. It makes me feel like I betrayed myself. It's just not worth it, even though I know it will make the weekend much easier."

Here is an interesting thing about using sex as emotional caretaking: rarely do we manage or caretake someone emotionally to try to help that person identify and express feelings. Most often, we are trying to get the person to *not* feel their feelings. We are perhaps afraid that it will negatively impact us if the person feels angry, frustrated, bored, or lonely. So, instead, we have sex, even though we do not want to, in the hopes that it will help our partner be more pleasant, engaged, faithful, etc. This fear-based coping technique perpetuates the problem (medicating feelings through escape behaviors) that recovery is trying to solve.

DUTY SEX AND THE CYCLE OF DREAD

Another pattern that can be present in relationships affected by cheating is duty sex and the cycle of dread. Duty sex and the cycle of dread evolve from the previously discussed patterns, particularly the patterns where sex is objectified or there is a lack of sexual interest from one partner.

Author and sex therapist Debby Herbenick, PhD, coined the term "cycle of dread"[1] to describe a pattern where sexual interactions shift from an enjoyable expression of play, connection, intimacy, and togetherness to a divisive issue that creates dread and turns sex into an obligation undertaken to avoid feelings of guilt. Sex that becomes a duty is not fun. Naturally, dread follows.

In these relationships, there is a lower desire partner and a higher desire partner who begin to react to one another—pushing each other further into their positions. Roles become rigid, with each person occupying their ground and defending their reality in a relational and sexual tug-of-war that eventually robs the relationship of joy. Couples lose the creativity, understanding, and resourcefulness necessary to navigate their sexual life together.

In this pattern, both partners come to feel that the other person is controlling the sexual relationship. The higher-desire partner feels like the lower-desire partner oversees the frequency of sex and whether they will get their sexual needs met. The lower-desire partner feels like the higher-desire partner's sexuality has taken over the relationship, and that the higher-desire partner's needs are more important and dominant. The higher-desire partner can become preoccupied with obtaining sex, and the lower-desire partner can become preoccupied with avoiding it.

In this scenario, both partners are caught in the cycle of dread. For the higher-desire partner, dread is about not knowing when sexual activity will happen and feeling fear that it may not happen for a long time. Feelings of being unwanted, undesired, or inadequate can haunt them.

Meanwhile, the lower-desire partner begins to react to the sexual pressure by losing connection to their own sexuality and instead becoming preoccupied with and reactive to the higher-desire partner's sexual interest. Dread grows as time passes and the pressure to reconnect sexually increases but they are unable to muster sexual desire of their own. They feel guilty and obligated to meet the sexual needs of the higher-desire partner. The lower-desire partner becomes focused on either avoiding sex or engaging in sex only to manage or appease the pressure they feel.

Below is a chart to help you see the way that each partner is reacting to the other partner and how this dynamic moves the relationship toward sexual extremes.

HIGHER-DESIRE PARTNER	LOWER-DESIRE PARTNER
Believes the other partner is controlling the sexual relationship.	**Believes the other partner** is controlling the sexual relationship.
Believes the other partner controls whether they get their sexual needs met.	**Believes the other partner's sexual needs** are more important and have taken over the relationship.
Loses connection to sex as expression of relational bond and becomes focused on physical release of sex.	**Loses connection to their own sexual interest and desire** and becomes preoccupied with and reactive to their partner's interest.
Becomes preoccupied with **obtaining sex.**	Becomes preoccupied with **avoiding sex.**
Dread is about not knowing when sexual activity will occur and feeling fear that it may not happen for a long time.	**Dread is about the pressure to reconnect sexually** as time passes but they are unable to connect to sexual desire.
Feelings of being unwanted, undesired, or inadequate can prevail.	**Feelings of guilt,** obligation, burden, and inadequacy can prevail.

Regardless of how it shows up, any dynamic in which a higher-desire partner pursues sex out of fear of deprivation, or a lower-desire partner engages in sex out of guilt and fear of abandonment creates loss of intimacy and safety in the relationship.

If duty sex and the cycle of dread feel familiar, you will want to work on it in couples therapy when the time is right. Duty sex creates emotional and relational distance. Seeking help with this pattern once you are ready to work on the sexual relationship is vital. Often duty sex requires expert outside help and support to move each of you out of the fear-based pattern you are stuck in. This allows you to broaden your lens, see the bigger picture, and get reconnected emotionally as you find a pathway out of the cycle of dread together.

HOPE IN THE DARKNESS

One of my professors in graduate school said something I have never forgotten: "No matter how hard or horrific the truth you are naming with your client, the act of naming what is true always brings hope." Over the last twenty-plus years of working with clients, I have found this to be a profound truth. Our willingness to look at the harm we have experienced and put words to how it impacts us is a key that unlocks the door to healing. By speaking the words and naming the harm, we introduce hope into our experience and move toward change.

In this chapter we have named some of the harm that sexual betrayal creates. This chapter may have been hard to read as you revisited painful memories or understood your story in a new way. My hope is that by looking squarely at the sexual injuries created by betrayal you feel validated, you know you are not alone, and you have new words and concepts to help you communicate your story to others.

Now that we have identified some of the common relational and sexual patterns that betrayed partners experience, in the next chapter we are going to turn our attention to the specific ways in which cheating injures the sexuality of the betrayed partner.

> Erotic injury means that
> the partner who has been cheated on
> experiences an undermining
> of erotic confidence
> because of the infidelity.
>
> TAMMY NELSON

CHAPTER FIFTEEN

LOSING THE SEXUAL SELF:

The Impact of Betrayal on Partner Sexuality

Cheating and secret-keeping hijack sex and cause significant injury to the betrayed partner's sexuality. In fact, many betrayed partners report trauma symptoms similar to those experienced by survivors of sexual abuse.

Below is a list of common sexual trauma symptoms described by therapist Wendy Maltz in *The Sexual Healing Journey*, her book for survivors of childhood sexual abuse. See if any of these items resonate with you regarding the impact of cheating on your sexuality:

- Avoiding or being afraid of sex
- Approaching sex as an obligation
- Experiencing negative feelings such as anger, disgust, or guilt with touch
- Having difficulty becoming aroused or feeling sensation

- Feeling emotionally distant or not present during sex
- Experiencing intrusive or disturbing sexual thoughts and images
- Engaging in compulsive or inappropriate sexual behaviors
- Experiencing difficulty establishing or maintaining an intimate relationship
- Experiencing vaginal pain or orgasmic difficulties[1]

Do you see yourself in this list? If so, you are not alone.

It may surprise you that a list of sexual trauma symptoms written for survivors of childhood sexual abuse hits so close to home for adults who have been cheated on. I believe the trauma symptoms experienced around cheating mimic sexual abuse symptoms because cheating violates consent.

When our partner breaks the sexual agreements in the relationship, we are now having sex under circumstances and conditions that we have not knowingly and with full awareness consented to. When our consent is taken away from us, sex moves from something we freely engage in with full agency to something that is being done without our awareness. Cheating mirrors sexual abuse in that it robs its victims of choice, self-determination, and agency. This is why the symptoms that betrayed partners experience can so closely reflect those of sexual abuse survivors.

In this chapter, we look at four ways cheating impacts a betrayed partner's sexuality. This is not an exhaustive list, but these are four of the most common impacts betrayed partners experience: loss of sexual voice and power, carried sexual shame, loss of sexual self-confidence, and the loss of sexual desire.

LOSS OF SEXUAL VOICE AND POWER

When betrayal enters our relationships and creates a sense of being one-down or less-than, it often robs us of our voice and power in the relationship. We feel constricted, small, and insecure. The relational threat directly lowers the sense of sexual safety, making it feel treacherous to share our sexual reality with our cheating partner. This less-than position makes it challenging to feel that we are entitled to use our sexual voice to communicate with our partner.

Using our sexual voice means being able to share our beliefs, preferences, turn-ons, turn-offs, thinking, desires, fears, needs, and vulnerabilities around sex with our partner. To co-create a sexual relationship that is fulfilling and enjoyable for both people, each partner must be able to voice their sexual reality and have it be heard and honored.

This does not mean there is no negotiation, and every sexual desire and whim gets met. Sex is just like all the other parts of our lives—there are boundaries that we work within. Just as we cannot purchase whatever we dream about or eat all we might wish to, healthy sex takes place within the boundaries of what is good for us and good for our relationships; it encourages a richer and more satisfying life. As a result, there will always be negotiation, compromise, and growth as we learn more about our partners and who they are sexually and share more of ourselves.

However, to grow together and create a satisfying and enlivening sexual relationship, we first must be able to share who we are sexually with our partner. To do this we must be able to use our sexual voice. Many betrayed partners report they have never known how to have a sexual voice in their relationships. This is particularly true for those who come from homes where sex was never talked about or where sexual abuse or violence occurred.

These sex-negative environments create an unconscious but deeply held belief that sex is taboo, not to be spoken of, shameful, or immoral. These environments make the task of sexual development incredibly challenging. Many people who grew up in these contexts find they still feel like confused young children or adolescents when trying to navigate their sexual relationships.

When we do not know how to use our voice, we limit our ability to bring our authentic selves to our relationships with any partner. Trust is harmed when we feel we must curb who we are or silence our true feelings.

One of the most important parts of using our voice and power within our sexual relationships centers around the ability to say both *yes* and *no* to sex. If we are unable to say *no* to sex, then we are unable to say *yes*. If we can't say *no*, then our *yes* is not full and freely given. It is a *yes* that comes out of duty sex or a *yes* that is coerced or a *yes* that is about avoiding conflict. It is not a *yes* that is rooted in our own relational and sexual desires that moves us toward true connection with our partner.

Saying *yes* and *no* to sex is about more than just indicating whether we are up for having sex. Saying *yes* and *no* to sex is about the full sexual experience. It is about choosing the activities and adventures we want to have, and it is about saying *yes* or *no* throughout the whole experience.

For example, we may decide to try something new with our partner that seems like it will be fun. But, once we are in the middle of it, we find that it is not fun, in fact it's a little awkward or painful or just doesn't do anything for us. We need to be able to access our *no* and tell our partner how we are feeling and then access our *yes* and share what we would like to do instead. Without this information, our partner may have no idea what is happening for us. Also, sharing our reality with our partner opens the door for them to do the same.

Using our sexual voice and power is about exercising our agency—our ability to make choices for ourselves—within our sexual relationship. To do this, we must be connected to ourselves in a way that allows us to know what we believe, think, and feel about whatever is happening. If we are focused on our partner and trying to figure out what is going on inside of them, it diverts us away from ourselves. The goal is for both of us, our partner and ourselves, to be operating from our authentic selves and sharing our sexual realities in a way that creates a level playing field where sexual power is shared.

CARRIED SEXUAL SHAME

In Chapter Five we explored the issue of carried shame. Carried shame occurs when the shameless behavior of one person (the cheating partner) spills over onto the offended party (the betrayed partner) who ends up carrying shame about the cheating.

Carried shame instantaneously adheres to betrayed partners, causing us to question our worth and value to the cheating partner. Rather than see the cheating as an indicator of issues our partner is dealing with, we often, without even realizing it is happening, begin to carry the shame instead.

This carried shame often attaches powerfully to our sexuality. We can begin to feel shame around sexual functioning, sexual desire, sexual preferences, sexual self-esteem, and body image. This distressing sense of self-doubt coats our sexuality in a black tar that resists removal, refusing to be scrubbed off no matter how unwelcome its presence.

For betrayed partners, one of the most devastating areas that shame attaches itself to is our sense of desirability. We all long to be wanted by our partner, and this includes feeling that our partner desires us sexually. Being desired by our partner makes us feel that we matter, are worthy, and belong (our core needs). Curt Thompson describes this phenomenon saying, "Embedded in the process of being known is our awareness that the one by whom we are known desires to know us. As such, a critical element of our desire is that of being desired. We long to be infinitely desired, wanted by the other . . ."[2] The loss or detouring of our partner's desire for us robs us of our sense of safe connection and importance.

In addition, comparison to the "other" feeds sexual carried shame. It doesn't matter what we look like, our gender, our sexual orientation, our age, or our sexual history. The fact that our partner has breached our sexual agreements and chosen someone else to be sexual with automatically creates self-doubt and raises questions about what that person or experience offers that we don't. Carried shame causes us to compare ourselves to the one(s) chosen by our partner in a game where the deck is stacked against us, and we are always losing.

Feeling desired is closely linked to issues of trust and mistrust in our relationships. Before discovery of the cheating, we trusted our partner when they told us we were sexy, beautiful, handsome, or hot. We trusted their words and felt the heated glow from knowing we are desired by the person we desire.

Now sexual betrayal has wiped out our trust. Carried shame can create self-contempt about believing we were in fact sexy, hot, or beautiful. We can cringe as we remember how we freely engaged sexually with our partner when we thought we were accepted, safe, and loved. This is one of the most heartbreaking impacts of carried shame as it robs betrayed partners of the joy of past sexual adventures and introduces the constriction of fear and shame into an experience that was once playful and free.

We know the way to heal carried shame is to give it back and release it. Carried shame is literally like taking someone else's sack of rocks and carrying it for them. In this case, we have taken the cheating partner's sexual and emotional issues and made them our own. We have taken on their compulsion, dysfunction, or bad choices instead of recognizing that these are theirs to reckon with. We have begun to carry their sack of shame rocks.

There is no denying how deeply painful it is to find our partner's sexual desire has turned to someone or something else. That hurts. Badly. However, our task is to acknowledge our pain and loss without taking on shame about their choices. We want to avoid allowing their behavior to become a referendum on our worthiness, desirability, and significance.

We need support to do this. Sexual carried shame is sneaky, ubiquitous, and grows in isolation. We need other eyes to help us spot it. We need others to broaden our perspective and help us with our fear and primal panic around the threat to our sense of self. We cannot manage carried shame alone. Reaching out to other betrayed partners and trained experts is our first step to help ourselves put down those rocks of carried shame.

LOSS OF SEXUAL SELF-CONFIDENCE

A third negative sexual impact for betrayed partners centers around loss of sexual self-confidence due to harm experienced around body image and self-esteem. The effects on body image and self-esteem are part of carried shame, but they deserve their own focus due to how painful and prevalent they are.

Regardless of gender, almost all betrayed partners experience loss of self-esteem and negative impacts to body image. Many partners have talked to me about how good they felt about themselves and their bodies until betrayal plunged them into self-doubt and insecurity. Others have talked to me about long histories marked by the struggle to accept their bodies and to feel worthy. For them, sexual betrayal confirms their biggest secret fear: that their body is not desirable or that they are in some way deficient or lacking.

This is, of course, all happening within a toxic cultural context where impossible standards around body size, aging, and beauty surround and impact us whether we want them to or not. Historically, women have been the primary targets of this cultural body shaming and youth bias. But today, that is changing, and all genders are increasingly encouraged to meet unrealistic standards and expectations.

When betrayal is layered on top of this toxic cultural foundation, many betrayed partners find themselves struggling with despair and self-doubt about body-size, age, and beauty. This negatively impacts sexuality. Anxiety about comparison shuts down desire and arousal, making sexual connection difficult or impossible.

When body shame and low self-esteem interfere, they separate us from our sexual selves. Instead of being connected to what we find arousing, what turns us on, turns us off, what we find pleasurable and fun, we are lost in anxiety about how our partner perceives us. We worry about what is happening in their minds, what they think about us and whether they find us desirable. This focus on them cuts us off from ourselves, and we lose our ability to bring our sexual selves to the relationship and co-create a sexual experience. Instead, we end up trapped in a constricted, fear-based dilemma where our anxiety about how our partner views us takes center stage. Sex can become awkward, stilted, and stunted by this anxiety or can disappear altogether.

For most betrayed partners, healing the damage done to body image and sexual self-esteem is a process that takes time. Even without the presence of betrayal, claiming our right to feel good about our bodies and ourselves within our cultural milieu can feel like trying to swim up a waterfall. Add betrayal, and the reclaiming takes focus, energy, and time.

LOSS OF SEXUAL DESIRE

The fourth impact on betrayed partners' sexuality is losing connection to sexual desire. Loss or diminishment of sexual desire can occur pre-discovery and/or post-discovery of betrayal. Let's look at each of these because they manifest in different ways.

Loss of Sexual Desire Pre-Discovery of Betrayal

Many betrayed partners have talked to me about losing connection to their sexual desire *before* they discovered the cheating. They talk about this with confusion and consternation, as though their sexual interest were a shoe that suddenly went missing and, despite diligent searching, they cannot find it. Diminishing sexual desire leaves partners confused and concerned, wondering what is causing this unwelcome change.

Many different factors can negatively impact sexual desire. Changes in health, chronic or heightened stress, childhood trauma, phase-of-life issues such as caring for babies, aging, etc. If you have experienced a loss of sexual desire, it can stem from many different directions, and more than one thing can contribute.

That said, nothing seems to impact desire more than sexual betrayal. This is because betrayal presents a tremendous emotional threat and danger to the relationship. And this is true *even when we are not yet consciously aware of the betrayal.*

We often think we only respond to threats we are consciously aware of. But this is not the case. We are highly sensitive creatures and, to survive, our threat systems are finely attuned to any changes in the environment around us—especially changes that might create danger. For example, we may find ourselves swerving out of the way of an oncoming biker before we consciously register that the biker was crossing into our lane. Our brain spotted the threat and primed us to act before we had any conscious awareness of danger.

This type of unconscious response can occur in both our situational worlds and our emotional worlds. Our unconscious mind can pick up on danger and prompt us to instinctually respond even though we are not yet consciously aware of the threat.

For many betrayed partners, our brain/body knows we are experiencing betrayal before our mind catches up. Our finely tuned threat system picks up on the sense that there is hidden danger. Subtle changes in behavior and emotional energy create free-floating anxiety. When this happens, our body registers loss of safety in our relationship and our threat center fires into protection mode.

One way the body protects against this type of murky relational threat is by overriding or shutting down sexual desire for the person who is no longer safe. Suddenly we find we are not initiating or responding to sexual overtures the way we used to. We are less interested, attracted, or turned on. We search for our missing libido but can't seem to find it and this leaves us confused and worried that something is going wrong with our sexuality.

Anytime we don't understand why something is happening, particularly physically or sexually, it creates anxiety for us. We can feel worried about our lack of desire for our partner, particularly because we don't understand why it is changing. Often, we will blame ourselves, not realizing that our threat system is registering external danger from the cheating and is shutting down sexual desire as a means of self-protection. Our body is not betraying us, it is protecting us.

When sexual betrayal is discovered, many partners realize that sexual desire began to wane as the cheating partner became involved in an affair or the sex or porn addiction began to escalate. This connects the dots, and we begin to see how the loss of safety in our relationship was impacting many different areas of our lives before we became consciously aware of the danger.

Loss of Sexual Desire Post-Discovery

When cheating is discovered and betrayed partners are thrust into pain and disorientation, their sexual desire for and attraction to the cheating partner often changes.

Many partners find that betrayal shuts down their sexual desire. Even if they do feel desire, they do not feel safe enough to connect sexually with the unfaithful partner. These betrayed partners enter a period where sex is put on hold while decisions about whether the relationship will survive the betrayal are made or time to heal is prioritized.

For some, even when the cheating partner enters recovery or closes the door on the affair and commits to the repair of the relationship, they are unable to find their desire. These partners regularly say to me, "They are doing everything right. They are going to therapy, going to twelve-steps, engaging with me differently . . . all the things! But I still want nothing to do with them. Will this ever change?"

Loss of sexual desire after betrayal can feel like being locked in a permanent winter where nothing is growing. There is brown and gray as far as the eye can see. Ice and snow coat everything. The ground is cold, hard, and unforgiving. It is hard to even imagine the lushness and beauty of spring or the fruitfulness of summer when you are stuck midwinter.

In fact, to their dismay, many partners discover that they cannot find their desire and actively feel disgust or revulsion for the cheating partner. They worry about how to overcome their distaste for their partner's behaviors so that they can feel desire or arousal once again.

The loss of sexual desire can persist even when we see our relationship changing and we *want* to feel sexual desire again; often, this occurs because we are in a state of freeze around sex. This can continue even if we have left the relationship with the cheating partner. Perhaps we are not able to be sexual with a new partner or are unable to venture into dating. Our threat system has shut down our sexual responses due to the sexual danger created by the cheating and lying. We are stuck where we can't find our sexual desire.

When stuck in a sexual freeze state, our biggest task is to help our body begin to feel safe enough to feel sexual pleasure once again.

In the next chapter, we take a deep dive into the topic of sexual safety. For now, I would like to introduce a few resources that can help us begin to build sexual safety with our bodies and to slowly fan the ember of our sexual desire back into a flame.

A couple of books are particularly helpful for female betrayed partners who feel stuck in the sexual deep freeze. Judith Leavitt's *The Sexual Alarm System: Women's Unwanted Response to Sexual Intimacy and How to Overcome It* spends the first couple of chapters helping us understand our sexual alarm systems and how they can become stuck, getting in the way of the sexual life we deserve. The rest of the book is full of exercises that help us reconnect to our bodies and reestablish a bodily-based sense of safety.

Another resource is *Better Sex Through Mindfulness: How Women Can Cultivate Desire*, which provides helpful information about female sexuality and how to use mindfulness to come into the present and connect to our bodies and ourselves in a way that creates safety.

A resource that is helpful to any gender is *Sensate Focus Therapy*, which is a technique that helps to build connections between awareness, presence, and pleasure in a way that can increase the sense of safety. Sensate Focus is often recommended for couples, but individuals who are needing to reestablish a safe connection with sexual pleasure can also use this tool.

Last, I want to introduce you to a sexual model that can help expand our thinking about sex and sexual desire. First, a little history lesson.

When Masters and Johnson did their groundbreaking research on sex, they identified the Human Sexual Response Cycle: it starts with excitement, moves to plateau, then orgasm, then resolution.[3] This placed quite a lot of emphasis on arousal and orgasm.

About a decade later, Helen Singer Kaplan, another sex researcher, offered a new model called the Triphasic Sexual Response Model.[4] This model begins with desire, then arousal, then orgasm. Kaplan's model upended things because it introduced the idea that desire precedes arousal, and that arousal doesn't just spontaneously happen.

Then in 2001, Rosemary Basson introduced yet another model called the circular or non-linear model of sexual response.[5] In her model, Basson points out that sexual desire is complex and can be experienced before or after arousal begins. In addition, orgasm adds to pleasure but is not necessary to experience pleasure. Finally, Basson looks at the wide variety of things that can impact sexual desire, from relationship satisfaction to health, etc.

Each of these models advanced our understanding of human sexual response and helped to broaden our ideas about what constitutes sexual health. However, one more model tucked into the middle of these advances doesn't get as much attention.

This model, created by JoAnn Loulan, begins with willingness (not desire) and ends with pleasure.[6] In this model, Loulan offers the novel idea that we don't have to feel sexual desire to engage in sexual play. We can start from a place of willingness to explore, experiment, or see what might develop. Instead of orgasm as the end goal, the end goal is to experience pleasure in whatever form or shape that may take.

For betrayed partners who have lost their sexual desire and are stuck in freeze, Loulan's willingness model can be particularly helpful. It can remove the pressure to feel sexual desire. When we feel pressure, guess what happens? Our sexual desire decreases. Pressure kills sexual desire. If we are putting pressure on ourselves and trying to find our desire for our partner or for sex at all, it can backfire by reinforcing the state of freeze that we are in.

If, instead, we understand that all we really need is a willingness to move toward experiencing sexual pleasure, that changes the game. Now we don't have to feel desire for sex to be willing to lay naked with our partner and hold one another. And we don't have to feel pressure to have sex and orgasm. Instead, with pleasure as our goal, we can just enjoy the skin-on-skin contact and the feeling of being held and see where it takes us. It may take us toward sex, or it may be enough for us at the time. Either way, our willingness has cracked open the door of possibility and removed the block that lack of desire can create.

Each betrayed partner's willingness will look different based on the unique situation. Some partners may want to consider willingness to simply reintroduce touch into the relationship after a long separation or period where all touch was off the table. Focusing on the pleasure that holding hands or receiving a hug or cuddling side by side on the couch can bring can begin to rebuild the sense that touch and pleasure are safe.

Regardless of our starting point, when we refocus on the ideas of willingness and pleasure, it can relieve the pressure to feel sexual desire and to have sex or an orgasm. Instead, we open the door to finding out what brings us pleasure and what our bodies like while also fostering safety. Willingness allows us to venture into possibility, which is what eventually enables us to fully move out of sexual freeze.

In the next chapter, we look more closely at the issue of sexual safety: ways to move toward safety and the challenges that can block our progress.

> **We need to develop
> safe ways to say "yes"
> to the kinds of sex that
> nourish and empower us.**
>
> GINA OGDEN

CHAPTER SIXTEEN

SEXUAL AND EMOTIONAL SAFETY:

Part One

Sex and safety go hand in hand. We need to feel safe with our sexual partner to expose our bodies and emotional selves to them during erotic play. When betrayal enters a relationship, emotional and sexual safety are severely damaged.

This interplay between emotional and sexual safety is even more significant if you are female. Because of our physiological sex differences, the female brain scans for danger and safety during sex in a different way than a male brain. Research shows that during sexual arousal, the judgment and control center in the female brain lights up in a way that it doesn't in male brains. This part of the brain is actively coming on board during arousal to scan for danger and to ensure that it is safe to continue into the vulnerability of full sexual desire and arousal.[1]

In this chapter and the next, we will explore four aspects of emotional and sexual safety, including places where betrayed partners can get stuck or blocked in the healing process: (1) the deep dive of couples therapy, (2) sexual reengagement with the cheating partner, (3) sexual safety with ourselves, and (4) dealing with triggers and flashbacks during sex.

DIVING DEEP IN COUPLES THERAPY

We have already talked about the lack of focus that sexuality receives in individual therapy for betrayed partners. The same is also true of couples therapy. While everyone in the room is clear that cheating is what brought the couple to therapy, the sexual impacts and sexual relationship of the couple are often ignored as the therapist attends to repairing the emotional bond.

The problem with this approach is that it is sexual betrayal that has created so much havoc, danger, and pain in the relationship. The sexual nature of the betrayal has directly impacted the sexuality of the betrayed partner, the cheating partner, and the sexual relationship between them. Direct attention to these sexual injuries is needed for healing to occur.

One of the pitfalls both betrayed partners and their helpers can fall prey to is the idea that disclosure somehow creates healing around the sexual wounds. Disclosure—where the cheating partner discloses the full scope of the cheating—does not heal the wounds of betrayal. Disclosure provides betrayed partners with clarity about the scope and depth of the betrayal, so it becomes contained and lays a foundation of honesty from which to rebuild trust. However, the disclosure process, the impact letters that partners write detailing how the betrayal has impacted them, and the amends letters that the cheating partner often writes detailing their understanding of the impact, and then making amends—while these are worthwhile parts of the process, they do not heal the emotional and sexual injuries. Too often, individuals and couples are left stranded post-disclosure with no further attention to the unhealed wounds that remain.

One of the most vital parts of the healing process for couples who are working to repair their relationship happens when they are helped to do a deep dive into the specific raw spots, vulnerabilities, and hurts that sexual betrayal has created. This includes both the emotional wounds as well as the specific impacts to each partner's sexuality and the sexual relationship.

Skilled therapists can help the couple move out of reactionary emotions into the deeper emotions that reveal the unique ways that sex and sexuality are intertwined with feelings of mattering and belonging. Betrayed partners need help articulating the pain and hurt they have experienced. Skilled helpers can then assist the cheating partner to access their own pain and sadness about the harm the betrayed partner has experienced and to express this in an emotionally connected way.

When couples can meet in this space where there is a felt sense of connection around the loss, sadness, loneliness, etc., that betrayal has introduced, true emotional safety begins to grow. When there is true empathic understanding of one another's experiences and a willingness to enter one another's emotional reality and hold space for each other's most tender, vulnerable parts, new neural networks develop that help each partner begin to see the other as a safe harbor once again.

This process requires a willingness to walk into the scary places where the hurt is big, and addressing it can feel threatening to the relationship. Most couples struggle with talking about sex, let alone the highly activating topic of sexual injury. This part of the healing process is overlooked because it can be so intimidating for everyone involved to face. However, when these sexual raw spots are left unaddressed, they can grow scar tissue that negatively impacts the emotional and sexual relationship for years to come.

For betrayed partners who are leaving their relationship, it is still vitally important that the sexual injuries sustained during the relationship with the cheating partner be examined and healed. Many partners can mistakenly believe that leaving their significant other will be enough. But the sexual wounds are still present and can be carried into the next relationship and negatively impact its potential if left untended.

SEXUAL REENGAGEMENT: HOW WE GET STUCK

After discovery, betrayed partners are often waiting for emotional safety to be restored enough to feel okay about venturing back into the sexual relationship. In this process, we can find ourselves getting stuck in a holding pattern that prolongs sexual disconnection longer than is helpful. Our bodies get mired down in fear, and we can't sexually engage. Our body's first job is to protect us. At all costs. And having sex with someone who has harmed us makes no sense to our body.

As we wait and assess our situation, we can start to believe that since we still feel fear around reengaging sexually it must mean not enough emotional safety has been rebuilt. We can fall into the trap of thinking we need to keep sex off the table until it no longer feels scary. We believe that if our partner will keep building emotional safety it will eventually take the risk out of having sex.

The problem is that there is no amount of emotional safety that will eliminate all the fear and risk around reengaging sexually with the cheating partner. When we decide to be sexual again with the person who cheated on us, we make ourselves vulnerable to the possibility of being hurt. I'm not talking about being cheated on again (though that can happen). Even without the possibility of further betrayal, when we reengage sexually, we may deal with memories, flashbacks, and intrusive images of our partner's cheating behaviors. We may be flooded with feelings of anger, pain, or sadness. We may doubt our own desirability and feel shame about our bodies or sexuality. We may struggle to relax, feel pleasure, or connect emotionally.

All of these are very real emotional experiences that accompany sexual reengagement for most betrayed partners. (And please note: these things can happen even if we have left the cheating partner and are developing a sexual relationship with a new partner). Betrayed partners know that reengaging sexually is going to be a process that includes risk and often brings us into difficult emotional terrain.

We can get stuck in the false belief that somehow, the cheating partner can create enough emotional safety that we won't have to walk through this landmine-laden field when it comes time to have sex. We mistakenly think that because there is still fear, pain, or risk, it must not be emotionally safe enough for us to reengage.

The reality is, reengaging sexually is always going to include some level of fear, risk, and vulnerability. At some point, we are going to have to make the leap, face our fear, and take the risk, trusting that we will have the resources and tools we need to help us navigate our way through reconnecting sexually. For many partners, the anticipatory fear around sex grows larger the longer the sexual hiatus lasts, making it even more challenging to take the risk and make the leap.

Taking the leap feels like flinging yourself off the edge of a steep cliff surrounded by giant waves and jagged rocks. However, here is why it is so important that we make the leap and take the risk: *sexual safety increases emotional safety.*

Doctors Bill and Ginger Bercaw, authors and sex therapists, created a sexual and emotional connection model called the Circulation Model of Sexual Intimacy.[2] Their model shows us that sexual connection and emotional connection feed one another. Emotional and sexual intimacy create a cycle where being together sexually heightens the sense of emotional connection and being more emotionally connected heightens sexual desire.

Think about the last time you made love with your partner. Did you feel emotionally closer and more connected afterward? Now, think about the last time you had a good conversation with your partner where you shared your inner emotional world and felt deeply understood and loved. Did this conversation make you feel more sexual attraction to and desire for your partner? Each form of connection often reinforces the other form of connection, creating a feedback loop that heightens intimacy and security in the relationship.

In the same way that sexual and emotional connection reinforce and enhance one another, sexual and emotional safety form the same symbiotic relationship. The more emotionally safe we feel, the more sexually safe we feel. And the more sexually safe we feel, the more emotionally safe we feel. Safety functions in much the same way that connection does, creating the same type of helpful feedback loop.

Creating Sexual Safety

What this creates is a paradoxical reality wherein sex with the cheating partner is what helps alleviate our fear, pain, and risk about sex with the cheating partner. I know. Stay with me. Don't throw your book at the canary yet. I promise it will all make sense.

To truly rebuild sexual safety with the cheating partner, we must rewire our neural networks so that instead of sex feeling like

SEXUAL AND EMOTIONAL SAFETY

a dangerous or painful activity or topic (which it can easily become after experiencing sexual betrayal), it feels safe, comforting, and enjoyable again.

Our neural networks get wired and rewired through repetitive experience. Our experiences are basically a combination of events or behavior and the feelings and emotions that accompany them. To rewire our brain, we need to have a different experience repeatedly that creates a different emotional pattern and begins to teach our brain new associations. If sexual betrayal and chronic gaslighting have created a pattern of mistrust, fear, and pain around sex with our partner, then we need to create new experiences that can generate a new emotional pattern and rewire our neural networks in a different direction.

The best way to do this is to have sexual experiences with the cheating partner (or with a new partner) that feel safe, loving, comforting, enjoyable, and fun. When we take the leap, face our fear, and begin to reestablish sexual contact with the cheating partner (and for some partners this starts with just allowing hugs or physical affection back into the relationship), we start the process of re-teaching our brain that we can feel safe with our partner. We rewire our brain for sexual safety and enjoyment again. The more times we have good sexual or physical connection with our partner, the safer we feel.

This sexual safety then feeds and enhances our emotional safety. When we experience sex with the cheating partner where we feel cherished, desired, attended to, and connected with, it builds the sense of emotional safety and security between us.

When we feel emotionally safe with the cheating partner, that emotional safety spills over and builds the sexual safety as well. When both the emotional and sexual parts of the relationship are online and safety is being actively attended to in both arenas, safety grows and expands more quickly than if just one part of the equation is being addressed.

This is a difficult and nuanced topic to discuss, and I feel trepidation as I write. Black-and-white thinking in either direction creates problems. There is absolutely a need for emotional safety to be rebuilt for there to be enough sexual safety to reengage. This requires significant emotional work on the part of the cheating partner who must shoulder responsibility for rebuilding the trust and safety they have broken. However, it is also true that betrayed partners can sometimes get stuck in a holding pattern of sexual disconnection for longer than is helpful because we have fallen prey to the idea that emotional safety can eliminate all sense of risk around sexual reengagement.

The challenge is that there is no objective measurement to tell us whether we are safe enough. Do we need to continue to hit the sexual pause button and rebuild trust? Or have we moved into avoidance to evade the discomfort and risk involved in re-adventuring into sex? Do we need to nudge ourselves forward or do we need to continue to hold the boundary? It can be difficult to discern where we are on the map of our sexual and emotional relationships and what we need in any given moment.

Most partners need help and support with this from others who understand the pitfalls and stuck places that can trap us. We need helpers who can support us as we explore our fears, listen to ourselves so we can determine where we are in the process, and make the choices that move us toward health and freedom. We need patience and kindness as we overcome our fears and reach for the sexual life we long for.

For those partners who are leaving their relationship, learning to date again and build trust with a new sexual partner, many of these same pitfalls around sexual and emotional safety exist. Our cultural norm brings the expectation that we have sex first and then we see if the person might be good for us as a potential partner. However, it can be difficult to feel emotionally and sexually safe with someone we don't know, particularly after having been through the wringer of sexual betrayal. For many betrayed partners, the road to developing sexual and emotional safety with a new partner means going slow, listening to our gut, staying in awareness, and allowing the emotional and sexual relationship to develop over time.

In the next chapter, we are going to continue discussing how to build sexual safety. We begin by looking at the role that sex with the self can play in healing and then move to explore how to deal with triggers, intrusive images, and flashbacks during sex.

Don't knock masturbation.
It's sex with someone I love.

ANNIE HALL

CHAPTER SEVENTEEN

SEXUAL AND EMOTIONAL SAFETY:

Part Two

BUILDING SEXUAL SAFETY WITH YOURSELF

Sometimes reclaiming sexual safety needs to start with us rather than with our partner. Because of the mistrust and hurt created by the cheating and lying, many partners find reclaiming authentic eroticism a very personal process—one that is best done alone at first.

For most partners, a significant part of healing betrayal trauma involves reclaiming our sexuality. Until we are clear about who we are sexually, what we prefer, what turns us on and off, what creates desire and arousal and what shuts us down, we will not be able to bring our full sexual self to our relationship, share it with our partner, and co-create a sex life that is satisfying and fulfilling for both of us.

For many partners, reinstating a sense of safety around sexual pleasure can feel easier to do by having sex alone for some amount of time.

When I introduce the idea of solo sex to my clients, I often hear the following response (and ladies I hate to say it, but I only hear this from you; I've never had a male betrayed partner say this to me): "Well since my partner is in recovery from sex addiction and can't masturbate as part of his sobriety definition, I can't masturbate either."

My response is to let that statement sit and breathe for a moment so they can take in what they just said. Then I ask them, "If your husband was told he was diabetic and had to radically change his diet, would you adopt the same restrictions? Would you begin taking insulin because he has to?" Or I'll say, "If both you and your spouse were avid runners and your spouse hurt their knee and had to stop running, would you decide that you also needed to stop running?"

My clients always see the absurdity in these situations, but when it comes to sex, it is harder for them to differentiate themselves from their significant other. The loss of ownership around sexuality can be deeply ingrained. However, it is this very loss of ownership that sex with self can begin to address.

It is impossible to feel sexually safe with our partner if we cannot feel sexually safe with ourselves. The purpose of solo sex is to create a safe space to reconnect with our own sexual pleasure and preferences.

When we explore sex with ourselves, we can do it without any sense of pressure or expectation from our partner. We can take the time and space needed to explore various forms of touch and sensation and to learn more about what we enjoy without the complexity that partnered sex can introduce.

Once we feel safe with and fully connected to our sexual selves, we can then move toward integrating sex with our partner. The more we know our sexual selves, the more we will be able to engage in sex with our partner with clarity and confidence.

Instead of returning to how we operated sexually within our relationship prior to discovering the cheating, we can now reassess and evaluate how we want our new sexual relationship to work. When we can use our sexual voice and claim our sexual selves, it creates the ability to discuss, negotiate, and explore with our partner in new ways. This allows us to co-create a new sexual relationship that maintains and builds upon the safety that has been established through sex with ourselves.

For some individuals, sex with self does not feel safe due to childhood messaging or traumas. In this case, working with an expert is vital to help explore the sense of danger that accompanies sex and to create new connections to your sexual self based on safety, presence, and acceptance.

If you are a partner who has left or is leaving the relationship with the cheating partner, sex with yourself is often a significant part of healing. As you work through the sexual injuries created by the cheating and gaslighting, you can begin to envision a new sexual relationship for yourself and a future partner. Sex with yourself gives you space to begin to learn your body in a new and different way, to connect to your likes and dislikes, and to tune into pleasure without the added dynamics that partnered sex introduces. As you reclaim your sexual self, it will equip you to bring yourself more fully to a relationship with a new partner and empower you to use your voice and presence to co-create something new and wonderful in the future.

Let me leave you with one last thought on this topic. If you are a more mature betrayed partner, it is still possible to create a new and wonderful sex life with and for yourself. Many of the partners who complete our *Braving Hope*™ online coaching program are sixty and older. I am always thrilled to see the sense of possibility that returns and the healing that begins as these courageous individuals forge ahead in creating the life they want for themselves. They are a testament to the reality that it is never too late to claim our sexual selves. No matter how deep the injury or how much time has been spent in unhelpful patterns, it is always possible to change the trajectory of your sex life and forge a new sexual self and relationship.

Now that we have looked at the helpful role that solo sex can play in our healing journey, I want to turn our focus to one last common issue that partners struggle with as part of the sexual injury: triggers, images, and flashbacks that arise during sex.

DEALING WITH TRIGGERS DURING SEX

If you are a betrayed partner, you have likely experienced intrusive thoughts, images, or painful emotions that flash in during sex. These intrusive images and flashbacks are trauma symptoms and create fear that hijacks sexual desire and arousal. These triggers can impact you regardless of whether you have needed a sexual hiatus from your partner, you have continued to be sexual with the cheating partner, or you have left your relationship and are with a new partner.

Experiencing these triggering events is no small matter. It often brings us right into the overwhelming feelings we felt when we first learned of our partner's cheating. When we decide to take the leap and reengage sexually with our cheating partner, ourselves, or a new partner, it can be profoundly deflating to land in the middle of what I call a "trauma-trigger-cascade" right when we are starting to enjoy ourselves. We were feeling pleasure, our arousal was building, and suddenly we are engulfed in feelings and images of the betrayal. Safety flees as our brains light up with threat and danger and sex once again feels profoundly unsafe.

Unfortunately, the coping strategies that betrayed partners often reach for in these moments can be unhelpful and even harmful to our goal of rebuilding trust and sexual safety. Most partners cope with these dysregulating triggers in one of two ways: we either push through the moment or we shut down and withdraw sexually. Below we look at each.

Giving It the Old "Push Through"
One of the most common ways partners deal with intrusive images and thoughts is to try to shut them out, push through, and keep going. We do this by trying to wall off the images and associated feelings. We focus our minds on the sensations in our bodies, or we dissociate altogether (sometimes through alcohol or other substances) to observe what is happening from a distance. In some way, we try to mentally push away the images and feelings that are coming up so we can complete the act of sex with our partner.

One reason this strategy is so common is that we don't feel we are allowed to stop once we have started down the sexy road. We mistakenly believe that it is better to just "get through it" so our partner does not become disappointed or angry with us. We don't know how to pause the action and take care of ourselves when we are in the middle of being sexual. Pausing to take care of us means pausing our partner's pleasure and arousal, and that feels unfair to them. We can feel uncertain about how they will respond and whether we will feel supported or unsupported during that difficult moment. As a result, we decide the best course of action is to just push on through.

What we don't realize is that the decision to push through is also a decision to disconnect from ourselves. To pull the plug on the intrusive images and feelings, we must disconnect from some part (or maybe all) of ourselves. When we disconnect from ourselves but continue to have sex, we are now having sex without our full self being present. If the goal is to bring our full sexual selves to our relationship and know and be known in a way that creates intimacy and connection, then giving it the old push through moves us in the opposite direction from our goal.

Not only that, but it also suspends the problem. Rather than pausing to deal with the issue in a way that increases trust and safety (and we will talk about how to do that in a minute), pushing through reinforces the lack of safety around sex. We have disconnected from the difficult moment rather than worked to alleviate and heal it. As a result, we are left with another unsafe or threatening sexual experience. If the goal is to create new experiences around sex that rewire our brains for safety and security, pushing through leaves us stuck in the old threatened, fearful neural networks. This leaves the problem intact and waiting to come right back and haunt us another day.

Shut Down and Sexual Withdrawal
Another way betrayed partners cope with the flashbacks and negative emotions is to avoid sex altogether. When triggers and flashbacks hijack our hearts and minds during sex, it can be so distressing that we don't want to try again. We can decide we just aren't ready or get so afraid of experiencing those feelings that we avoid sex altogether.

The drawbacks to this strategy are like those of pushing through. Avoidance freezes the problem in place and does not move us toward resolution and healing. It robs us of our right to sexual pleasure, connection, and fun. And it prevents us from having the safe sexual experiences that are the very thing we need to create new neural pathways for sexual safety and security.

It's an Us Problem

Both common coping strategies—giving it the old push through or avoiding sex—stem from the belief that the triggers, flashbacks, and intrusive images are our problem to solve. Betrayed partners can automatically assume that since it is happening to us, it is ours to deal with.

The reality is that even though it is our heads the circus has decided to visit, the animals and clowns that make up the acts all came from our partner's behaviors. We experience these trauma symptoms because of the cheating. Prior to discovering our partner's behaviors, we did not have pornographic images or imagined scenes of sex with the affair or acting out partners blasting into our minds and hearts during sex. Post-discovery, it is only after we move toward the vulnerability of sex with our partner that we experience these unwelcome symptoms.

To effectively deal with these trauma triggers, we must first accept that it is an "us" problem. We are intertwined in activity that is creating the intrusive sense of danger. Our partner and their history are very much a part of this. To truly begin to resolve and heal these symptoms they have an active role to play. We must move out of the belief that we need to stay silent about the spectacle unfolding in our minds and deal with it by ourselves. We need to learn to invite our partner into this moment with us, and our partner needs to learn how to enter in a helpful and supportive manner.

To shift from "my problem" to "our problem," it is best to talk about this outside of the bedroom, when you are not being sexual and both of you are rested and able to engage in a conversation that may bring up intense feelings. Talking about your experience and requesting that your partner begin to help you cope with those moments is a necessary first step. The cheating partner must recognize that reengaging sexually after cheating is a process and that there is healing work to be done. They must see themselves as a key actor in the healing drama and fully invest in the role of supporting you.

Once the two of you have shifted to understanding that this is a shared problem that you must join together to resolve, you can begin to approach it differently in the bedroom.

Coming into the Present

When we experience intrusive images or flashbacks, they are the past intruding on the present. We are jerked out of the present moment where we are having sex with our partner into the past horror of discovering the cheating. When this happens, we need help coming mindfully back into the present and reassurance that we are safe.

This is where your partner plays a pivotal role. The two of you need to agree that pushing through or avoiding sex are not helpful for your sexual relationship. Instead, when these triggers happen, you are going to let your partner know. You are going to pause the sexual action and say, "Hey, can we stop a minute, I'm struggling with flashbacks and images right now and I'm not here anymore." This will cue your partner for their role in helping you move out of the past and come back into the present.

As the two of you slow down and pause sexual activity, your partner can do things like look into your eyes and hold your gaze as they say to you, "I'm here with you, we are here together, come back to me." They can rub your back or hold your hand or remind you to look around the room and name the colors on the walls, or five things that you see around the room—a grounding technique that can help you come back to the present moment. They can reassure you by saying, "I love you; I am with you and only you, we are here together."

What works will be different for each partner and each couple, and you will need to experiment to find what is right for you. However, just the act of bringing what is happening out of the isolation of your mind and body into the relationship to be held by the two of you will create change. This choice creates a moment of true co-regulation as the cheating partner becomes aware of your emotional dysregulation and brings their presence and support to help you move back toward safety.

Sometimes you will not be able to continue being sexual. Sometimes the flashbacks will have triggered so much emotional load that tears come, or you are just simply not able to get reconnected to your arousal and desire. That is okay, and the cheating partner must be in a place where they can hold sex loosely and know that the process of working through these types of trauma symptoms works best when there is plenty of room and space and very little pressure. Slower is often faster in this process.

Other times you will be able to talk for a few minutes, receive reassurance, and ground yourself in the present in a way that allows you to resume sexual activity from a place of connection and emotional safety.

Whether you can resume sexual activity or not, you and your partner will rebuild sexual safety by working through these trauma symptoms together. Instead of shouldering the burden alone and disconnecting from yourself to cope, reaching for your partner and inviting them to join you in loosening the grip of the intrusive thoughts and images builds trust and security in your relationship.

A common treatment for flashbacks and intrusive images is Eye Movement Desensitization and Reprocessing (EMDR). This is a highly effective form of trauma treatment that can reduce the emotional charge and frequency of flashbacks. If you are struggling with these issues, a trauma therapist trained in EMDR can be very helpful. However, even with this treatment, you will still need to work with your partner to rebuild sexual and emotional safety whenever triggers surface during sex.

The Belligerent Cheater

For some of you, the cheating partner may be unwilling to support you in dealing with flashbacks and intrusive images. They may get defensive, angry, or impatient when you raise the topic. They may belligerently demand that you deal with it yourself and ask why you can't get over it already.

In this case, the cheating partner is creating more emotional damage. Their lack of empathy and awareness about the loss of safety created by the cheating and lying exacerbates the sense of threat in the relationship. Unwillingness to accept responsibility and accountability to repair and rebuild security within the relationship leaves betrayed partners without any path toward healing.

If your partner has adopted this stance, it is vital that you carefully consider what is best for your health and healing in terms of engaging sexually and emotionally with the cheating partner. This can be painful and may bring you into primal panic as you consider whether you can stay in the relationship. Getting expert help, either individually or as a couple, is vital and can help you determine how to move forward.

Flashbacks with a New Partner

If you are in a sexual relationship with a new partner but still have flashbacks and intrusive images from your previous relationship, consider a couple of things:

You may be reengaging sexually too soon. Perhaps you need more time to grieve the loss of your previous relationship and fully heal the sexual injuries. Remember, our culture tells us we get over the loss of one attachment by replacing it with a new one. But this leaves us to work out our unfinished healing on our new partner, which is not fair to them. So, you may need more time.

If you feel like you are ready to be sexual again but are still dealing with this trauma symptom, you may want to slow things down with your new partner and ask them to work with you to help you resolve such issues. Only by taking the time to work through what is happening will you be able to be fully free to move forward in your new relationship. It can be difficult to ask a new partner to do this type of healing work; however, without it, you suspend the problem and prolong the suffering for yourself and your relationship. Even though your new partner has not caused the issues creating the trauma triggers, it is still an "us" problem, because they are your sexual partner. Hopefully, they want you to be fully present and able to connect with them. They have the same role in helping you come back to the present when you get stuck in the past.

SUMMARY: JUST THE BEGINNING

Are you out of breath yet? We have covered an enormous amount of ground in exploring the sexual injury created by intimate betrayal. And yet, what I am aware of, and likely so are you, is that there is so much more to be said. How cheating impacts sexuality is an enormous topic. Each person's sexuality and sexual expression is unique, and the variety and permutations in our world are endless and fascinating. No single book can do justice to this complex topic, let alone one section of a book.

My hope is that these chapters have at least introduced the topic to you and addressed some of the key experiences that shape partner sexuality after betrayal. You may not see your experience represented here or examined as fully as you would like. I can only say yes, yes, yes to that, and apologize for the limitations of space to address it all here.

Whatever your experience has been, know that you are not alone. Others have experienced the same. And whatever the sexual injury that follows betrayal has looked like for you, please know that your experience is valid. When we bring our sexual injuries out of the shadows and into the light, we can begin to share our experiences with each other, speak our truth, name the carried shame, identify toxic beliefs, and release it all. This releasing creates room for us to reclaim and recreate our sexuality, choosing what we want to think and believe about ourselves and others, and opening space for profound healing to take place and new life to grow and flourish.

ADDITIONAL RESOURCES FOR YOU

To learn more about the role the cheating partner can play in the healing process, watch the free video **When You Are Both the Problem and the Solution: The Cheating Partner's Dilemma** by Michelle Mays. Visit michellemays.com/cheating-partner-video to watch.

PART FOUR

Betrayal

Dynamic

Multidimensional

Attachment Injury
The overwhelming experience of damage to the relational bond through sexual behavior that violates the trust and safety in the relationship.

Emotional & Psychological Injury
The confusing experience of being lied to, manipulated, coerced, and intimidated by the cheating partner in their efforts to protect their secret behavior.

Sexual Injury
The impact to the betrayed partner's sexuality resulting fom the cheating partner's betrayal of the sexual agreements within the relationship

Past — Present — Future

INTRODUCTION

THE ATTACHMENT-FOCUSED PARTNER BETRAYAL MODEL

Thus far, we have taken a deep dive into the three injuries created by partner betrayal: the attachment injury, the emotional and psychological injury, and the sexual injury. Along the way, we have identified the attachment-based dynamics that motivate the emotional responses and behavioral reactions experienced by betrayed partners.

Now we turn our attention to the healing process. The following four chapters look at the key elements vital for effective recovery. We will explore in detail the goals, tasks, and outcomes involved by looking at the six phases of the healing journey. Finally, we wrap up by coming full circle to where we started in Chapter One: the journey to becoming the hero of your betrayal story.

Only in relationships
can you know yourself,
not in abstraction and
certainly not in isolation.

TIAN DAYTON, PhD

CHAPTER EIGHTEEN

RELATIONAL RECOVERY:

Attachment-Based Treatment for Partner Betrayal

Healing sexual betrayal is not a linear process. Betrayed partners find themselves in the middle of a multidimensional, dynamic, emotional rodeo that pushes and pulls their attachment systems in opposite directions while catapulting them into severe nervous system dysregulation. To effectively wrangle their experience, they need attachment-based treatment.

In this chapter, we explore the five factors that form the foundation for effective attachment-based treatment:

1. Defining Our Outcome: Secure Bonding
2. Understanding Our Attachment-Based Motivations
3. Accessing Validation, Articulation, and Specificity
4. Core Self Connection: Tracking and Deepening Emotions
5. Facing Fear and Building Resilience

DEFINING OUR OUTCOME: SECURE BONDING

In 2011, I founded the Relational Recovery Institute (RRI) to provide treatment to those dealing with sexual addiction, trauma, and relationship issues. RRI's tag line is . . . *because change happens in relationship*. This pithy little phrase can fool us because it is so simple. But it contains all that we understand about how human transformation takes place. It captures the truths revealed in science and research, the principles guiding religious and spiritual teachings, and the lived experience of humanity. Those five little words zero in on who we are, how we function, what gives life meaning, and the primary motivator for all evolution and change: relationship.

If our most significant wounds happen in relationship with others (and they usually do), then doesn't it make sense that our healing and restoration must also happen in relationship? If our attachment system influences all areas of our lives and the health and happiness we experience, then attachment and secure bonding must be at the center of any treatment approach that addresses relational problems and traumas.

When our attachment system is placed at the heart of the healing process, the outcome we are seeking becomes clear: *secure bonding with ourselves, others, and our higher power*. I call this process *relational recovery*.

Relational recovery is the imperfect, courageous, and vulnerable act of allowing ourselves to know and be known in relationships in a way that heals past wounds, transforms our life, and matures and ripens us into the authentic self we were created to be. Relational recovery applies to our relationship with ourselves (how securely we are attached to our core self), our relationships with our partner and others (how securely we are attached to those we love), and our relationship with our higher power (how secure we feel in the world at large and in our relationship with a divine being).

Growing our ability to be securely attached is the *one thing* that changes everything else. It affects our emotional lives, how we handle stress, how fulfilled we feel, our level of joy, our sense of safety, the risks we can take and the adventures we are able to have, along with our physical, mental, and spiritual health and *all* our relationships. Literally everything in our lives is impacted by our desire for secure bonding. Relational recovery is our goal and the outcome we are working toward.

UNDERSTANDING OUR ATTACHMENT-BASED MOTIVATIONS

This book provides an attachment-based model and map for betrayed partners and helpers alike. When viewed through the lens of attachment, betrayed partners' responses and reactions make sense in ways that open fresh language, concepts, and pathways for treatment and healing.

To heal the emotional and behavioral reactions that follow betrayal, we must clarify the experience of attachment distress. While we know betrayal creates a profound loss of safety and our reactions and responses are driven by this loss, we must go further with our understanding of these dynamics.

We have a clearer roadmap to healing when we identify the thinking and behavior patterns that evolve as we cope and are given language and concepts to describe the relational and attachment-based motivations that drive our responses. Concepts like *attachment ambivalence*, *attachment shame*, *betrayal blindness*, and *fear of loss* help us distill the experience of betrayal so that it becomes understandable and containable.

When our reactions are normalized as predictable responses that occur when attachment systems enter distress because of the impossible choices created by partner betrayal, relief is immediate and palpable. When our experience is organized and mapped, it becomes less threatening and more contained. We develop hope that there is a pathway through the disorganized emotional chaos to clarity and wholeness.

ACCESSING VALIDATION, ARTICULATION, AND SPECIFICITY

Betrayal plunges partners into a profoundly disorienting experience riddled with loss. In the middle of this reality fragmentation, one of the most helpful interventions is the validation of our emotions, thinking, and behaviors.

Rather than rushing toward change or healthier coping, we first need our pain, shock, anger, and sadness validated. We need to feel heard, seen, and acknowledged. When we feel truly held within another person's empathic recognition and acceptance of our distress, it provides a soothing balm that helps us to regulate our over-activated, over-aroused nervous systems.

Validation of our experience pulls us out of the loneliness and isolation that can accompany betrayal. When our support system creates space to help us hold our pain, anger, and despair without judgment or agenda, it forms a cradle for healing to grow. Acceptance and acknowledgment reach in and touch our core needs—to belong and to matter—at the very moment when these needs are under siege, and we struggle with feeling rejected and unworthy.

Articulation is one of the most effective forms of validation. We need language and concepts that help us put words to the felt experience occurring in our bodies. Language helps us begin to contain our new and overwhelming reality. We reach for words and models that help us locate ourselves on the map of our own experience and point us toward healing.

Specificity is also vital. Simply being told we feel unsafe or that our behaviors are about safety-seeking is not enough. We need clear definitions and astute explanations that pinpoint the specific moments of exquisite pain, panic, and distress that we are traveling through. We need help making sense of our reality as we are often encountering new and strange versions of ourselves and our partner as our coping is stretched beyond its normal limits.

Lastly, we need concrete suggestions and ideas that support our forward movement. Because betrayal has overwhelmed us, our best thinking is not available. We need our support system to help us create a short list of potential requests to make or boundaries to set within our relationship. We need specific options spelled out so we can choose the one that feels best. We may even need to be walked through a role-play where we practice how we are going to say something important or ask for a key need to be met.

Being told we must set boundaries, without detailed ideas about what those boundaries should be, leaves us wandering in the dark; we have no real understanding of how to put that advice into action. The ultimate choice of how to handle the situation is ours, but suggestions, options, and ideas from our support system help us determine which direction is best.

Support that helps us validate and articulate our experience with specificity and concrete suggestions forms the first step on the path to healing. And taking this first step begins the process of integrating the new experience of betrayal into our understanding of ourselves, our relationships, our histories, and our futures.

CORE SELF CONNECTION: TRACKING AND DEEPENING EMOTIONS

A key element in understanding how our threat response and attachment systems respond to betrayal lies in recognizing the difference between primary (core) and secondary (reactive) emotions and how these two different emotional states impact our thinking and behavior.

Emotions are not neutral events. They automatically move us in a direction—toward what we find pleasurable or enjoyable or away from what we find dangerous or distasteful. Each emotion carries within it an action tendency.[1] As a result, emotions drive our thinking and behaviors, even when we are unaware of or disconnected from them.

To understand coping behaviors, we must first define core and reactive emotions and understand their specific role.

Primary (Core) Emotions

Primary emotions are what we feel first: the core emotional response rooted in our deepest attachment needs. These are related to both our sense of self and our sense of self with others. Am I lovable (sense of self), and can I count on others to love me (sense of self in relation to others)? Our core emotions are connected to our deepest longing to be safe, fully accepted, known, to matter, and to be loved.

For example, discovering our significant other has cheated on us activates our attachment fears, creating primal panic as we lose our connection with our partner. This panic spurs the most important questions of our existence: Am I loved, wanted, worthy, safe, and secure? The emotions that accompany our threatened attachment needs—panic, shame, fear, sadness, and anger—are overwhelming and can leave us feeling raw and vulnerable.

Secondary (Reactive) Emotions

When we are feeling tender and exposed in our primary (core) emotions, secondary emotions ride to the rescue. Secondary emotions are reactive. They rush in and move us toward emotions that help us feel more in control. Reactive emotions protect our vulnerability by moving us into a defensive emotional stance.

With secondary emotions, we become enraged, jealous, terrified, panicked, or heartbroken. From this emotional space, we begin to make meaning about what we have discovered. Meaning about ourselves ("I'm a good wife, I don't deserve this!"); meaning about our partner ("She's a narcissist and always has been!"); meaning about the world around us ("No one can be trusted!"). We move into reactive secondary emotions to avoid the overwhelming pain of primary emotions.

This means that our core emotions (and the wisdom they contain) get suppressed and pushed down. Instead, we speak and act from our reactive emotions. We do this because we feel safer and more in control in this space.

The Same but Different

We can feel the same emotions as primary or secondary. We can feel anger as a core emotion or as a reactive emotion. Same with fear. Same with sadness. What helps us know whether we are connected to our core emotional experience or in reactive emotions is the level of vulnerability we are leaning into, and how closely connected we are to our deepest attachment needs.

When launched outside our window of tolerance, we automatically move into secondary defensive and reactive emotions. We do this to cope with something unmanageable at a time when our normal resources are overwhelmed. As a result, we disconnect or dissociate from our core self.

As we are overwhelmed with chaotic feelings and unable to process our experience, we turn to reactive emotions as a coping mechanism.

This process is an emotional roller-coaster that swoops and rolls as we hurtle through one reactive emotion after another. All the while, we are separated from our core emotions. This is nature's design to protect us from emotional pain. However, that separation can (and usually does) increase our sense of distress and dysregulation—our sense that we don't know who we are.

Healing for betrayed partners centers around learning to widen our window of tolerance to where we can hold our big hot primary emotions, connect to them, process them, and integrate them into our understanding of our lives. Author and researcher Daniel Siegel, PhD, says, "In many cases our well-being depends on widening the window of tolerance so that we can hold the elements of our internal world in awareness—without being thrown into rigidity (depression, cutoffs, avoidance) or chaos (agitation, anxiety, rage)."[2]

When we come into connection with our core emotions, we also connect to our core self. This allows us to process our experience in a way that creates new meaning and understanding of both ourselves and others.

When stuck in our reactive emotions, however, we recycle our experience in endless loops of reactivity that take us nowhere new. Instead, our traumatic responses heighten as we are left in activated distress without the relief that processing our core emotional experience provides.

Connecting to My Core Self

When I began therapy to deal with my betrayal trauma, I was living in chronic hyper-arousal, disconnected from my core self and my primary emotions. I walked into therapy amped up, knee ricocheting up and down, hair standing on end with anxiety. I sat down full of stories to tell and all manner of thoughts about what it meant about me, my spouse, our relationship, and the world around me. I could have talked for *days* about my racing thoughts.

Fortunately, my therapist knew not to get sidetracked by the drama. Instead, she began our sessions by validating my experience. This was one of my therapist's most powerful and loving actions because she helped me feel normal. She helped me understand that the emotional ride that often made me feel crazy wasn't crazy at all. She created space for my reactive emotions by helping me to look at how those emotions were impacting my thinking and behavior.

This was all enormously helpful, and it was essential that my treatment began there. It was equally essential that treatment did not stop there because real healing lies in connecting to our core emotional experience.

In session after session, my therapist helped me come down into my body and articulate what was happening for me emotionally at the deepest levels. She would bring me into the core of my experience, helping me name it, feel it, and let it move through me. These core emotions were harder for me to feel. They were quieter but also fiercer. They were connected to my vulnerability and my deepest fears about whether I was worthy, acceptable, and lovable. They were about a lack of safety that started in infancy, accompanied me through my entire childhood, and shaped my adult relationships.

Would I ever feel safe and securely held by my primary attachment figures? My parents had failed me profoundly in this regard, and now my spouse was too. What did this say about me? What did this mean for me? These questions brought me into contact with enormous sadness, loneliness, and grief as I acknowledged all I had lost as both a child and an adult and how gravely significant those losses were to my sense of self.

These core emotions were the very feelings that my knee-bobbing and drama-talking were trying to avoid. These emotions were more intense, scarier, and more vulnerable than my reactive emotions. But they were also the pathway that brought me back into connection with myself. Feeling and processing my core emotional experience brought me back into my window of tolerance, grounded me, resourced me, and opened new ways of thinking, being, and doing. This is the paradox of core emotions. While they initially feel too big and overwhelming to go near, when we do draw close and touch them, we find it relieving, grounding, and clarifying.

Each time we did this work, I left my therapist's office in a completely different emotional state than when I arrived. I felt calm, grounded, back in my own skin, and available to myself in ways I was not just an hour earlier. I began to learn that the way back to feeling connected to myself, resourced, and whole was through connecting to my deeper, more vulnerable core feelings instead of avoiding them. I learned that the way I was coping when I was revved up and hyper-vigilant perpetuated more anxiety as I worked to avoid the feelings that I thought would destroy me. Paradoxically, when I dug down and found those scary feelings and invited them in to be felt, cried, grieved, and raged over, I landed back in my window of tolerance. Better still, I was able to stay there longer and longer as my window expanded and enlarged.

The Magic of Co-regulation

I could not have connected with my core emotions and expanded my window of tolerance by myself. I needed someone there with me, someone to create safety by connecting to me emotionally and holding the big feelings with me. Safe connection with another person, whether a therapist, friend, spouse, family member, or spiritual leader, is always needed for us to face the primary emotions that otherwise drive us out of our window of tolerance. Learning to come back into our window of tolerance is *always* a relational task. We need another calm, safe, accessible nervous system to soothe our own nervous system, to help regulate our affect, and to bring us back to our window of tolerance and therefore to ourselves.

Over time, as I continued working with my therapist on connecting to my core emotions and giving them space to be listened to and processed, I began to be able to do this work on my own. I was in a highly relational process with myself. I learned to move from reactive emotions to core emotions in a very intentional and mindful way. I was present to my emotional world. My newfound stable connection with myself was proof of the changes that were taking place.

My hope is that you will experience this same transformation.

Betrayal trauma is an experience that leaves us stranded in the disorganized emotional storm of secondary reactive emotions. This is normal. Healing involves learning how to validate our reactive emotions, understand the relational patterns those emotions are creating in our lives, and then, with support, come down into our core emotional experience and create new relational patterns that factor in the vulnerable underbelly of our deepest needs and longings.

FACING FEAR AND BUILDING RESILIENCE

In Chapter Twelve, we explored the profound impact that fear of more relational loss can have on our healing trajectory. We get stuck, unable to use the tools of recovery because we fear that using our voice, setting a boundary, or asking for what we need will create more relational distance or disconnection. We fear the primal panic that loss of our safe base creates inside our bodies, so we stay frozen, looping around in patterns driven by powerlessness and shame.

Working with our fear is one of the most delicate but vital parts of our healing process. We cannot truly make a choice about our relationship until we are fully free to either stay or leave. If we are staying because we are too terrified to leave, that is not full choice. If we are leaving because we are terrified of staying, that is not full choice.

We must come to a place where we have built up our internal strength, resourcefulness, and resilience enough that we can tolerate the risk of loss that comes with movement toward healing. If we fully and freely choose to stay, we risk relational loss as we advocate for change and repair in our relationship. If we fully and freely choose to leave, we will encounter the profound grief and loss of our primary attachment figure. There is no forward direction for betrayed partners that does not include the risk of relational loss. Learning how to lean into our fear of relational loss is one of our core healing tasks.

For many betrayed partners, the fear of relational loss is unconscious. In our *Braving Hope*® online coaching program, we work with fear of loss every week. Over and over as I coach partners, they tell me that they are not afraid of losing their relationship or creating relational distance with their partner.

However, just like poker players, betrayed partners have a "tell" (a signal that what is happening on the surface is not the real story). For betrayed partners, the tell is behavior patterns that are repetitive, unproductive, and rooted in powerlessness.

As we lean into their experience together and start to peel back the reactive emotions and probe for what is underneath, we almost always arrive at fear. This fear is so big that it is often held out of conscious awareness. It is the primary (core) emotional experience that is too overwhelming to feel. It is only when we move the reactive layers out of the way that we see this fear, pulsing and throbbing at the heart of the partner's experience.

For most betrayed partners, a significant part of the healing work is learning how to face and feel the fear (the abandonment terror) that is blocking their path forward. This work should always be done with expert support, as it is almost always too dysregulating for partners to do by themselves.

Here is the secret to shifting the fear: We do the thing we are afraid to do.

I know, this is another book-throwing moment, so go ahead and swear or throw something and then let's unpack this together.

If we adhere to the false belief that we cannot make forward progress until the fear goes away, we will forever stay stuck. Waiting for the fear to go away is a false promise that yields nothing but more pain and suffering.

So, we must learn to move through fear by doing the thing we are afraid to do and then finding out we were able to do it. We see that we are still standing, we are still intact, and, in the famous mantra coined by author Glennon Doyle, "we can do hard things." When we do move toward our fear and do the hard thing in front of us, it builds our confidence in ourselves, our sense of resilience, and our inner strength and resourcefulness. Best of all, *it builds trust with ourselves.*

We start to trust our ability to take care of ourselves, make wise choices, advocate for ourselves, set boundaries, use our powerful and effective voice, and ask for what we need. Facing our fear is the antidote to staying stuck. Every. Single. Time.

The key to working with our fear is what I call "the nudge." We do not rip the blanket off the baby and leave it howling in the wind. No. Slowly and gently, with support, we nudge ourselves forward. We are like the rock climber scaling the face of a mountain. We know where we are going and what our goal is (secure bonding with ourselves and others), but we can't just leap to the top. Instead, we climb steadily, looking for the next toe hold, the next place to grip, scanning for what will hold us and what will move us toward our goal. We gather our courage each time we reach for the next incremental step in our journey.

Do you know the difference between free climbing and free solo climbing? Free soloists are those risk-loving adrenaline junkies who rock climb with no rope attached to catch them if they fall. Free climbing is scaling the surface with just your hands and feet (no other accoutrements), but you are attached to a rope to catch you if you fall.

In facing our fear of loss, we are free climbing, not free soloing. We have the rope of our relational support system to catch us when our partner responds poorly, or the relationship moves closer to ending, or we are betrayed again. That support helps us restabilize and reorient so we can continue facing our fears and moving forward.

As we nudge ourselves forward, facing manageable fears and taking risks we can tolerate, we build trust in ourselves, our core self expands and enlarges, and we forge internal resilience and resourcefulness that will be with us for the rest of our lives.

These are the critical interventions vital to support our healing: identifying secure bonding as our goal, understanding our attachment-based motivations, accessing validation, articulation, and specificity, connecting to our core emotional experience, and facing our fear and building resilience.

In the next two chapters, we distill the healing journey further by looking in detail at the six phases of healing.

> Everything that has happened
> to us up to this point
> is rehearsal for us to act, now,
> as our true self and to find
> and speak in our true voice.
>
> STEVEN PRESSFIELD

CHAPTER NINETEEN

BRAVING HOPE® AFTER BETRAYAL:

The Six Phases of Healing

One of my favorite moments as a therapist is when new clients come into my office and tell me their story. As I listen, I begin to see in my mind's eye the ways in which their lives will change, the freedom they will encounter, how much better their relationships will be, and how comfortable they will feel in their own skin if they enter fully into the transformation process. I start to glimpse a vision of what is possible for them, and it is an exciting and hopeful image.

The clients, however, are usually having a very different experience. They are entirely focused on the crisis or problem that has brought them to my office. For them, there is no vision and very little hope, as they are mired in their troubles and struggling without success to find a way out. For those dealing with betrayal trauma, the shock, pain, and anger tend to overwhelm everything else, making even the possibility of hope seem doubtful and unlikely.

Nevertheless, I and many others know there is an enormous amount of hope for betrayed partners. Hope for you. Hope for your significant other. Hope for your relationship. Sometimes not all three, but *always*, at a minimum, the first one.

This hope is not just a Hail Mary. It is grounded in the fact that there is a process available for healing from betrayal. There are steps, tasks, tools, and information to guide you from the initial chaos and devastation of betrayal to a place where you are actually—dare I say it—flourishing.

Below, I have outlined the six phases of this journey: *devastation, realization, stabilization, reimagining, creating,* and *flourishing*. Each phase has a goal, with tasks to be accomplished and outcomes to be achieved. These six phases are called the Braving Hope™ Process and form the foundation for The Braving Hope™ Treatment Model.

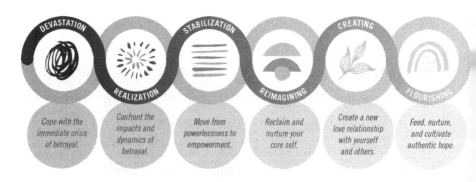

BRAVING HOPE

Let's start by defining what it means to brave hope. Braving hope summarizes the core action that betrayed partners engage in repeatedly through the recovery process. We are braving hope anytime we risk doing something new and untried as we move toward healing. Braving hope is accessing our courage and bravery after disappointment or heartbreak and allowing ourselves to hope for healing, transformation, and redemption.

We brave hope each time we walk through the door of the therapist's office and open ourselves to new ways of relating, thinking, and behaving. We brave hope each time we get out of bed during the dark days after discovery and show up for our kids, jobs, and friends while trying to sort out how to move forward. We brave hope when we get curious about ourselves, our relationships, and the history that shaped us. We brave hope when we show kindness to the partner who hurt us, when we engage in our own recovery alongside theirs, and when we hold hope for the restoration of our relationship. We brave hope when we identify and work through our fears of abandonment or loss and choose to leave our relationship and reimagine a new life for ourselves. All these actions, from the small to the momentous, are what it means to brave hope.

WE BRAVE HOPE TO ACHIEVE AUTHENTIC HOPE

When we brave hope, the result of daring to risk and long for more is that we get to experience authentic hope. Authentic hope is different from the false hope that our culture and those around us sometimes peddle. False hope embraces toxic positivity—trying to talk ourselves into a reality that doesn't exist using platitudes and affirmations that do not account for where we really are. False hope directs our focus toward our partner, who we cannot control, rather than helping us move toward our own empowered decision-making. False hope settles for short-term change rather than long-term transformation. False hope is what we experience when we are mired in betrayal blindness, carried shame, and fear.

Authentic hope, on the other hand, is grounded in the following core beliefs about what creates true possibility and transformation in our lives.

- **Our ability to choose our response to any situation is where our true power as human beings lies.** We do not always get to choose our circumstances. We are all amid life and experiencing the joys and tragedies of being human. However, no matter our circumstances, we can hold on to the true center of our being and choose how we respond. Utilizing our power to choose creates authentic hope and connects us to our true self.
- **We must always stay connected to our reality, even when our reality is painful and distressing.** The reality of betrayal is challenging, thrusting us into unwelcome and unchosen circumstances. Avoiding, denying, and distorting reality are normal human responses to traumatic events. However, working to stay grounded in the reality that is unfolding so we can stay in awareness, be present, and make good choices is vital to the healing process. Authentic hope is grounded in reality.
- **Deep, long-lasting personal and relational transformation is possible.** It is possible to change your life (your sense of secure connection with yourself, others, and your higher power) in significant and permanent ways. Transformation is possible and ongoing if you allow life to be your teacher, if you allow yourself to be stretched and grown through each challenge and joy presented, including the challenge of betrayal. Conviction about the possibility to truly change creates authentic hope.
- **Change that arises out of connection to our heart's longings and desires is more transformative and longer lasting than change that**

comes through pain and suffering. Pain and suffering will always challenge us to grow. However, we grow in more meaningful ways when we connect to the deepest desires of our hearts and allow those longings to stir us to action. Our inner longings tell us the truth much more than pain and suffering do. If we create space for what we long for and listen closely to it, it will guide us into a new and better way of living. Our longings lead us toward authentic hope.

Each phase of the Braving Hope® Process has its own goals, tasks, and outcomes. My hope is that by laying out the phases and steps you will see that there is a clear path to healing from partner betrayal—there are specific skills, tools, and relational abilities that, when developed, will move you out of pain and confusion into a place of being connected, empowered, grounded, and whole again.

The phases of the Braving Hope® Process are both linear and nonlinear. Most betrayed partners tend to experience a progression through the phases. At times, however, you may find yourself experiencing more than one phase simultaneously or doubling back and revisiting previous phases. For instance, it is not unusual to experience more and more flourishing (the last phase) while still occasionally feeling the pain of devastation (the first phase).

With this in mind, please know that however you experience these six phases, you are normal. Do not judge yourself about where you are in the process or how your journey is unfolding. While the phases are similar for everyone, each person's journey through them is unique.

Below are descriptions of the phases of the Braving Hope® Process. Please read through them with patience, kindness, and curiosity. Give yourself plenty of space and time to be where you are while still being open to and curious about what lies ahead as your healing journey progresses. In the remainder of this chapter, we focus on the first three phases: devastation, realization, and stabilization.

PHASE 1: DEVASTATION

The devastation phase follows the initial discovery of betrayal and can last a few weeks to many months. Some partners reexperience the devastation phase multiple times as new instances of betrayal are discovered—sometimes days and sometimes years after the initial discovery.

In the aftermath of betrayal, you are likely to experience some (and possibly all) of the following hallmarks of the devastation phase:

- All the symptoms of complex trauma that we talked about in Chapter Two are experienced, including high levels of anxiety, fear, anger, confusion, and pain; reduced functioning and an inability to focus or concentrate; loss of security and safety in the relationship; and deep mistrust of and disconnection from partner, friends and family, higher power, and self.
- Attachment Ambivalence that cycles quickly and chaotically, pulling you toward and away from the cheating partner almost simultaneously and leaving you reeling and confused. Your need for safe connection with your partner and your inability to obtain it are at a peak.
- Attachment shame overwhelms your self-esteem as fear that some lack in you has caused the cheating becomes a central haunting question.

- Betrayal blindness is active and present as you bargain with your new reality. Hope that it is not as bad as it seems, that the relationship is still salvageable, that your partner has not really been capable of hurting you this deeply. Gaslighting by the cheating partner is often at a peak during this phase, contributing to the crazy-making and reality fragmentation as you struggle to determine what is real and what is not.
- Coping is stretched to its limit as you operate outside your window of tolerance and your attachment system moves into high distress over the loss of safe connection to your partner. As a result, early attempts to cope are often reactive, inconsistent, and of limited help. You find yourself stuck in activated emotional states.
- Desperate searching for information (Sherlocking) begins as you try to find a way to contain and put limits around the threat and danger. Seeking the extent of the betrayal, you go to any and all lengths to try to find out exactly what your cheating partner has been doing. In addition, seeking expert guidance about the emotional experience of betrayal begins as you search out blogs, books, groups, therapists, coaches, and podcasts to try to understand and manage your experience.

The devastation phase is the most chaotic and emotionally charged phase of the Braving Hope® Process because of discovery's blindsiding and shocking nature. You believed you were living in one reality, only to discover a second unknown reality was running parallel to your experience.

Many partners look back on this phase and are shocked by the way they behaved and reacted when in extremis. It is important to remember that you (and by "you," I mean your body, brain, and mind) are experiencing a survival-level threat. Discovery of betrayal puts you in a fight to survive, and we all fight dirty and chaotically when backed into a dark corner. This is not to say that you are not responsible for yourself; we are all responsible for our adult selves. You may have some amends to make down the road. However, it is important to recognize the level of emotional disorganization that betrayal initially creates and to offer yourself grace and compassion about how you weather this phase.

Each phase of the healing process includes a specific *goal* along with *tasks* and *outcomes* that support the accomplishment of the goal. Our *goal* is our desired result. The *tasks* are what we do to accomplish the goal. The *outcomes* are the benefits and transformation that we look for in our lives and relationships due to taking action.

On the facing page is an outline of these important elements for the devastation phase.

PHASE 2: REALIZATION

The realization phase is when the initial shock of discovery begins to wear off and you start to more fully recognize the scope and depth of the betrayal and what it means for you and your relationship. During this phase, there are several key realizations that you will likely grapple with and process.

Realization #1: The problem is bigger than I thought.

For most betrayed partners, the initial discovery of the cheating reveals only a portion of the full story. In your relationship, you may have initially discovered a single affair, or an emotional

DEVASTATION PHASE GOAL:
Cope with the Immediate Crisis of Betrayal

TASKS	OUTCOMES
Learn to recognize partner betrayal trauma.	**Experience relief as you learn terms and concepts** to help you understand and articulate your experience; and recognize that you are normal, the range of reactions and emotions you are experiencing is to be expected.
Identify where and how to get expert help and build your alternative safe base.	**Begin to feel connected** to a stable source of support and help that you can depend upon.
Develop skills and utilize tools to calm, comfort, and soothe your activated nervous system.	**Move toward your window of tolerance, feel longer periods of calm,** and gain better access to clear thinking and decision-making.
Access help from your support team managing any immediate crisis issues (legal, financial, parenting, health, etc.). To access the free Betrayal Trauma Crisis Assessment Tool to assist you and your support system in this process, go to: www.michellemays.com/crisis-and-risk-assessment-tool/	**Resolve immediate crisis issues** to the degree possible to free up mental and emotional resources to focus on healing.
Learn about the attachment injury at the heart of betrayal and the role of attachment ambivalence and attachment shame in activating relational trauma symptoms.	**Move into awareness about the deeper relational needs and motivations** driving your thinking, feeling, and behaviors as you respond to the loss of relational connection and safety.
Identify the core attachment needs reflected in specific common behavioral patterns following betrayal such as battling for empathy, repudiating shame, and declawing the tiger.	**Begin to trade unhelpful reactionary coping strategies** for new coping skills that better meet your needs for relational and emotional safety.

affair that your significant other swears never turned physical, or a pornography issue, or any of a million other possibilities. And this initial discovery was without doubt terribly painful.

Unfortunately, most of the time the initial discovery is only part of the story. Often, over time, more discoveries are made, and the truth slowly trickles out in a death-by-paper-cut vortex of ever-deepening betrayals. Sometimes what is revealed over time is a sexual addiction that requires serious and intense treatment. Sometimes what is revealed over time is infidelity that is broader in scope than first anticipated. Other times, what you discover initially really is the whole story. In that case, what is revealed over time is the level of damage this has caused to your relationship. Whatever the case, there is a deepening understanding of the significance of the problem being faced. Which leads to the next realization . . .

Realization #2: This is not something I/we can just get over and move on from. After initial discovery, most partners go through a phase where they hope the relational breach can be patched up and worked through relatively quickly. They desperately want to escape the pain of the betrayal and move back into relational connection. As a result, they look for ways to quickly repair the damage and get the relationship back on stable ground. Usually, cheating partners also want to move the relationship out of crisis. To this end, they will apologize and make heroic promises for change.

However, when more lies and betrayals come to light, or the significance of the lies and cheating becomes clearer, the hope for a quick resolution fades and betrayed partners begin to realize they are not going to be able to easily move on from what has happened.

At this point, there is a deepening awareness of the level of damage that has been done and the fact that serious work and effort are going to be required to heal. Sometimes there is the possibility of repairing the relationship and moving on together. Sometimes there is the unwanted realization that your relationship must end. Which leads to realization number three...

Realization #3: Healing from betrayal trauma is a process that takes time. As betrayed partners develop a fuller understanding of the scope of the issues confronting them and their relationship, they begin to recognize that the quick fix they were hoping for is not going to happen. They start to understand that healing from betrayal is a longer-term process of learning about and repairing the wounds that have occurred.

This realization is a big one because it requires betrayed partners to reorient themselves and adjust their expectations. It asks them to take the long view about what has happened and the type of healing that might be possible. It changes the lens from a close-in immediate view of the situation to a bigger-picture examination of what might be possible over time. It asks them to accept that their individual healing and the potential healing of their relationship are processes that must unfold.

The realization phase is a pivot point for many betrayed partners. It is the phase where many partners make the decision to seek out help and fully enter a healing process. They adjust their expectations and commit to the deeper level of healing and restoration needed for themselves and potentially their relationship.

In the realization phase, as the initial devastation starts to lessen, partners begin to absorb new information and recognize how their sense of reality has been altered by betrayal. The following are the common experiences of the realization phase.

- Intense feelings of loss, uncertainty, anger, and pain wash through in waves as the depth and scope of the betrayal becomes clearer and is further absorbed and processed.
- Attachment ambivalence is ongoing, but a growing awareness of the cycle of connection and disconnection begins to create opportunities to slow the cycle and make choices regarding the need for emotional and physical connection and safety.
- Betrayal blindness creates a danger point as partners who are overwhelmed with painful emotions and fear of abandonment move into "knowing but not knowing" as a way of preventing loss and lessening fear.
- The question, "Should I stay or leave?" becomes central and attachment shame is felt acutely and wrestled with around issues of self-respect, dignity, and the opinion of others. Options like therapeutic separation, divorce, or continued relationship are weighed and assessed.
- Attempts to manage trauma symptoms lead to both healthy and unhealthy coping behaviors rooted in attachment needs as partners struggle to weather the lack of safety created by the chaotic period that follows discovery.
- Awareness of the negative impacts of sexual betrayal to the partner's sexuality grows, and partners struggle with managing sexual self-esteem and knowing how much or little to engage in the sexual relationship with the cheating partner during a time when emotional safety is significantly lacking.

- Increasing recognition of the cheating partner's lies and secrets creates an acute need for a full disclosure of the scope and depth of the betrayal. Sherlocking behaviors continue but often decrease as partners begin to understand the role that full therapeutic disclosure plays in the healing process and set expectations and boundaries with their partner around receiving disclosure.

As you can see from this list of common experiences, the realization phase is marked by increasing awareness and understanding of both the problem itself and what it will take to deal with and repair the damage done. As your new reality begins to sink in and you start to process different parts of your experience, you can expect to feel the acute crisis of the devastation phase lessen. You may still move back into crisis at times, but there will be longer periods where you feel more accessible to yourself and able to think about and process what is happening.

On the following page are the goal, tasks, and outcomes of the realization phase.

There is a specific danger point in the realization phase that I want to draw your attention to. This is where betrayed partners can veer off the path of healing and find themselves circling the proverbial drain for months and sometimes years before they find their way back.

Sexual betrayal is a difficult challenge to face, and sometimes partners choose to not face it. When betrayed partners are presented with the severity of their situation, they sometimes give in to the temptation to avoid fully looking at what has happened and instead move into betrayal blindness.

REALIZATION PHASE GOAL:
Confront the Impacts and Dynamics of Betrayal

TASKS	OUTCOMES
Develop skills to slow the cycle of attachment ambivalence and identify safe zones within the relationship where connection is possible and danger zones where boundaries are needed.	**Accept your attachment needs as normal and healthy and make positive choices** about how to get those needs met in your current situation while also protecting yourself from further harm.
Learn about the emotional and psychological injury at the heart of betrayal including the types and impacts of gaslighting and the attachment-based role of betrayal blindness.	**Experience clarity and decreasing confusion** as you identify gaslighting when it is happening and remove yourself from the path of danger. Experience growing tolerance for uncomfortable emotions and fear as you learn to stay connected to your reality even when it is scary.
Identify and release cultural carried shame, sexual carried shame, and carried shame related to the infidelity.	**Increase self-worth and expand your ability to hold the cheating partner accountable**. Experience freedom from attachment shame and make the decision that is best for you regarding staying in or leaving the relationship.
If you need or want to leave your relationship but are unable to due to fear, develop a plan for working through fear and developing internal resilience and resourcefulness. Understand that you must be able to leave the relationship before you can make a choice to stay.	**Welcome a growing sense of resilience and connection** to your core self as you work through your fear and become able to make a fully free choice to stay or leave your relationship.
Learn about the sexual injury at the heart of betrayal and identify ways in which sexual betrayal has impacted your sexuality and your sexual relationship.	As you grieve the losses around the sexual injury, you also **experience a new understanding** of your worth and value as a sexual being. Your expectations for a healthy sexual self and a healthy life-giving sexual relationship expand and enlarge.
Become empowered to learn the whole truth about betrayal through requesting a full therapeutic disclosure.	**Experience the relief of limiting further emotional harm to yourself** from staggered discovery by decreasing Sherlocking behaviors and setting boundaries around receiving a full therapeutic disclosure.

Partners who experience betrayal blindness move into a version of denial—ignoring, devaluing, refuting, or minimizing information. When this happens, they are susceptible to believing ongoing lies and gaslighting from the cheating partner. They mistakenly hope that an appointment or two of couples therapy is all that is needed for healing, or that a few big fights and conversations with their significant other will set things back on track, or that everything they currently know about the betrayal is all there is to know.

Betrayal blindness tempts us to slap a Band-Aid on a gaping wound and ignore the fact that it is seeping around the edges. Sometimes, betrayed partners will discourage their significant other from getting help or insist that they and their partner exit therapy. They take these counterproductive steps because they are afraid to face the full reality of the problem and what it might mean for their life and relationship.

The fear and panic that follows betrayal is common and very real, and the desire to avoid something so scary and potentially painful is understandable. However, my experience working with betrayed partners tells me that this avoidance usually turns out to be a temporary detour that eventually brings them back to the same frightening spot and the same potentially painful choices.

If you can be aware of this very real temptation to avoid your new painful reality and go for the quick fix, it will help you stay with the natural and necessary unfolding of the realization phase and to eventually move through it. And this is a very good thing, because after realization comes the stabilization phase.

PHASE 3: STABILIZATION

Many betrayed partners report that the stabilization phase is the longest phase in the healing process. This is because the stabilization phase is an acute skill-building phase. Partners begin to learn new coping skills and develop new understandings of themselves, their partner, addiction, infidelity, sexual health, and relational health. The stabilization phase often continues even as partners also move forward into the later stages of healing. Remember, the phases are not linear, and most partners tend to experience multiple phases at one time.

One sign that you are entering the stabilization phase is that you start to feel like you have more emotional space. Instead of feeling pushed to the emotional wall, you find that you are not quite as short-tempered or exhausted or prone to teary outbursts. The painful feelings do not completely go away, of course. You are still going to catch yourself asking, "How did this become my life?" But as you start to wrap your mind around what has happened and to understand your experience, the most severe symptoms of shock—emotional and mental fragmentation, difficulty concentrating, and impaired functioning—begin to recede and improve.

You also start to ask different questions. In the devastation and realization phases, your questions were about how to survive and what to do in the moment to manage your overwhelm. In the stabilization phase, your attention turns to deeper matters: to your future, and to the future of your relationship. Common experiences of the stabilization phase include:

- Periods of overwhelm and activation decrease as a growing ability to healthfully manage trauma symptoms develops, and

tools to help calm and soothe yourself and your nervous system are utilized more regularly.
- Clarity increases as there is a growing understanding of the role of gaslighting and betrayal blindness and an increasing ability to identify gaslighting when it occurs and hold onto your reality.
- Decisions to stay (for now) or leave the relationship create a sense of direction and clarity about the skills and resources needed to either repair the relationship or grieve the relational loss and create a new life.
- There is continued pain, anger, and fear but the confusion and shock significantly decrease as your understanding about the cheating grows and you are also clearer about the steps you need to take to heal.
- Conflict between you and the cheating partner improves as communication boundaries are implemented, and support for the relational dynamics is put in place through couples therapy or check-ins with individual therapists.
- Daily functioning improves as your nervous system becomes more stable and you feel better resourced to handle the challenges you face by drawing on your support system.
- Pursuit of details (Sherlocking) regarding the cheating decreases significantly as either a decision to leave the relationship is made or agreement that a full therapeutic disclosure will be provided is put in place.

The stabilization phase is where you start to make decisions, ask for change, use your voice, and set boundaries. All these things help you make one of the most significant shifts in the healing process: the shift from powerlessness to empowerment.

In the stabilization phase, you move out of this powerless "one-down" position by learning to operate from your personal power center. Your personal power center is your core truth about what you need, what you want, what you value, what is important to you, what you are willing to sacrifice for, and what is truly meaningful in your life. It is your belief in your inherent worth and your acceptance of your human imperfections and character defects. You operate from this place by learning to listen to yourself, trust yourself, and use your voice effectively to communicate with your partner and others.

Below and on the following page are the goal, tasks, and outcomes of the stabilization phase. In the next chapter we continue our exploration of the Braving Hope™ Process by looking at the final three phases: reimagining, creating, and flourishing.

STABILIZATION PHASE GOAL:
Move from Powerlessness to Empowerment

TASKS	OUTCOMES
Learn to effectively set and maintain boundaries and bottom lines.	**Experience an increased sense of safety and empowerment** in all your relationships.
Learn to hold your reality in conscious awareness as you step out of the gaslighting dance and move away from betrayal blindness.	**Experience clarity and decreasing confusion as you identify gaslighting** when it is happening and remove yourself from the path of danger. Experience growing tolerance for uncomfortable emotions and fear as you learn to stay connected to your reality even when it is scary.
Learn to use your effective powerful voice to communicate and ask for what you need.	**Decreased conflict along with increased relational risk** as you more clearly communicate what you need and wait to see how your partner responds.

STABILIZATION PHASE GOAL:
Move from Powerlessness to Empowerment *(continued)*

TASKS	OUTCOMES
Learn to rescue yourself from the trauma trigger cascade by identifying powerless behaviors and exchanging them for empowered beliefs, thinking, and actions.	**Increased knowledge of and trust in yourself** and your ability to handle challenging situations expands your capacity to face fears, take risks, and do what is best for you.
Identify where fear of loss is creating paralysis and patterns of powerlessness that prevent you from utilizing the skills you are learning. Begin to work through fear by taking manageable risks with support.	**Get unstuck, experience forward movement and increased healing** as you build trust in yourself, internal resilience, and resourcefulness.
Identify the difference between reactive emotions and core emotions and learn to experientially differentiate when you are in each.	**Begin to experience the relief and emotional grounding** that occurs when you access and process your primary emotional experience.
Complete a full therapeutic disclosure with the cheating partner (if you are staying in your relationship).	**Full confidence that you know the scope of the betrayal** and have established a baseline of honesty and trust within the relationship to begin to build upon.
Create a plan for handling relapses or slips that may occur.	**Decreased fear of relapses/slips along with increased empowerment** to handle any sobriety challenges that occur with self-care, self-compassion, appropriate boundaries, and bottom lines.
If you are leaving your relationship, create a support team to provide you with community, guidance, and nurture as you enter the grieving process.	**Experience support** that allows you to truly separate from and divorce your partner both legally and emotionally, freeing you to move forward.

Hope is being able to see
that there is light
despite all the darkness.

DESMOND TUTU

CHAPTER TWENTY

THE BRAVING HOPE® PROCESS:

Imagining a New Life

The first three phases of the Braving Hope® Process center around understanding and coping with the immediate personal and relational impacts of sexual betrayal. Grieving losses, letting go of hopes and dreams, and accepting the new and very challenging reality that you now find yourself in are key steps along the path of recovery. After taking these important steps, it is vital that you begin to develop a vision for a new, post-betrayal future and life.

Phase four, reimagining, marks a shift in the process—a transition into looking forward toward the future and starting to think about life after betrayal and the possibilities that healing might hold.

PHASE 4: REIMAGINING

Phase four is called reimagining because in this phase your energy shifts from the narrow focus of coping with sexual betrayal to a broader view of yourself and your relationship. You begin to get curious about and explore the ways in which your history has shaped your present story. As you learn more about yourself, you begin to imagine a new and different future.

When you experience partner betrayal, there is no going back. You will never again have the relationship you had with your partner pre-discovery—even if you decide to stay with them and repair the relationship. Sexual betrayal creates a seismic reordering within relationships. The crisis created by sexual betrayal pushes most relationships to the very edge of survival. As betrayed partners evaluate their decision to stay or leave, those who choose to stay do so with vigorous expectations that if they stay, things must be different. Not only must the cheating and lying stop, but the entire relationship needs to up-level and things that were previously tolerated must now change.

You will also never again be the same person you were pre-discovery. The core of who you are does not change. If you were funny before, you will still be funny. If you were creative, outdoorsy, or loved animals, those parts of your essential self will remain. However, the version of yourself that you were pre-discovery is altered. You will never again be the version that had not experienced betrayal.

The reimagining phase is exactly what it sounds like. It is where you begin to consider who you are now, what you want for yourself, what you want for your relationship, how you want to craft and live your life going forward. You examine what you want to change, what old baggage from your history needs to be healed so you can be free of it, and what you hope for and want for yourself and those you love.

These are the hallmarks of the reimagining phase as you begin to think bigger picture about your life and relationships:

- The new skills, tools, and resources learned and accessed during the stabilization phase continue to grow and are utilized more regularly with increasing comfort.
- Your relationship with yourself is stronger as you trust yourself more, listen to yourself better and can make decisions, take good actions, and move you toward what you want.
- You begin to be curious about your history and what has shaped you and brought you to this point in your life. You start to explore relational and emotional patterns, often rooted in childhood, that have not served you well, and you begin to create new ways of relating to yourself and others.
- You begin to explore your sexual history and learn about what has shaped you sexually. The tools that you have learned in stabilization regarding boundaries, asking for what you need, speaking effectively, etc., all begin to be utilized within your sexual relationship as you learn more about yourself and (if you are ready) your partner.
- If you have stayed with your partner and have completed a full therapeutic disclosure, you begin attachment-focused couples therapy. This type of couples therapy helps you and your partner enter the places of deep wounding that have resulted from the betrayal and begin to emotionally connect to one another and hold the pain together in a way that creates healing and repairs the damage to your relational bond.
- You alternate between periods of hope when things are going well and periods of despair when you lose progress and old

issues resurface again. This back-and-forth between hope and discouragement is a common part of the growth process for individuals and couples. It is at its highest during the reimagining phase, where real change starts to take root, and you can see progress, but at times you (and your partner) revert to old patterns.

- If you are leaving your relationship, grief is often at a peak during the reimagining phase as you are beginning to sever the emotional bond with your partner permanently. Allowing room to process the sadness around the loss of the relationship is vital. At the same time, there is a sense of possibility that starts to emerge as you begin to imagine your new life as an individual, separate from your relationship.

The reimagining process starts with an examination of trauma. Many betrayed partners have experienced what I call multilayered trauma. What this means is that before they experienced the trauma that results from being cheated on and systematically lied to, they had other experiences of betrayal trauma, either in their childhood or in previous adult relationships.

Betrayal trauma encompasses far more than the sexual and relational infidelity. Betrayal trauma also includes the traumatic impact of someone you depend upon betraying you through neglect, abandonment, or physical, sexual, emotional, or spiritual abuse—especially during your developmental years. This includes a full range of experiences from what we might typically think of as overt abuse, like being slapped or hit or verbally abused, to more covert experiences, such as not getting your emotional, intellectual, or spiritual needs fully met, or being expected to behave like a little adult instead of a child.

If you experienced betrayal trauma in childhood, that trauma reverberates when you encounter fresh betrayal trauma as an adult. New trauma awakens the emotions of your childhood trauma and layers them on top of the reactions triggered by your current sexual and relational trauma. Suddenly, you're dealing with a double whammy of trauma responses.

For example, if you had a father who was busy being a provider and was often absent or distracted when he was present, you may have wounds from not getting your needs for attention, affirmation, direction, care, and nurturance met. In your adulthood, when you experience your partner as disconnected, withdrawn, preoccupied, or in some way abandoning or rejecting, you are likely to have feelings about that plus feelings from the wounds with your unavailable father. This is the experience of multilayered trauma with which many betrayed partners must cope.

During the reimagining phase, attention turns to exploring and beginning to understand and heal these past traumas along with the current trauma. In this phase, most betrayed partners start to identify and connect with the longing they feel for something more. They realize they want and need something more than what they had even before they found out about the cheating and lying. This is a gift hidden in betrayal, and partners come to recognize, over time, that even though they did not choose betrayal and they are still mad as hell that they are dealing with it, the betrayal has opened a doorway leading to the possibility of a much deeper healing and freedom than they previously imagined.

The reimagining phase can be a pivot point in reclaiming your sense of self. Your focus shifts from an emphasis on your cheating partner and what they are or aren't doing to understanding more about who you are, what has shaped you, and what your emotional and relational life could be like as you heal and shed the restrictions created by past and present wounds.

This is a phase that includes intensive work on past and present trauma to reclaim your sense of self and to move out of old patterns that perpetuate harmful behaviors in your life and inhibit you in your relationships. Hopefully, this work is done with an understanding that the pathway leading you through your past traumas eventually leads to a changed and happier future.

On the following page are the goal, tasks, and outcomes of the reimagining phase.

The reimagining phase is where some of your deepest healing happens. In this phase, sexual and relational wounds are emotionally engaged in a way that allows transformation of not just the mind but the heart.

For couples who are staying together and repairing the relationship, the reimagining phase is where the work to restore secure bonding really takes off.

Up to this point, if you are like most betrayed partners, you are waiting for the type of healing to occur that will truly change your felt sense of safety with the cheating partner. You may see and appreciate the efforts your significant other has made to repair things while also feeling that they have fallen short.

This assessment does not discount the tremendous effort that your partner has likely made. They may have started to attend weekly therapy, group therapy, and twelve-step meetings, done homework, attended classes, and put all that they are learning into practice. But that is not enough. Certainly, all this work is vital to the healing process, and betrayed partners whose significant others do these things experience

THE BRAVING HOPE® PROCESS

REIMAGINING PHASE GOAL:
Reclaim and Nurture Your Core Self

TASKS	OUTCOMES
Identify and understand your attachment style and your partner's attachment style (if staying).	**Increased compassion and empathy** as you better understand your (and your partner's) relational patterns and how they came to be.
Identify the beliefs, feeling states, and behavioral patterns that shape your sense of self (i.e. I believe I am not worthy of getting my needs met. So, I feel deprived and exhausted and operate in an anti-dependent manner in my relationships).	**Welcome a new understanding** of the patterns that have shaped your relationship with yourself and others.
Identify the beliefs, feeling states, and behavioral patterns that shape how you see others (i.e. I believe others are not reliable and I cannot depend on them. So, I feel alone and I expect others to disappoint me or not treat me well).	**Allow yourself to grieve** the negative beliefs and patterns that have limited your ability to have secure relationships with yourself and others.
Identify the origin story behind these beliefs, feeling states, and relational patterns by exploring family of origin dynamics or childhood trauma impacts.	**Experience growing compassion, knowledge, and self-love** as you better understand your story.
Access and process your core emotional experience related to the partner betrayal trauma as well as childhood betrayal trauma.	**Experience healing and freedom** as old emotional wounds are processed and transformed, creating space for your core self to emerge and develop.
Learn to reparent yourself to heal old wounds, develop secure bonding, and create new healthy relational patterns with yourself and others.	**Become empowered** to operate from new powerful beliefs, supportive emotional states, and healthy behavioral patterns that honor your core self and build positive relationships with others.
Practice operating from new beliefs, feeling states, and behavioral patterns in relationship with yourself and others.	**Experience the benefits of vulnerability and risk-taking** as your core self gets stronger and your capacity for secure bonding with yourself and others expands.
Participate in attachment-focused couples therapy to heal relational injuries and reshape and repair the secure bond between you and your partner.	**Experience deep healing, rebuilt trust, and renewed love for your partner** as the wounds created by betrayal heal and recede from the forefront of the relationship.

much greater hope and earlier stability in their relationships. But in some important ways these efforts inevitably fall short.

If you're like most betrayed partners, you have watched and participated in this journey and wondered why their efforts aren't resolving the core pain you still feel when the cheating partner is obviously trying so hard.

Well, here is why: To truly heal the heart of betrayal, emotional connection, empathy, compassion, regret, remorse, and guilt must be felt and experienced together, simultaneously by you and your partner, in a meaningful and intentional way. Your partner must be willing to hold your pain while feeling their own pain about the damage and loss they have created. Your partner must be willing to feel their guilt and remorse and vulnerably share it with you. At the same time, you must be willing to let down your guard and talk about the rawest places in your heart, taking the risk of opening yourself and being vulnerable with the one who hurt you.

You may be saying to yourself, "But I have done that. I've talked about how much my partner has hurt me until I had no words left, and it didn't help." If so, you're not alone. Most betrayed partners have talked about their pain at length with their cheating partner (and others). However, this typically happens early in the healing process, shortly after discovery when emotions are running high, and the cheating partner is defensive. Most of this talking is about expressing reactive emotions rather than your core emotional experience.

What I am talking about here is a different and deeper level of communication about these issues. And that typically cannot happen until this later stage of the recovery process, when both of you have done some individual healing, learned to connect to your core emotional selves, worked through defenses that come up, and can stay present with one another in the face of conflict. These are the tasks that pave the way for the possibility of true repair, restoration, forgiveness, and reconciliation. For couples who are staying together, this deep, emotionally connecting work is a vital part of the reimagining phase.

PHASE 5: CREATING

If the reimagining phase is a turning point for betrayed partners as you start to think about what your post-betrayal future might look like, the creating phase is where the work of building your new future gathers momentum and takes off. Betrayed partners in the creating stage often experience the following:

- Your sense of self has grown strong, and you are clearer about who you are, what is good for you, what you like and don't like. Out of this newfound sense of self, the creation phase is often marked with venturing into new activities, hobbies, friendships, and adventures as you try new things and reach for new dreams.
- If you have stayed in your relationship, the creating phase often marks a turning point as you more fully let down your guard and risk love and connection again with your partner. The relationship improves; there is less conflict as your communication skills grow, your ability to feel emotional safety and share your inner worlds increases, and your ability to regulate yourself and each other expands.
- Sometimes during the creating phase the relationship stalls. This happens if either the cheating partner sabotages safety in some way or if the betrayed partner is too fearful to risk vulnerability.

In either case, the forward movement can be hijacked and a return to earlier phases can occur.

- If you are leaving your relationship, you are often dealing with legal issues, custody arrangements, learning how to be a single parent at times and co-parent with your soon-to-be ex-partner at others, managing telling friends, family, and children, moving into a new home, etc. All these details are part of the transition from life with your partner to a new life without your partner. The creating phase is full of change and opportunities to begin to make choices to shape the new life that you want.
- If you have fully left your relationship, grieved its loss, and processed the learning and growing that it held for you, then you may be ready to risk again by venturing into dating and exploring a new relationship. If so, this phase is where you envision a new fulfilling partnership as you get clear on what you are available for and what you are not available for in a new relationship.
- Sexuality is embraced as you reclaim your sexual self, take risks, explore, learn, and venture into creating the sex life you long for.
- Family dynamics, either with your immediate family (partner and children) or with extended family, begin to change as you practice using boundaries, asking for what you need, speaking from your effective voice, and sharing your authentic self with others.

Even as a new vision for the future unfolds in the creating phase, you must continue to grieve and accept the losses that have occurred because of the betrayal. Often, one of the most interesting and poignant things about healing from betrayal trauma (or any trauma, for that matter) is that as you come more fully into connection with your emotions, you find that the sadness, grief, and loss lay right next to something else inside of you. Something very surprising. That something else is *longing*.

Grief awakens not just your sadness about what is lost, but your deeply held inner yearnings and desires. As you count the cost of the betrayal, you also begin to feel the stirring of your longing for joy, aliveness, connection, intimacy, fulfillment, meaning, purpose, etc. Things you thought were dead and gone slowly awaken, raising their sleepy heads to peer around and see if it might be safe to send out tendrils, dig in, and start to grow and bloom.

There are only two things in life that motivate us to do the hard work of changing. The first is suffering and pain. The second is our longing for something different. Authentic hope is grounded in the belief that the most sustainable, longest-lasting changes are changes that are connected not to your pain, but to your longings.

Nevertheless, for most betrayed partners change starts because of the pain and suffering caused by infidelity. The change is not chosen and is often about surviving and coping with the trauma of betrayal. However, by the time you move into the creating phase, a profound shift in your motivation occurs. Now, instead of being in the process because you had no choice and needed to cope with the pain and loss and take care of those who depend on you, you are in it for yourself and for the new life and relationships you long for. You continue the work because you see the potential for a life you never thought was possible. You dig into your learning and healing because you want something more and better than what you previously had.

Each betrayed partner longs for different things. Some want the freedom to live from their authentic self without feeling the need to people-please or experiencing shame attacks when they are seen and known by others. Some want a new and improved relationship with their cheating spouse. They have glimpsed the potential for true honesty, intimacy, and connection, and they want to go for it. Others want to break generational patterns of dysfunction and betrayal in their families, creating a new opportunity for their children and grandchildren. Still others want a new relationship with someone different. They want to learn how to pick a healthy, available, present partner, and how to be healthy, available, and present for that relationship themselves.

In the creating phase, betrayed partners move toward dreams they may never have dared to acknowledge, let alone pursue in the past. Slowly, step-by-step, they create a new life guided by the deep longings and yearnings that are only revealed through the grief and losses of betrayal.

And here is the mystery: that out of something so awful and life-wrecking could come such powerful and positive life-altering possibility. This is the essence of authentic hope.

The creating phase is where all that you dreamed of and thought about in the reimagining phase begins to take shape. In this phase, the changes that you have been making, the new skills that you have been learning, and the self-knowledge that you have gained start to add up to a new way of life and a new way of being in relationship with both yourself and others.

On the following page are the goal, tasks, and outcomes of the creating phase.

THE BRAVING HOPE® PROCESS

CREATING PHASE GOAL:
Create a New Love Relationship with Yourself and Others

TASKS	OUTCOMES
Practice operating from new beliefs, feeling states, and behavioral patterns in relationship with yourself and others.	**Experience the benefits of vulnerability and risk-taking** as your core self gets stronger and your capacity for secure bonding with yourself and others expands.
Continue building safe connection in your relationship and repairing wounds that still need tending.	**Enjoy increasing connection** with your partner as the betrayal begins to recede from the forefront of the relationship.
Repair sexual wounds and create a healthy sex plan for yourself and/or your relationship.	**Welcome a new understanding and acceptance of your sexual self** and grow in your ability to co-create a fulfilling and life-giving sex life with yourself and/or a partner.
Transform fear, anger, and bitterness through a deeply personal experience of forgiveness.	**Experience the freedom** of releasing yourself from the emotional prison of resentment, anger, or bitterness while continuing to hold the cheating partner accountable.
If newly single, learn about healthy relationships and sexuality, and develop a dating plan with bottom lines and boundaries (for yourself) if you have left your relationship and are ready to date.	**Adventure into the experience of sharing your authentic self** with new potential partners who are available for safe and secure connection.
Create a vision for the life and relationship you long for and venture toward new dreams that arise from deeper connection with your core self.	**Experience the joy** that comes from listening to your longings and allowing yourself to move toward new relationships, hobbies, careers, and adventures.

PHASE 6: FLOURISHING

While flourishing is the final phase of the healing process, it is by no means the end of the journey. As we have discussed, healing from betrayal is not a linear path. It is a road that winds around, revisiting familiar territory, sometimes going slow and then speeding up and then slowing down again.

So, do not look at the flourishing phase as a place you arrive at, never to return to the earlier phases. Rather, it is a place you come to while still experiencing and occasionally returning to other stages of the healing process. Over time, you will find yourself spending more and more time in the flourishing phase, and eventually, it will become your new normal.

The flourishing phase is where you begin to live beyond the trauma of sexual betrayal. The changes that you have made, the new relationship with yourself, the new connections with others, and the new ways of being have become your new normal.

Below are the hallmarks of the flourishing phase, as you begin to relax into your "new normal":

- You have developed a sense of safety and security with yourself. You trust yourself and know yourself much more than before. You can rely on your core self, and your trust in your resourcefulness and resilience forms a solid foundation of support for your life and relationships.
- You know how to balance vulnerability and protection. You set boundaries as needed and take risks as you share your authentic self with others (partner, friends, family, co-workers, etc.).
- When challenges arise, you can draw on your relationship with yourself and the secure relationships you have developed with

others (partner, friends, family) to support you as you navigate the rough waters that life can bring.
- You have learned how to care for yourself and grieve when losses occur. Life brings loss regularly and you have learned to tolerate loss and cope with it in healthy and life-giving ways.
- Living life in community with others is standard practice and you reach for others in moments of joy, celebration, difficulty, or hardship.
- Eroticism and healthy sexual expression play a vital role in both individual life and romantic relationships.
- If you have stayed in your relationship, shared recovery and healing are an ongoing part of life as the betrayal recedes into the background and new exciting parts of life take precedence.
- The intense healing phase concludes as you graduate out of therapy, group, etc., and begin to use your long-term supports to maintain progress and continue your growth journey.

If you have wholeheartedly committed yourself to the process of healing from betrayal, digging deep and doing the work, then you are engaged in what is called "second-order change." First-order change is when you tinker with the existing structures in your life and relationships. You tweak things here and there to achieve a better result or to bring your life back into alignment and balance.

Second-order change is when you go below the structures and change the foundational beliefs, feelings, and thinking that guide your behaviors. Second-order change is deep, and it is long-lasting. It changes things at the core, and these changes then weave and wind through your life, rising up to create all kinds of additional changes in different areas.

Second-order change takes time. It is not a short, quick fix. It's a process that must be slowly and intentionally undertaken with diligence and attention. It requires risk-taking and the willingness to be uncomfortable—because all change requires you to leave your comfort zone to experience something new. And the deeper the change, the more profound your discomfort will be.

Second-order change is also experiential. You cannot think yourself into a new state of being. You must live your way to second-order change by doing new things and having new experiences that challenge your old beliefs and convince you in your cells and bones that something new is possible.

When you get to the flourishing phase, all the second-order change that you have been working toward begins to feel comfortable. You are well on your way to creating a new normal for yourself through hard work and metamorphosis, and you can now start to experience the joy of living in this new life.

On the following page are the goal, tasks, and outcomes of the flourishing phase.

CONCLUSION

These are the six phases that betrayed partners travel through as they heal from sexual betrayal. These phases—devastation, realization, stabilization, reimagining, creating, and flourishing—provide a roadmap of hope, leading you out of the darkness that betrayal brings into the fresh air and sunlight once again.

In the next and final chapter, we wrap up our journey together by returning to where we started: my personal story of betrayal.

THE BRAVING HOPE® PROCESS

FLOURISHING PHASE GOAL:
Feed, Nurture, and Cultivate Authentic Hope

TASKS	OUTCOMES
Maintain connection and interdependence with your community of support.	**Life a life that is enriched** by a strong sense of community and relationships.
Maintain long-term self-care priorities, rituals, and practices.	**Experience the emotional and relational stability** that consistent self-care and emotional self-nurture create.
If staying in your relationship, determine long-term supports needed (i.e. twelve-step meeting participation) to continue to cultivate and maintain gains.	**Enjoy the sense of accomplishment** that comes with graduating from therapy and moving into a new phase where growth is less intense but is an ongoing part of life.
Increase intimacy with your partner and more easily and confidently repair relational breaches, triggers, or conflicts.	**Experience the relief that comes when the relationship is no longer under threat** and you and your partner are able to weather bumps in the road constructively.
Continue to learn about yourself, healthy relationships, and sexuality as you venture into dating and building a new love relationship.	**Enter dating or romantic relationships with new confidence** in your ability to share your authentic self with a partner and to make wise choices about who you choose to partner with.

This is an invitation
to allow everything to fall away
in order to be left holding
what can never be taken.
The invitation in this pain
is the possibility of discovering
who I really am.

GLENNON DOYLE

CHAPTER TWENTY-ONE

DON'T WASTE A GOOD CRISIS:

Endings and New Beginnings

I was beginning to acknowledge defeat. I desperately wanted to save my marriage. I wanted nothing more than for my story to end in renewal, hope, and restoration. I had worked as hard as I knew how in my own therapy, making hard choice after harder choice, all in the hope and belief that miracles could and would happen. I had stood at the fork in the road and risked it all on the possibility of resurrection.

Instead of miracles, however, I saw the mundane same old same old of addiction and dysfunction, day in and day out. And yet, long after everyone around me was saying "enough already," I continued to hold out, waiting to see if things would change.

Until...

Finally, even my ride-or-die self had to acknowledge that my relationship was not salvageable. Not if I wanted to keep me. Not if I wanted to honor the self I had worked so hard to discover and to rescue.

Not if I wanted to live in the light of truth, honesty, and the integrity of being whole.

I did not move quietly into acceptance. I did not go down without a fight. One of the biggest fights of my life, in fact. And if you are going to have a big fight, you might as well have it with a big Being, so I chose my higher power (God) to rumble with about the loss of my dream.

One day, at the start of this fight, I sat across from my therapist, a woman who had walked me through the past few years of my life, patiently unwinding the layers of lies, shame, and betrayal that I had been wrapped in. I crossed my arms, glared at her, and said, "I am so angry that I need a new word for anger. *Rage* is not even big enough. I am jumping up and down spitting mad with every fiber of my fucking being." Normally, I loved this woman. Today, I hated her. She was just another part of the grand betrayal I was experiencing.

I told her, "I have done everything right. I have made the hard choices, I have been honest, I have not sought revenge, I have tried to offer grace in the face of abject cruelty. I have done my part even though it has made my teeth hurt, and what do I get in return? I get the ending of my marriage. After all my sacrifice and hard work, what I get is a divorce. I am pissed at God. I am pissed at you. I am pissed at everyone!" I sat back, arms crossed, tears streaming down my face, wrapped in a fury so deep I was shaking with it.

At the bottom of my rage and anger I felt tricked. Duped by a healing process that asked me to offer understanding to my addicted spouse, to take responsibility for my own healing, to look unflinchingly into the dark corners of my own heart, to grasp with both hands the truth of my own deep worth and lovability in the face of mountains of rejection. Now, as the finale to the drama that had been my relationship, the curtain was going to come down on my marriage. *Ta-da!*

This was unacceptable to me.

Every cell in my body screamed in protest about the unfairness of what was happening. Somewhere deep inside, I thought that if I were a good girl, if I did what was right, if I did what was hard, if I stayed the course, I would be worthy of the outcome I wanted. I think I thought I could earn my marriage. Turns out, this is not how life or relationships work.

To suddenly discover that I was losing my marriage and, even worse, that I was the one who was going to have to walk away, shattered my entire paradigm. I felt like I was being stripped of everything I wanted. Instead of healing, I was getting destruction. Instead of restoration, brokenness. Instead of resurrection, death. This was not how it was supposed to work, and I was undone by my confusion and outrage.

My Yoda therapist listened to me and looked at me with clarity and confidence in her eyes. My anger did not ruffle her one bit, and she sat with openness and attentiveness while I unloaded my cart full of grievances. And then she said, "Michelle, it is your turn right now. You need to say everything you have to say. Let it all out. Do not hold anything back. Be as angry and enraged as you need to be. Say everything you need to say. God can handle it, and so can I. So say it all."

I listened to this, and I believed her. Partly because I had no way to keep it in. My anger was boundless, and no dam could hold it. My type A efforts had availed me nothing, so what did I have to lose if I let God know how I really felt about the very bad job S/he was doing?

And then Yoda spoke again. This time she said, "When you are done, when you have said everything you need to say, then it will be God's turn. God will show up and meet you in some way. I do not know how, but God will show up and touch you and you will perhaps have a limp to show for it."

She was referring to the story of Jacob in the Old Testament. I will not recap the whole thing here; you can google it if you are curious. The micro version is that Jacob had a wrestling match with God that left him with a limp for the rest of his life—a permanent reminder of what had passed between him and his Creator.

The idea that God would hit me with a limp fit right into my understanding at that time of God as a punishing, unfair, unjust, and unloving Being, so I looked my therapist in the eyes and said, "Let God bring it."

I walked out of her office that day, climbed into my Jeep Wrangler, and commenced taking my turn. When I am angry, I cuss like a trucker. Also, when I am being funny. This, however, was all about fury. Pure, white-hot rage. I drove my Jeep over the bridge toward Seattle and let my anger fly. "Fuck you, God. Fuck you. You are stripping me of everything I want. That is not love. If this is love, then fuck you, keep your goddamned love. You are going to show up and talk to me? I dare you. I dare you to have something to say to me in the face of all that has happened here. I. Fucking. *Dare. You.*"

For the next several weeks, I drove around with the top off my Jeep, looking skyward and ranting my pain and anger at a God who I felt was just like my husband. A big fat betrayer.

Eventually I ran out of words and ran out of steam. The anger moved through me and left me with sadness and grief as I faced this final impending loss. The last one in the long heart-wrenching stream of losses that had gone before it. I moved on with the task of making decisions. My focus shifted and my anger faded into the background as other things arose that needed my attention.

Until...

There is a beach north of Seattle in a town called Mukilteo, where the ferry boats leave to cross Puget Sound to Whidbey Island. When I lived in Seattle, this beach was where I went to church.

I went there whenever I could snatch a window of time to make the half-hour drive and sit awhile. I would pack my trail chair, a fleece, a blanket, and a backpack full of pens, paper, and some books, and I would head north.

There is a coffee shop as you enter Mukilteo, right at the top of the hill that takes you down to the water and the ferry. I would stop there and get a cup to keep me warm and then head down the hill to my spot.

If you are imagining a beach with sand and seashells, waves, and warmth, let me introduce you to the beaches of the great northwest. This beach had some sand, very brown sand, that was covered in small but beautiful and colorful rocks. There were large logs and pieces of driftwood all over the beach, grouped together in various places creating a perfect opportunity to plop your blanket and your butt down and do some leaning.

If you happen to be there in summer when the sun is out, you might be able to take your fleece off and just sit in your T-shirt. But most of the time, some layers with a good thick zip-up fleece on top are called for.

Once you have your spot picked out and your log to lean against, with your fleece and your coffee, you are ready for church.

The sanctuary is a spread of water—deep blue, sometimes green, reaching out from the shore to islands covered in green pines and land rolling beneath the curved outline of mountains that play hide-and-seek in the cloud cover so prevalent in Seattle. Because it is a Sound, there are no big oceanic waves; instead, there is a gentle, steady lapping that can reach all the way inside of you and soothe even the most ragged situation.

During those Seattle years, I was in the most wretched and heartbreaking experience of my adult life. Most of the time I was in a whirlwind of pain and panic, sprinkled with rage and fear. I needed an escape, a place to go where I could leave the hurricane behind for a while and find a moment of calm.

This beach became the cloister that I took myself to over and over, looking for solace, comfort, and wisdom. I spent hours there journaling, reading, thinking, crying, but most of all sitting, watching, and listening while the lapping water worked its magic on the torn edges of my heart.

This day, I had packed my backpack with my journal and some books to read, but I was not interested in any of that. It was warm and beautiful. The sun was shining on the water, creating a ribbon of diamonds, making the water dance and sparkle as though it was overcome with joy in response to the sun. (Which is kind of how everyone in Seattle feels when the sun finally comes out.)

I was sitting on my blanket letting the bright light warm me, listening to the waves, soaking in the beauty and peace of my spot on the beach, and letting my mind float in no particular direction.

As I watched the brilliance of the water, mesmerized into a bit of a trance, a movie began to play in my mind. One I had not seen before. This movie started back at the beginning of my relationship and unfurled in front of me with scene after scene of constriction, betrayal, and reduction. I saw not just the lies and sexual betrayal but the constant struggle to be allowed to be myself in my relationship. To be allowed to know myself or claim myself in any way. I saw the hollowing out of my core, the conviction of my worthlessness, the spiritual abuse and the self-loathing and contempt fed to me at every turn by a steady diet of lies and manipulations.

Suddenly the movie changed, and I started to see scene after scene of my current life, the life I had grown into during my years of healing and recovery. I saw my sense of self emerge and my newfound belief in my own worthiness and lovability. I saw that my journey through dealing with betrayal actually had very little to do with my partner's addiction, other than to learn to see it accurately and deal with it appropriately. Instead, I realized, my journey was about going in and rescuing a girl/woman who was entangled in the lies that her family and then her husband had told her about herself.

As this movie unfolded, scene after scene of freedom, light, laughter, and love played out on the screen of the water in front of me. Somewhere in that moment I became aware of a loving presence there with me, and a voice in my head said very gently but clearly, "This has not been about stripping you, taking away from you, robbing you of what you desire. This has been about saving you. I am giving to you, not taking away."

I sat on that Mukilteo beach and tears began to stream down my face as I heard this refrain over and over in my head as the movie continued to play. "I am saving you. I am freeing you. This is about love and hope and freedom." My body filled from head to toe with a sense of overwhelming love. I felt loved in every cell and fiber of my being as I sat in the light and listened and once again understood things in a completely new way.

As I sat there, my anger disappeared like water droplets evaporating off my skin. In that moment, everything changed. I no longer understood myself to be sustaining loss after despairing loss. Instead, I understood that each of those losses opened a space for me to receive something new, to be given something that my soul needed much more than whatever I was losing.

I no longer understood myself as betrayed by everyone dear to me; instead, I saw myself as guided with a steady, purposeful love. I no longer felt abandoned and alone. Rather, I felt held, comforted, and deeply protected.

Somehow in my grief I had forgotten what it was like before. Because my newfound way of being had become my new normal, I had forgotten the desperation and darkness of the years that came before. Until that day on the beach when I was helped to remember and see all I had gained as I walked through the pain and loss of betrayal.

RECLAIMING OURSELVES

When we make the commitment to heal from partner betrayal, we are choosing to embark on a journey to learn how to become securely attached to ourselves and to others. We are entering a process that offers us far more than just the alleviation of our trauma symptoms. Healing offers us the priceless joy of learning how to get our core needs—to matter, to belong, to be safe—met consistently.

Betrayal disconnects us from ourselves, our significant other, and those around us. We experience a profound relational rupture that affects every one of our sources of security and safety. Healing this relational trauma requires that we rebuild the lost connections.

We must reclaim and reshape our relationship with ourselves, moving toward authenticity and trust. We must either risk the restoration of our current romantic relationship or grieve its loss, grasp all the lessons that it offers and venture into a new relationship. We must learn how to bring our authentic selves to relationships with others, risking vulnerability to gain true intimacy and connection.

In their brilliant tome *Attachment Disturbances in Adults*, authors and researchers Daniel P. Brown and David S. Elliot outline the five key conditions that promote secure attachment. These five conditions include:

- A felt sense of safety
- Feeling seen and known
- A felt sense of comfort/soothing and reassurance
- Feeling valued and delighted in
- Feeling "a sense of support for being and becoming one's unique best self"[1]

Moving toward and increasing these five conditions for secure attachment are what the healing process is all about. All our therapy, learning, growing, and risking is at the core about developing these five things and increasing our ability to be securely attached with ourselves and others.

This change process is the pure gold that is surprisingly spun from the wreckage of betrayal.

Who would have thought it was possible?

Yet when we stepped out and declared our commitment to become the hero of our betrayal story (remember Chapter One?), we launched ourselves into a change process that does not just rescue us from betrayal, it transforms our core self and all our relationships.

This is the invitation hidden in the life-altering experience of partner betrayal. An invitation to develop a new securely bonded relationship with ourselves and others that allows us to venture into life with confidence, security and trust in our resilience and resourcefulness.

ADDITIONAL RESOURCES FOR BETRAYED PARTNERS

The 5-Step Strategy to Take Back Your Life After Betrayal is a free online masterclass by Michelle Mays.

Discover a step-by-step game-plan to heal sexual betrayal by reducing trauma symptoms, restoring your personal power, and grounding your healing in authentic hope that creates *real change*.

Visit michellemays.com/masterclass to watch
The 5-Step Strategy to Take Back Your Life After Betrayal.

ADDITIONAL RESOURCES FOR THERAPISTS & COACHES

For information about training and certification in **The Attachment-Focused Partner Betrayal Model: Attachment-based healing for partner betrayal** developed by Michelle Mays LPC, CSAT-S please visit michellemays.com/professionals.

ACKNOWLEDGMENTS

My deepest gratitude to my writing partners. To Steve Brock, who hired me to do one project, which turned into many, which turned into a twenty-three-year friendship and a fifteen-year writing partnership that has been both a wild ride and a complete joy. This book (and so much more) would not exist without you. Also, I just want to remind you of what you said when I told you I was closing my consulting business to do counseling full-time: "What a waste."

To Kelly McDaniel who reached out to me after reading a blog post that resonated with her seminal work around *Mother Hunger*. I have enjoyed every minute spent writing, talking, and thinking together about attachment and what it means in each of our lives personally and professionally. Thank you.

Thank you, Scott Brassart, for your wise and informed editing support as I wrote the manuscript. Your encouragement is so appreciated. Mary O'Donahue, thank you for the invaluable media expertise and preparation. Kathryn Goldman, you are a treasure, and your mix of legal advice and sharp wit have been so helpful.

I have been blessed with extraordinary mentors who have entered my story at pivotal moments to teach, coach, counsel, and guide me. Thank you from the bottom of my heart: Teri Larsen—you saved my life. Dan Allender and Precious and Liam Atchinson—you gave me permission to leave and that has made all the difference. Barbara Giuliano—for mothering me when I sorely needed it. Glynn Ford (RIP)—you were my true Oracle. Sandy Gray—for all the things, but most of all for modeling what it means to live a playful, robust life. Lou Argow—for training and mentoring par excellence when I was a baby therapist. Sharon Bauer—for calling me sweetie while guiding me through it all. Mark Sanna—for being so much more than a business coach. Lisa Toste, Jayne Jewell, Russ Ruffino, and Marc Von Musser—for life-changing modeling, mentoring, and coaching.

This book has been twenty years in the making and would not exist without the consistent nurturing provided by my friends. To my Seattle peeps who held me during the darkest days of my journey as we biked, hiked, camped, and road-tripped our way through grad school. And to my East Coast peeps for being a collective source of incredible wisdom and insight wrapped up in fun. I treasure you all: Brooke Kennaugh, Bill Bedell, Mikey G and Laurie Caniglia, Kari Hingst, Sandy Flewelling, Dennis Marceron, Jason (RIP) and Linda Francis, April Ispas, Rebecca Brittle, Denise Forsythe, Andrea Anderson Polk, Cyndi Wagner, Julie McCarter, Tonia Manning, Denise Hirschlein, and Lynda Carter.

Thank you, Beth Ratchford, best friend extraordinaire for journeying alongside me through an ever-changing landscape of marriage, divorce, dating, singlehood, deaths, births, celebrations, successes, and failures.

ACKNOWLEDGMENTS

You are who I call when I need to play the "best friend card" and be a pain in the ass and when I need to connect to unconditional acceptance. Thank you for helping me stay grounded in my true self. May we laugh until we snort, wheeze, and cry to the nursing home and beyond.

This book would have remained a dream without a remarkable team who stayed on mission and on purpose while I was at home on the sun porch writing. Deepest gratitude to Angela Cook and Melissa Howard—your commitment, sense of humor, amazing skills, and support are invaluable. Thank you, Bruce Butler, Lauri Barton, Aja Murillo, and Jenna Young for your dedication to serving our clients. And thank you to Derek Rippe and Joel Markquart for the marriage of design and technology that sings.

To my siblings who grew up in the same family I did, where counseling was never mentioned and insight into oneself was not encouraged. Thank you for supporting me in work that flies in the face of everything we were taught.

My love to chosen family Becca, Tam, Amias and Tobi, and Rachael, Robert, and Lilou. Chosen family is something special. I recommend it.

I owe a debt of gratitude to all those whose research, writing, and innovation have laid the foundation for my own learning and thinking about the issue of partner betrayal.

Last, thank you to each individual and couple who have dealt with the issue of sexual betrayal in some form or fashion and have invited me into your healing process. You have been my greatest teachers and it has been my privilege and honor to learn from you and journey with you. The last sentence of our mission statement at the counseling center says, "The human spirit's ability to create, heal, and generously give in the face of enormous adversity is a miracle we love being a part of." Amen.

ENDNOTES

INTRODUCTION
1. Barbara A. Steffens & Robyn L. Rennie (2006) The Traumatic Nature of Disclosure for Wives of Sexual Addicts, *Sexual Addiction & Compulsivity*, 13:2-3, 247-267, DOI: 10.1080/10720160600870802
2. Barbara A. Steffens and Marsha Means, *Your Sexually Addicted Spouse: How Partners Can Cope and Heal* (Far Hills, NJ: New Horizon Press, 2010).
3. Pamela J Birrell, R. E. Bernstein, and Jennifer J. Freyd, "With the Fierce and Loving Embrace of Another Soul: Finding Connection and Meaning after the Profound Disconnection of Betrayal Trauma," in *Reconstructing Meaning after Trauma* (Academic Press, 2017), 29–43.
4. Ibid.
5. Ibid.

CHAPTER TWO
1. Rachel E. Goldsmith, Rose M. Barlow, and Jennifer J. Freyd, "Knowing and Not Knowing about Trauma: Implications for Therapy," *Psychotherapy Theory: Research, Practice, Training* 455, Vol.41, No. 4 (2004): 448–63.
2. J. L. Herman, J. L., *Trauma and Recovery: The Aftermath of Violence—From Domestic to Political Terror* (New York: Basic Books, 1992), 121.

CHAPTER THREE

1. Robbie Duschinsky, "The Emergence of the Disorganized/Disoriented (D) Attachment Classification, 1979–1982," *History of Psychology* 18, no. 1 (2015): 32.

2. Amir Levine, and Rachel Heller, *Attached: The New Science of Adult Attachment and How It Can Help You Find—and Keep—Love* (New York: Penguin, 2010).

3. Mario Mikulincer and Phillip R. Shaver, *Attachment in Adulthood: Structure, Dynamics, and Change* (New York: Guilford Press, 2007), 16.

4. Mario Mikulincer and Phillip R. Shaver, *Attachment in Adulthood*, 18.

5. Levine and Heller, *Attached*, 2.

6. Mikulincer and Shaver, *Attachment in Adulthood*, 18.

7. Sandra Naaman, James D. Pappas, Judy Makinen, Dino Zuccarini, and Susan Johnson-Douglas, "Treating attachment injured couples with emotionally focused therapy: A case study approach," *Psychiatry: Interpersonal and Biological Processes* 68, no. 1 (2005): 55–77.

8. Mikulincer and Shaver, *Attachment in Adulthood*, 23.

9. These attachment styles are often referred to by other names. For example, avoidant attachment can be called dismissive attachment or anxious can be called preoccupied attachment. For clarity I've used the simplest terms for each type of attachment style.

10. Ibid, 19.

11. Levine and Heller, *Attached*.

12. Mikulincer and Shaver, *Attachment in Adulthood*, 25.

13. Levine and Heller, *Attached*.

14. Mikulincer and Shaver, *Attachment in Adulthood*, 20.

15. Bowlby, John, *Attachment and Loss: Volume I: Attachment* (New York: Basic Books, 1969).

16. Levine and Heller, *Attached*.

17. Ibid.

ENDNOTES

CHAPTER FOUR

[1] Judith Solomon, Robbie Duschinsky, Lianne Bakkum, and Carlo Schuengel, "Toward an Architecture of Attachment Disorganization: John Bowlby's Published and Unpublished Reflections" *Clinical Child Psychology and Psychiatry* 22, no. 4 (2017): 539–60.

[2] Mikulincer and Shaver, *Attachment in Adulthood*.

[3] Robbie Duchinsky, "The Emergence of the Disorganized/Disoriented (D) Attachment Classification," *History of Psychology* 18, no. 1 (2015): 32.

[4] Daniel P. Brown and David S. Elliott, *Attachment Disturbances in Adults: Treatment for Comprehensive Repair* (New York: W.W. Norton & Company, 2016), 540.

[5] Susan M. Johnson, *Attachment Theory in Practice: Emotionally Focused Therapy (EFT) With Individuals, Couples, and Families* (New York: Guilford Publications, 2019.)

CHAPTER FIVE

[1] Patricia A. DeYoung, *Understanding and Treating Chronic Shame: A Relational/Neurobiological Approach* (Oxfordshire: Routledge, 2015), 18.

[2] Ibid, 22.

[3] Ibid, 19.

[4] Ibid, 20.

[5] Sue Johnson, *Hold Me Tight: Seven Conversations for a Lifetime of Love* (New York: Little, Brown Spark, 2008), 57–58.

[6] DeYoung, *Understanding and Treating Chronic Shame*, 21.

[7] Ibid, 24.

[8] Ibid, 31.

CHAPTER SEVEN

1. Sue Johnson and T. Leanne Campbell, *A Primer for Emotionally Focused Individual Therapy (EFIT): Cultivating Fitness and Growth in Every Client* (New York ; London: Routledge, 2022), 39.

PART 2, INTRODUCTION

1. M. Scott Peck, *The Road Less Traveled: A New Psychology of Love, Traditional Values, and Spiritual Growth* (New York: Simon and Schuster, 2002).

CHAPTER TEN

1. M. Rose Barlow and Jennifer J. Freyd, "Adaptive Dissociation: Information Processing and Response to Betrayal," in *Dissociation and the Dissociative Disorders: DSM-V and Beyond* (2009): 93–105.

2. Robyn L. Gobin and Jennifer J. Freyd, "The Impact of Betrayal Trauma on the Tendency to Trust," *Psychological Trauma: Theory, Research, Practice, and Policy* 6, no. 5 (2014): 505.

3. Jennifer Freyd and Pamela Birrell, *Blind to Betrayal: Why We Fool Ourselves We Aren't Being Fooled* (Hoboken, NJ: Wiley & Sons, 2013), 93.

4. Ibid., 119.

5. Ibid.

6. Ibid, 56.

7. *Diagnostic and Statistical Manual of Mental Disorders: DSM–5*, (Arlington, VA: American Psychiatric Association 2013, 291.

8. Jennifer Freyd and Pamela Birrell, *Blind to Betrayal: Why We Fool Ourselves We Aren't Being Fooled* (Hoboken, NJ: John Wiley & Sons, 2013), 86.

9. Ibid., 92.

CHAPTER ELEVEN

1. Ibid., 115.

ENDNOTES

CHAPTER THIRTEEN

1. Curt Thompson, *The Soul of Desire: Discovering the Neuroscience of Longing, Beauty, and Community* (Westmount, IL: InterVarsity Press, 2021), 21.

2. Even if we lucked out and had caregivers who were consistently attuned to us and helped us form a secure sense of belonging and significance, we still live in an imperfect world filled with imperfect people and, as a result, we will still feel the impact of our core needs going unmet at times.

CHAPTER FOURTEEN

1. Debby Herbenick, *Because It Feels Good: A Woman's Guide to Sexual Pleasure and Satisfaction* (New York: Rodale), 2009.

CHAPTER FIFTEEN

1. Wendy Maltz and Carol Arian, *The Sexual Healing Journey: A Guide for Survivors of Sexual Abuse*, Third (New York, NY: Morrow, 2012).

2. Curt Thompson, *The Soul of Desire: Discovering the Neuroscience of Longing, Beauty, and Community* (Westmount, IL: InterVarsity Press, 2021), 22

3. William H. Masters and Virginia E. Johnson, *Human Sexual Response* (New York: Little, Brown, 1966).

4. H. S. Kaplan, *Disorders of Sexual Desire* (New York: Brunner, Mazel, 1979).

5. R. Basson, (2001). "Human Sexual Response Cycles," *Journal of Sex and Marital Therapy*, 27 no. 1 (2001), 33–43.

6. S. Iasenza, *Transforming Sexual Narrative: A Relational Approach to Sex Therapy* (New York, NY: Routledge, 2020).

CHAPTER SIXTEEN

1. *At Attachment Perspective on Sex–Both Soporific and Splendid* by Dr. Sue Johnson at the International Institute for Trauma and Addiction Professionals Symposium, May 2, 2020

2. Bill Bercaw and Ginger Bercaw, *The Couples Guide to Intimacy: How Sexual Reintegration Therapy Can Help Your Relationship Heal* (Pasadena, CA: California Center for Healing, Inc., 2010).

CHAPTER EIGHTEEN

[1] Susan Johnson, (2009) "Extravagant Emotion: Understanding and Transforming Love Relationships in Emotionally Focused Therapy," in *The Healing Power of Emotion*, ed. D. Fosha, D. J. Siegel, and M. F. Solomon (New York: W. W. Norton & Company, 2009), 257–79.

[2] Daniel J. Siegel, *Mindsight: The New Science of Personal Transformation* (New York: Bantam, 2010).

CHAPTER TWENTY-ONE

[1] Brown, D. P., & Elliott, D. S. (2016). *Attachment disturbances in adults: Treatment for comprehensive repair.* W W Norton & Co., 288.

www.ingramcontent.com/pod-product-compliance
Lightning Source LLC
LaVergne TN
LVHW041623120425
808494LV00022B/140